Unsettling "Sensation"

Rutgers Series on the Public Life of the Arts

A series edited by
Ruth Ann Stewart
Margaret J. Wyszomirski
Joni M. Cherbo

Unsettling "Sensation"

Arts-Policy Lessons from the Brooklyn Museum of Art Controversy

edited by
LAWRENCE ROTHFIELD

RUTGERS UNIVERSITY PRESS
New Brunswick, New Jersey, and London

Library of Congress Cataloging-in-Publication Data

Unsettling *Sensation* : arts-policy lessons from the Brooklyn Museum of Art controversy / Lawrence Rothfield, editor.

p. cm.—(Rutgers series on the public life of the arts)

Essays based on the conference "Taking Funds, Giving Offense, Making Money," held Feb. 12, 2000, at the School of the Art Institute of Chicago.

Includes bibliographic references and index.

ISBN 0–8135–2934–4 (cloth : alk. paper)—ISBN 0-8135-2935-2 (pbk. : alk. paper)

1. Art and state—United States. 2. United States—Cultural policy.
3. Brooklyn Museum of Art. I. Rothfield, Lawrence, 1956– II. Series.

NX730 .U57 2001
700'.1'030973—dc21

00-045896

British Cataloging-in-Publication data for this book is available from the British Library.

Manufactured in the United States of America

For Penelope

For Penelope

Contents

Illustrations

Preface

This volume on the controversy that erupted in reaction to *Sensation: Young British Artists from the Saatchi Collection,* an exhibition at the Brooklyn Museum of Art in the fall of 1999, is the second in the Rutgers University Press series "The Public Life of the Arts," which presents works in the emerging field of cultural policy. These essays are the product of "Taking Funds, Giving Offense, Making Money," a conference held on February 12, 2000, at the School of the Art Institute of Chicago and organized by the Cultural Policy Program at the University of Chicago. Close to four hundred people (well over our most optimistic estimates) attended the nine-hour conference, listening and responding with remarkable attentiveness. A number had flown in from around the country. In the final days before the event, we were inundated with calls from those who had heard about it and wanted to attend, and we came near to running out of space (like the airlines, we overbooked but fortunately did not have to turn anyone away). Why this burst of interest on the part of so many, and why the desire to spend an entire Saturday listening to museum directors, academics, lawyers, and journalists talk about yet another chapter in the culture wars?

In part, at least, it is because this conference raised questions and examined issues in a way somewhat different from the format our audiences were used to. This was not simply a group of academics talking to one another, nor was it simply a convening of specialists from the museum world. We designed this particular event to do what a number of newly emerging research centers around the country are beginning to do: to focus on the actions and decisions of all those who influence how the public experiences and participates in the arts and cultural activities more generally. In its most general incarnation, our center examines the role of the arts and humanities in public life.

Using as a model the work done in the relatively new field of environmental studies since the mid-1970s, we seek to foster working collaborations between academic and arts communities, between researchers and practitioners. These communities do not have a strong tradition of collaboration. But we believe that effective partnerships can be forged among those who think about, engage in, and support cultural activities of all kinds. The result will be more robust and immediately useful research. Work of this kind will better enable governments (local, state, and federal), foundations and philanthropists, cultural organizations, and schools to establish clear priorities, formulate policies and programs, and allocate critical resources. It will also enable community organizers, arts advocates, and artists themselves to argue more forcefully on their own behalf. All these groups, and the public more generally, stand to benefit from a closer look at what Richard Epstein in this book calls "the grubby engines" that power cultural institutions and generate controversy.

The conference and this publication would not have been possible without the generous support of Richard Behrenhausen and the Robert R. McCormick Foundation, Provost Geoffrey R. Stone, Dean Janel Mueller, Dean Robert Michael, and the Smart Museum of Art. We thank the following panelists for their important contributions to the conference: Joan Harris, Lewis Manilow, Hamza Walker, Margaret O'Brien Steinfels, Thomas Blackman, Gregg Bordowitz, Thelma Golden, and moderator John Callaway. Crucial support was also given by Carol Becker, Sarah Mallin, Katie O'Reilly, Greg Downs, and others on the staff of the School of the Art Institute, and by Christopher Perrius, Mario Pereira, Christine Coch, Shaleane Gee, Anthony Lichi, Kristin Scott, Rebecca Zorach, Jenny Adams, Philip Gossett, Jamee Rosa, Abby O'Neil, Conor O'Neil, Arthur Fournier, Lawrence Arbeiter, and Froeter Design.

Unsettling "Sensation"

LAWRENCE ROTHFIELD

Introduction
The Interests in "Sensation"

On September 22, 1999, New York's mayor, Rudolph Giuliani, strode into a press conference to publicly attack the Brooklyn Museum of Art's (BMA's) not-yet-opened show of Charles Saatchi's collection of British artists. The mayor's threats ignited a firestorm of controversy that finally burned itself out six months later, when a settlement was reached in federal court that ended legal hostilities; the museum's free speech rights were affirmed and its funding was saved, at least for the immediate future.

For many arts supporters and arts advocates, the entire episode seemed like a recurring nightmare. Once more, as with Robert Mapplethorpe, Andres Serrano, Karen Finley, and David Wojnarowicz, cutting-edge art—in this case, Chris Ofili's *The Holy Virgin Mary*—had provoked anger from the usual suspects: religious conservatives and their right-wing political representatives. And, once again, the anger expressed itself in threats to cut public funding, First Amendment be damned.

For their part, religious conservatives also viewed the *Sensation* controversy as a sobering replay from the past. Once again, as with Mapplethorpe, Serrano, Finley, and Wojnarowicz, religious sensibilities had been trampled on by the usual suspects: morally suspect artists promoted by elite liberals in the art world. And, once again, efforts to withdraw public funding for patently offensive art had been thwarted by the American Civil Liberties Union, while those brave souls who objected to having to pay for such hateful speech were smeared as McCarthyist philistines.

The "chilling inexorableness" of this latest confrontation, the staleness of the rhetoric from both sides, and the similarity of the denouement to that of previous controversies, all seemed to imply that what happened in Brooklyn was a nonevent.[1] Had those in the midst of the fray learned no new offensive or defensive strategies, either rhetorical or practical, in the past decade that would move them past stalemate? Had those who were not direct combatants learned nothing since 1989 to help bring the warring parties to the peace table? Was the history of arts controversy in the United States doomed to repeat itself?

The answer to this last question may well be yes if one accepts the pessimistic view that conservative attacks express a deeply rooted and intractable American predisposition against state-sponsored art.[2] But it may make better sense to take a more dialectical view of what seems, at first glance, to be simply more of the same. If the history of arts controversies in America repeated itself in Brooklyn, it did so there in classic Marxist fashion, first as tragedy and then as farce.[3] Compared with the life-and-death struggles of the earlier controversies—in which the institutional survival of the National Endowment for the Arts and the literal survival of people with AIDS were at stake—the *Sensation* controversy was strangely bloodless and bizarre. The cast of characters included David Bowie, aging-rocker-turned-cicerone for the exhibition's audio tour (his arch voice-over included questions like "Is it art?"); Charles Saatchi, advertising mogul turned collector, whose desire to remain anonymous as a financial backer of the exhibition of his own collection did not preclude his brazen interference in the Brooklyn Museum's curatorial efforts; Dennis Heiner, an iconoclast who vandalized the offending image with washable, slow-drying white paint that was immediately removed; a mayor who professed himself shocked, *shocked,* to find such goings-on in a museum whose board included his commissioner of cultural affairs, Schuyler Chapin; and a titillating marketing campaign by the museum that promised ticket buyers the possibility of "shock, vomiting, confusion, panic, euphoria, anxiety." That neither the museum director nor the mayor had bothered to see the exhibition prior to judging it "visually powerful and intellectually challenging" (Arnold Lehman) and "sick stuff" (Giuliani) only added to the postmodern sense of unreality surrounding the whole controversy, which Lewis Lapham likened to a piece of performance art.[4]

Describing the *Sensation* controversy as farcical may seem only to underscore its frustrating pointlessness, its failure to advance beyond the sorry spectacle of earlier controversies. As Marx noted, however, political farce is an essential prelude to real and effective political action. For Marx, of course, such action would be revolutionary. Readers of this volume, however, will probably be satisfied with something less grandiose, yet still material: policy analysis and recommendations that constructively anticipate controversy, recognize its potential impact, and provide a framework for managing it. The essays that follow offer a range of such policy assessments and advice.

In breaking down the Brooklyn controversy into distinct policy domains, each of which calls for several quite different kinds of expertise, this book marks a departure from the valuable books published in response to earlier controversies.[5] If a more differentiated, analytical, and multi- (if not non-) partisan approach toward arts controversies is now emerging, I would suggest that it is in part because of the farcical quality of this latest round of cultural fisticuffs. For the first time, an arts controversy had arisen in which the various stakeholders—the museum itself, the mayor, the Catholic League, the collector, and the media, as well as the public—could be understood as acting primarily not out of ideological orientation or passions or commitments (with all the tragic irrationalities these imply) but out of the stuff that policy, like farce, is made of: intense but calculated, or at least calculable, interests.

Take the painter at the center of the controversy, Chris Ofili. Unlike artists caught up in previous controversies such as Mapplethorpe, Finley, and Wojnarowicz, Ofili is no militant voicing a queer nation's desire for inclusion in American political life. Even in Britain, he hardly stood out as a radical, even during the intense outcry over another *Sensation* artist's portrait of a notorious child killer. (Tellingly, the protest that did emerge in England against Ofili came from a disgruntled artist, angered at Ofili's winning the prestigious Turner Prize in 1999, who dumped a pile of dung on the steps of the Tate Gallery and implanted a placard in the heap that read "Modern Art is a Load of Bullshit.") Among artists whose work had drawn fire in America, Ofili had the most in common with Serrano, whose works over a long period deliberately aimed at provoking a response from the Catholic Church. Both artists had juxtaposed a Christian icon to bodily waste in their art. But while Serrano's title, *Piss Christ* (figure 1), forced the recognition on viewers, Ofili's title, *The Holy Virgin Mary*, occluded it, and Ofili himself refused to be drawn into arguments about what his work meant politically.

That Saatchi himself became as much a lightning rod as Ofili again marks a departure from earlier arts controversies, in which debates focused on the meaning of the artists' works rather than on the motives of their patrons. As a collector, Saatchi might in an earlier era have been spared interrogation, his collection taken as a reflection of personal taste,

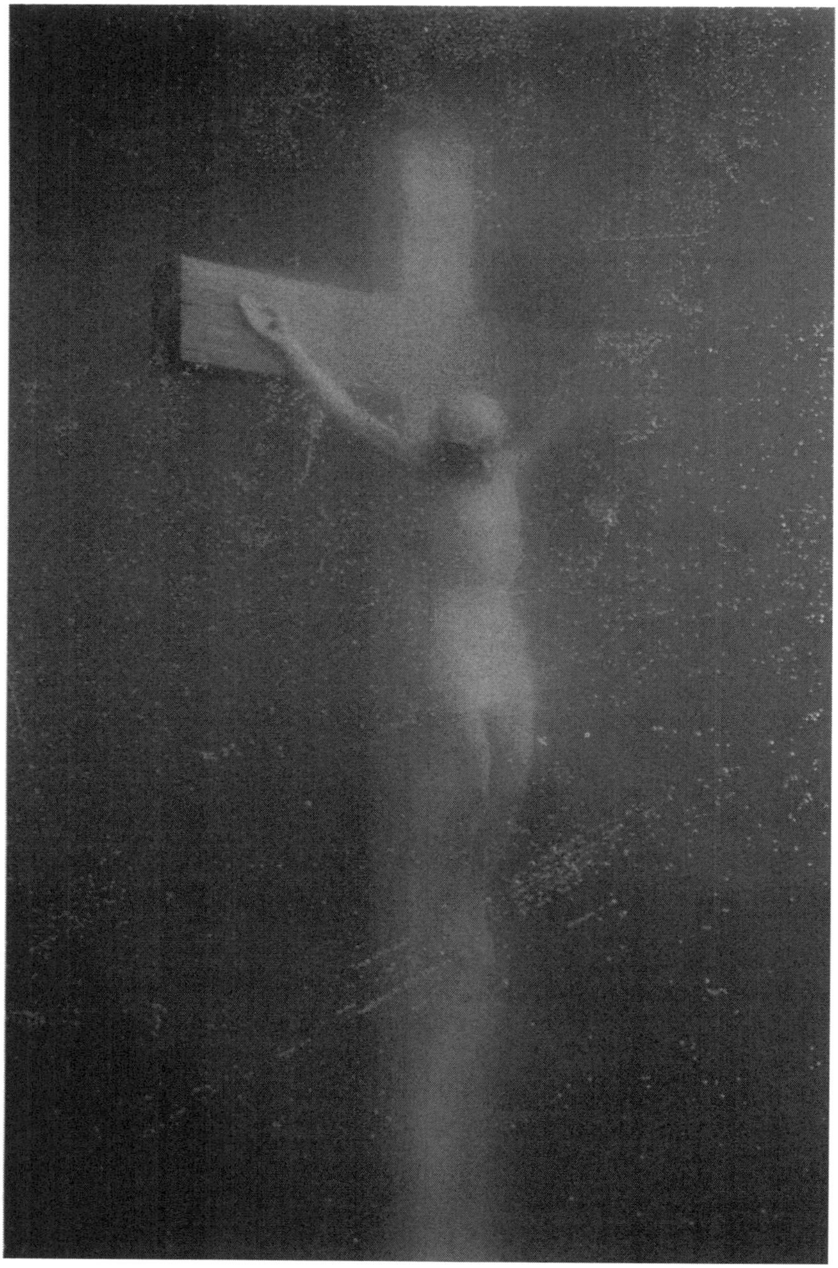

Figure 1. Andres Serrano, *Piss Christ*, 1987. Cibachrome, silicone, Plexiglas, wood frame. 60 × 40 in. (65 × 45 1/8 × 3/4 in., framed). *Courtesy Paula Cooper Gallery, New York.*

his financial support as generosity making possible the showing of what he loved. But such motivations were difficult to apply to a collector who seemed also to be a speculator in the art market, who was not merely feeding an appetite for art but investing in artists, and who in some cases liquidated his portfolio with devastating effects on the careers of the artists involved.[6]

Like the artist and his backer, the institution responsible for bringing controversial art to the public was not engaged in a political crusade or even an aesthetic one. The Brooklyn Museum was honorably candid in articulating its own motivations—which were, above all, material: to increase the museum's visibility, attendance, and membership. "We want to establish the BMA," Director Lehman wrote, "as a primary art destination for every tourist and every resident in New York City, reflecting the ethnic, racial, national, religious, economic, and lifestyle diversity of our population. . . . As part of our mission 'to serve the public as a dynamic and rewarding destination for personal connection to the past, present and future through art,' we must compete for new, expanded, and more diverse audiences. We must reinvent what we offer to our public in order to make the BMA more intellectually accessible to all audiences."[7] While Lehman went on to claim that the *Sensation* show was meant to speak "to the topical sociocultural issues, expressed through art, that drive our daily lives," his phrasing made clear that these issues were raised as a means to a marketing end, not as an end in themselves. In earlier controversies, self-described "activists for public art and community"[8] such as Cincinnati's Contemporary Arts Center Director Dennis Barrie might have understood "diversity" as a goal, something to be brought to the consciousness of audiences through the art of a Mapplethorpe. For the Brooklyn Museum, in contrast, diversity was a demographic feature of the audience it sought to reach.

A similar shift occurred in the way conservative opponents of immoral art understood their task. Rather than framing their objections as concerns about "family values," as Protestant fundamentalists such as the Reverend Donald Wildmon and the Christian Coalition had done in the early 1990s, Catholics, spurred by William Donohue, president of the Catholic League, attacked Ofili's painting as an affront to their religion. Speaking as a defender of the faith rather than a religious zealot, Donohue could claim to be the protector of the interests of Catholics, interests much more narrowly defined but also as a consequence more easily translatable into political action. Because he represented an institutionally unified constituency, rather than a coalition, Donohue had the ear of elected officials in a direct way that Wildmon and other fundamentalist firebrands simply did not, and he used this direct access to bring straight to the mayor his group's views of *Sensation,* views the mayor promptly acted on.[9]

The mayor's action itself reflected the general shift from ideology to interest that distinguished the Brooklyn Museum controversy from previous ones. When Cincinnati officials were driven to act against the Mapplethorpe exhibition, they attempted to make offensiveness a criminal offense; when Congress took its turn in 1989, it tried to force grantees to swear that they would not be obscene on government time; and when black aldermen in Chicago objected to a depiction of revered Mayor Harold Washington in drag, they stormed the School of the Art Institute to "arrest" the painting. Mayor Giuliani's actions were more prudent and calculated: temporary impoundment of operating funds, along with threats to withdraw funding and evict the museum from city-owned land. As a former prosecutor, Giuliani surely knew that the courts were highly unlikely to allow him to punish the museum in this way, but as a savvy politician he just as surely knew that making such threats was an effective political gesture.

For all these various stakeholders, then, an arts controversy that in an earlier incarnation might have been driven by passions (moral, aesthetic, political) was reduced, as it were, to a more rationalized conflict of interests and interest groups. Thanks to this rationalization, policy experts can more easily model how interests take shape, interrelate, converge, or balance each other. It is easier as well to chart the possible ways in which controversies can play out, and to help policymakers understand what can and cannot be done to control the outcome.

As matters have become clearer, however, the complexity of policy issues in arts controversies has become more, not less, evident. The First Amendment issues discussed in Part II of this volume, for example, appear less stark, and more technical, than had previously been assumed. It is now clear that government can control artistic speech not merely by defunding or protecting offensive speech *tout court* but by exercising a range of options. As Cass Sunstein shows, government can do more than just censor or pull funding to penalize art it doesn't like. It may seek to control art by regulating the subjects art may treat, the viewpoints of a subject artists may offer, or even the form or genre that artists may work in, with each of these efforts more or less likely to stand up to constitutional scrutiny. Government may also simply decline to fund at all if public opinion does not support arts funding. This last prospect makes most First Amendment victories hollow ones, according to David Strauss. Politicians may choose to lose in court in order to erode long-term public support for the arts. But the most radical option open to government may be the one that Stephen Presser suggests and that Mark

Schuster argues is already on the horizon: redefining the relationship between government and grantees as a partnership, with all the accountability such arrangements impose on recipients of funding. Since this is more and more the reality in practice, at least with regard to museums, holding the line against further encroachment of such mechanisms of arts funding may be the next mission of free speech advocates.

If the arts-funding system is evolving in ways that will fundamentally change the terrain on which First Amendment questions will be engaged, the public served by the arts is evolving as well, with a resulting change in the terrain on which questions are engaged about how museums should manage controversy. Even without the government looking over their shoulders, museums have always pursued exhibition and education policies meant to affirm standards—of excellence, beauty, taste, decency, or representativeness—shared by the public. But the notion of a unified public itself, always a myth, has over the past several decades given way to a more nuanced recognition that America contains multitudes of cultural communities, each with its own distinctive mores, sense of impropriety, and demand for respect.

In the first phase of this evolution, museums found themselves between a rock and a hard place. For those privileged communities whose standards had previously stood unchallenged as public ones, efforts by museums to respond to other sensitivities were seen as abandonments of all standards whatsoever. Already in the 1960s, critics like Hilton Kramer and John Canaday complained bitterly that the Metropolitan Museum of Art's groundbreaking *Harlem on My Mind* exhibition represented a "politicizing" of the museum.[10] Versions of this argument would reemerge more virulently in the late 1980s with the declaration of cultural war by conservatives, who seemed willing to destroy museums in order to save them from going over to the cultural enemy. Yet even as they were being charged with offending the dominant culture, museums also were charged with offending the emergent groups they were trying to serve. The *Harlem* show, for instance, earned criticism from within the African American community for giving an outsider's view of black culture. Even an institution as progressive as the School of the Art Institute of Chicago found itself accused of racist insensitivity in the 1988 fracas over the Harold Washington painting.

Reflecting on that controversy shortly afterward, Carol Becker decried the absence of "built-in avenues of trust and negotiation between the Art Institute and the community, which could have been employed to de-escalate the event."[11] Since then, building such avenues has become easier. As the new century begins, cultural pluralism has become a more or less settled phenomenon, and communities themselves have become more organized, coherent, and adept at representing their interests. Thanks to surveys like the one conducted by David Halle, summarized in this volume, even the tastes of hybrid demographic groups are beginning to be mapped, with surprising and potentially useful findings. (Who knew Asians would like *Sensation* less than Caucasians, or that Republicans are just as opposed to the government's banning art in public museums as are Democrats?) Unfortunately, museums and museum associations have not yet made use of such policy tools to develop carefully thought-through guidelines about how negotiations with communities should be framed or about how community perspectives should be incorporated into a museum's institutional structure. As first steps in this direction, Teri Edelstein urges museums to more fully diversify not just their offerings but their own policymaking bodies, including trustees, and David Ross recommends proactive measures to educate boards, communities, and the media about museum activities in general.

W.J.T. Mitchell cautions us, however, that such measures can go only so far, given the nonverbal nature of images. Because pictures don't directly say anything, yet seem to be saying *something*, spectators are driven to project statements onto them. At the very least, then, museums need to think carefully about the psychological mechanisms motivating outrage at controversial art, if only to gauge the power of the forces with which they are grappling.

But even if museums could avoid or de-escalate controversies, doing so might be bad policy. Indeed, in a democracy, one might argue, the aim of publicly funded art should be to generate dissent purposefully, to bring the moment to its crisis, to redirect or bring to the surface issues in need of escalation. As Mitchell puts it, "Demonstrations in front of museums are a sign of a healthy state of affairs, not a regrettable anomaly that should be averted by fine-tuned policies." It is not clear whether museum policies could be devised to go even further in order to deliberately incite (rather than avert) a reaction they control and to channel its energy toward productive dialogue. What is clear is that absent careful crisis-management thinking before the fact about the array of interests and sensibilities within the public, the very communities that should be drawn into discussion will either reject it altogether or enter it enraged.

No crisis-management plan to defend First Amendment rights or sooth offended sensibilities, however, could have prepared the Brooklyn Museum for the unanticipated assaults on its funding arrangements for *Sensation*. With a front-page exposé in the *New York Times* darkly reporting that, "far more than has been previously disclosed, the '*Sensation*' exhibition . . . has been financed by companies and individuals with a direct commercial interest in the works of the British artists in the show," a new front had been opened in the culture wars.[12] At issue were not conflicts of taste or rights, but conflicts of interest. For those upset by the revelations about the museum's quid pro quo deals with donors, what was really at stake in Brooklyn was divorced from any question about the morality or immorality symbolized in the art or even about the aesthetic quality of the art itself; at stake was what James Cuno calls "the principle of disinterested inquiry" guiding the museum, which Cuno more or less equates with the interests of the public. One might share the museum's taste or agenda, then, while decrying its interestedness. As details about the financing and commercial tie-ins for the exhibition leaked out, the museum began to look, Cuno writes, like "a 'hired hand' for private interests if not an 'interested party' itself."

Where conflict of interest is an issue, as all lawyers know, the appearance of conflict of interest also will surface as a problem. Hence it was unsurprising that the charges in the press against the museum included not only selling out to commercial interests but also deception, covering up the truth about the extent and nature of its dealings with misinformation and disinformation. As András Szántó points out, the best way to counter such charges is to adopt a policy of full disclosure. Even if Brooklyn had welcomed journalists into its boardrooms, of course, the increasing pressures of twenty-four-hour news cycles, pack journalism, ignorance about the arts, and the crushing need to keep "on story" might still have driven coverage. But in the absence of such a policy, Szántó shows, journalists are free to indulge in the worst tendencies of their profession, substituting outrage for analysis, a quick verdict for research into "what kind of lending practices are customary in arranging museum shows, what sort of individuals foot the bill, how curators work with private patrons in mounting exhibitions, and how museum shows influence the art market."

Not that such research would necessarily reveal a scandal-free picture, or even a clear one. As Gilbert Edelson of the Art Dealers Association of America reveals, in a paper that left even some art-world professionals at the conference stunned, museums have shown important artworks even though collectors were offering them for sale at the time of the exhibition; museums have taken commissions on sales of works they exhibit; and some museums have directly sold not just the original craftworks and prints commissioned for their gift shops but artworks from their walls. What's more, such practices may be perfectly justifiable under certain conditions. Edelson's lesson is that a one-size-fits-all policy toward the market is probably a bad idea.

As the essays in this volume make clear, however, thanks to the interests so baldly revealed in the Brooklyn Museum controversy, museums can go beyond ad hoc, case-by-case reasoning not only about their commercial dealings but also about their dealings with the public and the state. The more transparent the interests, the easier it will be to formulate sensible policies regarding the rights, responsibilities, and reputation of American museums.

NOTES

1. The phrase "chilling inexorableness" is Caryn James's, in "Recalling the Obscenity Case at the Start of It All," *New York Times*, May 26, 2000, p. B26.
2. For a brilliant exposition of this thesis, see Lewis Hyde, "The Children of John Adams: A Historical View of the Fight over Arts Funding," in Brian Wallis, Marianne Weems, and Philip Yenawine, eds., *Art Matters: How the Culture Wars Changed America* (New York: New York University Press, 1999), 252–275.
3. Actually, in this particular case, one could argue that before the farce of the Ofili case and before the tragedies of the early 1990s, there was an earlier historical moment—at the very origin of publicly funded avant-garde art—when arts controversy over an offensive Madonna took the form of romance:

   > In the summer of 1932, Village authorities set up an open-air market on Washington Square. The outdoor show was the first of the annual Greenwich Village Art Festivals, but at the time the more modest intention of the founders was to assist some of the fourteen hundred unemployed artists in New York City to show their works. Some 275 artists enrolled for the exhibition, among them Alice [Neel]. [Joseph] Solman's gouaches hung less than ten feet away from Alice's exhibit, and as he studied her paintings of the Well Baby Clinic and the Ninth Avenue El, the elevated train, he admired the talent.
   >
   > The young girl with the "dairy maid appearance" attracted him in unexpected ways. He watched, fascinated, as the local and irate Catholic priest demanded that she take down her portrait of Nadya, with hanging breasts and a baby on her lap, which Alice had provocatively entitled "Degenerate Madonna." He knew few people were bold enough to hang that painting with that taunting title, but especially not this seemingly shy, harmless-looking young woman.

   Gerald L. Belcher and Margaret L. Belcher, *Collecting Souls, Gathering Dust: The Struggle of Two American Artists, Alice Neel and Rhodary Medary* (New York: Paragon House, 1991), 160.

   Before tragedy, romance.
4. Lewis Lapham, "Performance Art," *Harper's*, December 1999, 12. That the mayor had not actually seen the painting he disliked so much did not prevent the director of the Metropolitan Museum from praising him for having "shown astute critical acumen. . . . I find no fault with the Mayor's aesthetic sensibilities, only with his effort at censorship." Philippe de Montebello, "Making a Cause out of Bad Art," *New York Times*, October 5, 1999, p. A25.
5. Richard Bolton, ed., *Culture Wars: Documents from the Recent Controversies in the Arts* (New York: New Press, 1992); Wallis, Weems, and Yenawine, *Art Matters*.
6. Saatchi has been criticized for buying and later selling in bulk works by artists such as Sandro Chia and thus adversely affecting the artists' reputations. See Richard W. Walker, "The Saatchi Factor. Is He the Ultimate Advertisement for the Latest Artist or Trend?" *ArtNews* 86 (January 1987), 117–121.

7. Arnold L. Lehman, a letter to museum supporters on *Sensation,* December 14, 1999, http://www.brooklynart.org.
8. Quoted in Erika Doss, *Spirit Poles and Flying Pigs: Public Art and Cultural Democracy in American Communities* (Washington, D.C.: Smithsonian Institution Press, 1995), 203.
9. Obviously, the Christian right in the late 1980s and early 1990s wielded considerable political power. But, as Smith has shown, that power was exercised in concert with an array of think tanks that did the ideological work necessary to find the one salient work of art out of one hundred thousand funded by the National Endowment for the Arts and to transform that finding into soundbite-sized bombshells for Republican senators. James Allen Smith, *The Idea Brokers: Think Tanks and the Rise of the New Policy Elite* (New York: Free Press, 1991).
10. Quoted in the Introduction to Allon Schoener, ed., *Harlem on My Mind: Cultural Capital of Black America, 1900–1968* (New York: New Press, 1995), n.p.
11. Carol Becker, "Private Fantasies Shape Public Events: And Public Events Invade and Shape Our Dreams," in *Art and the Public Interest, edited with an introduction by Arlene Raven (Ann Arbor, Mich.: UMI Research Press, 1989),* 251.
12. David Barstow, "Brooklyn Museum Recruited Donors Who Stood to Gain," *New York Times*, October 31, 1999, p. A1; David Barstow, "Artistic Differences: A Special Report; Art, Money and Control: Elements of an Exhibition," *New York Times*, December 6, 1999.

PART
I

Mapping the Minefield

CAROL BECKER

The Brooklyn Controversy

A View from the Bridge

Dennis Heiner, a dapper, seventy-two-year-old devout Catholic, feigning illness, leaned against a wall in the Brooklyn Museum near the much-maligned Chris Ofili painting, *The Holy Virgin Mary.* He waited for the guard to look away, took out a plastic bottle, then slipped behind the protective shield, and, with shaking hands, squeezed and spread white paint over the face and body of the image of Ofili's black Madonna (figure 2). When the police asked why had he done this, Mr. Heiner responded softly, "It was blasphemous." With this enactment Ofili's work entered a historical body of defaced art—from works vandalized during the French Revolution to Michelangelo's *Pietà,* Andres Serrano's *Piss Christ,* and David Nelson's infamous portrait of the late Mayor Harold Washington, *Mirth and Girth.* Heiner was charged with a Class D felony for "mischief making, possessing instruments of graffiti, and graffiti."

Let's begin with the Brooklyn Museum, about which *New York Times* art critic Michael Kimmelman wrote: "Playing on the implications of cultural elitism, the Mayor of New York, Rudolph Giuliani has in fact threatened one of the least elitist of New York cultural institutions." While I was growing up in Brooklyn, the Brooklyn Museum was the beloved museum of my working-class neighborhood. It was always "our" museum. Through such recent comments as "That's my museum. Take your hands off it," spoken by Brooklyn residents, we see that it is still "our" museum to the people of Brooklyn. This is enviable loyalty to a museum

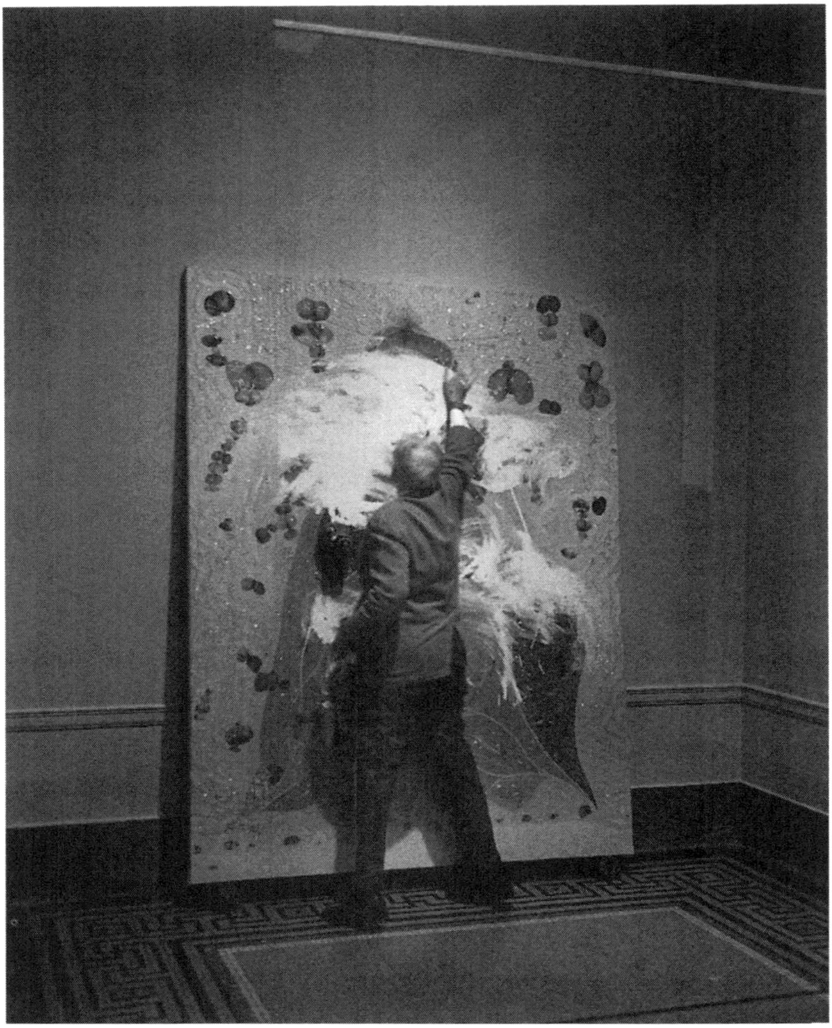

Figure 2. Dennis Heiner defacing Chris Ofili's *The Holy Virgin Mary*, 1999. *P. J. Griffiths / Magnum Photos.*

that probably serves the most ethnically and racially diverse population of any major museum. And it has done so since 1823. What was Museum Director Arnold Lehman thinking when he committed his institution to *Sensation*—a show that other museums in the United States had refused and for which he could find no institutional partners? Whom was he attempting to please, and what audience was he hoping to attract?

Lehman knew the history of the show's reception at the Royal Academy of London—its controversies and its vandalisms, particularly in response to Marcus Harvey's rendering of the face of Myra Hindley, the notorious child murderer, in what appears to be small children's handprints. That painting was splattered with ink and eggs in London. But he was also aware of the show's record-breaking attendance. Certainly he was hoping to draw similar, large crowds and also to attract a new audience—younger, more hip, first-time museumgoers from Sheepshead Bay, Canarsie, Bensonhurst, and East Flatbush. Perhaps he also thought that this show could entice those from Manhattan to cross the famous bridge that separates the boroughs and the classes and could pull art lovers a little farther than the Brooklyn Academy of Music. Wanting to position the museum as a player in the contemporary art conversation, he was also appealing to his own new constituency—the hundreds of young artists displaced by Manhattan's high-cost real estate and the numerous not-so-young artists and professionals who are increasingly making Brooklyn their home. He was probably hoping this show was dynamic enough to do all this, and he was right—much to the surprise of the more jaded art-world establishment.

Did Lehman go too far? Did he compromise his institution and overly sensationalize *Sensation*? The preshow publicity and the signage at the show warned that the exhibition "may cause shock, vomiting, confusion, panic, euphoria, and anxiety." The show was presented as if it were some drug with possible side effects or an amusement park ride to be entered at one's own risk. But the only one who suffered all these symptoms was probably Lehman himself. The day I was there no one fainted; in fact, everyone seemed to be having a great time.

There were the well-documented, endless compromises with collector Charles Saatchi: How much money would he give and under what conditions? How should the show be hung? How big and how close would the shield be to protect Ofili's *Virgin*? And what about David Bowie's contributions and Christie's expectations about deacquisition prospects, future sales? Everyone, it seemed, would make a profit from this venture. And, of course, in the end, perhaps the worst of it all was Lehman's unfortunate misrepresentations—actually lying about Saatchi's financial involvement—which probably proved the most damning to his reputation in the art world and most threatened his colleagues' willingness to support him in the future.

But I do not think Lehman should be on trial here, or Ofili, or even Giuliani. What does seem central to this discussion is what these events tell us about the desperate financial situation of many museums in the United States and society's unwillingness to adequately fund the making and showing of art. Also at issue is society's addiction to entertainment. So deluged is the public with images, so overstimulated by the media, that museums now position art as entertainment. Certainly Lehman is not the first. Without some dramatic hook—motorcycles, blockbuster favorites, old-master must-sees, or artists who make death masks out of their own blood—it is increasingly difficult for museums to bring in the crowds they need to generate the revenue the shows demand. And these practices are not just intended to attract younger audiences.

Also in question is how and by whom artwork is contextualized. Who has the power? Once Giuliani targeted the image of Ofili's *Virgin* and misrepresented it as irreverent, as blasphemously splattered with dung, there was no turning back. He seized control, set the terms in the public arena, and constructed the painting's meaning from his own ignorance. Everyone then had to scramble to recontextualize, redefine, redescribe, and reinscribe it with the meaning the artist had intended. The polarizations were in place: either one expressed reverence for the image of the Virgin and then acted appropriately outraged by Ofili's interpretation as presented by Giuliani, or one was willing to contemplate the artist's intent and risk being labeled as elitist and blasphemous. These reactions shocked Ofili, who had no power in this public situation. From there it was only a few steps to this question: Does anyone have the right to imagine such an image, or to show it in a public institution? And if it is shown, is it any wonder someone felt obliged to deface it? These issues battled themselves out in the public sphere, interpreted on one side by a sensationalizing press—the *New York Post*—and on the other by a newspaper that, in this instance, was remarkably determined to educate its readers about the history of art, religion, transgression, and bodily fluids—the *New York Times*.

Surprisingly, there was little discussion about the actual image of a black Virgin: spotted with small cutouts from pornographic magazines and with carefully placed, lacquered dung, perhaps a representation of the Virgin as sacred and profane, capable of manifesting herself as white, black, and brown. There was little speculation about whether the race of the Madonna provoked Giuliani, perhaps even more than the elephant dung. Nor was there much discussion of the color of paint finally thrown at Ofili's *Virgin* to cover her up, to make her pure, to make her white. Why was the issue of her race avoided?

Most good artists, and there were several in the *Sensation* show, do not set out to shock. They might attempt to challenge or provoke, but this is out of their own need to reflect on and give shape to their interpretation of the world. If they interpret an iconic image in a radically new way, is this not one function art should serve? If they challenge our assumptions about art, why do we not welcome this challenge and the dialogue that surrounds it?

Few New Yorkers were deceived by Giuliani's theatrics. Among the exhibition's attendees, 85 percent polled simply wanted to be left alone to formulate their own response to the art, as was witnessed by the show's large attendance. Most saw Giuliani's actions for what they were—a political move to control, to polarize, to seduce, to appeal to a certain conservative constituency. And for the most part such strategies left New Yorkers cold.

In New York, the so-called art and culture capital of the world, the art community proved to be a great disappointment, unable to effectively mobilize itself in response. After all the previous incidents of this kind, what had the art world learned? Apparently not much. When it finally did react, it could only present the argument of freedom of expression without truly articulating the right and necessity of a democratic society to support the work of artists whose interpretations of the world allow us to evolve visually and intellectually.

Why did it take so long for New York museum directors to respond? Was it because they didn't much care? Because it wasn't their museum? Because they too are dependent on New York funds and therefore afraid of Giuliani and the potential for retaliation? Because they were in shock that something so banal could occur in New York—a city that prides itself on its sophistication, savvy, and inability to be shocked? Because they are implicated in and therefore uncomfortable with the ambiguous role of donors, patrons, and issues of conflict of interest? Were they like Philippe de Montebello, adverse to defending this show and self-righteous in dissociating himself from it and from Brooklyn's exhibition practices, as he made so clear in his egregious op-ed piece in the *New York Times*? Perhaps they moved slowly because it was the *Brooklyn* Museum, somewhere "over there," in a borough only a few New York art museum directors ever choose to visit?

At the core of the cynicism around this event is the fact that a general audience does not understand the inner workings of the art world—the world of patronage, of the buying and selling of art. Art, most people believe, is committed to higher values and therefore antithetical to commerce; it is independent and should stand above the capitalist quagmire. But, alas, little can. In this instance the veil was ripped away, as art came dangerously close to being marketed as entertainment and associating itself with the worst of mercenary attributes—greed. Long articles took delight in exposing the relationship between the show and those who might have reaped financial gains from its success. But it must be said that many exhibitions in other museums are compromised in similar ways—if not to such an extent then to some extent: a catalogue paid for by the artists' dealer or by one of his or her collectors; a contribution by the dealer directly to the bottom line of the exhibition; board members who collect artists shown in their museum. Or consider Dior, Faberge, and Cartier, all of whom have been involved in supporting major shows focused on the history of their designs at the Metropolitan Museum of Art, shows that enhance their name and the value of their products. Lots of people are making money on art, but it is usually not the artists. All of this is common practice. The *Sensation* fiasco was more extreme, more overt, more crass, involving the likes of Saatchi and even a rock star David Bowie. And of course it was Brooklyn, already a bit déclassé. Would Giuliani have dared to assert himself as he did had it been the Metropolitan Museum of Art, whose board includes powerful members of his own party? The Brooklyn Museum was abandoned by its colleagues, left to stand alone and explain itself as if it were unique in engaging in such practices and not perhaps just a bit more hungry and more desperate.

A general audience in the United States also does not necessarily understand the role of art in society or the role of the avant-garde—its mandate to raise complex issues and express divergent points of view. Nor do most people think about why we need and want art to do this for us. And we in the art world have not done a good job of educating them or ourselves about such issues. But it would be interesting, just once, to have to defend work which does not focus on religious or sexual taboos but rather on ideological taboos like capitalism, race, class. Such work is not as easily targeted, not since 1934, when Nelson Rockefeller had Diego Rivera's mural *Man at the Crossroads* painted over and then destroyed in Rockefeller Center. Work which takes on more secular, societal issues, although arguably more directly challenging to the fundamentals of capitalism, is harder to sensationalize and exploit in a sixty-second soundbite.

What is fascinating about the Brooklyn Museum controversy is that it created a cathexis of issues begging to be unraveled: the relationship of art to society, issues of freedom of expression, the use of taxpayers' dollars, the ways in which difference is addressed in a democracy. Do the freedoms guaranteed exist only for those whose representations of reality match our own or align with those of people in power? What is the purpose of art in a democratic society?

There is much to be said about a situation in which a seventy-two-year-old devout Catholic inadvertently becomes a graffiti activist. But the complexity of such events often results in such absurd moments—like the Chicago alderman's attempt to burn Nelson's infamous portrait of Mayor Harold Washington in women's underwear on the front lawn of the School of the Art Institute of Chicago. The alderman's aggressions led the police to "arrest" the painting, for its own good. Heated human passions and the laws we have put in place to contain them often bump up against each other in the public arena. When they do, public intellectuals need to come forward to discuss how art becomes a magnet for the issues and politics of its times and how even democratic societies expose their fear of the human imagination when they act out the desire to repress and punish it simply because some feel it has gone too far.

RICHARD A. EPSTEIN

The Marriage of Art and Business

I had originally thought that the function of this essay was simply to welcome the reader. But we have already been treated to Carol Becker's rare and extraordinary rapid-fire critique of everything that has gone on in the art world. So complete was her introduction that it might, if we think deeply about it, render the rest of the volume superfluous. Carol and I have crossed swords on these issues already on public radio, courtesy of Gretchen Helfrich and Odyssey, and with the participation of Homi Bhabha, another contributor to this volume. Although I would always speak about the virtues of a market economy, Carol exhibits a certain pointedness about the defects of the capitalist system. Nevertheless, it is always wonderful to observe that the choice of terms used to describe various kinds of institutions gives some sense of the attitudes that the speaker has toward them.

With that disclaimer in place, I will now attempt to set up in a convivial style some of the issues that are raised in the following pages. My mission is to relax the reader for the essays that follow. So, as I was ruminating about this topic, I asked myself what comparison would help advance the understanding of the structural problem. And I decided, in effect, to take a page from one of my favorite justices of the U.S. Supreme Court, before he became a member of the Supreme Court, when he sat on the New York State Court of Appeals. That justice was Rufus Peckham, who is remembered (and reviled by many) for writing in 1905 the opinion that struck down New York's maximum (ten) daily hours of work for bakers in *Lochner v. New York*. But, in his earlier incarnation, Peckham was struggling with a complicated matrimonial dispute, and, as I recall, in the course of his opinion, he declared that, "whenever we approach marriage, we have to remember that it has both its sentimental and its business side." And what we as lawyers and ordinary citizens have to do is to figure out how these two impulses may be properly reconciled.

In dealing with marriage, there is a familiar lecture that all divorce lawyers like to deliver to married couples or to people in general. I am now going to give that advice free of charge. When you start thinking about marriage the first time through, your natural tendency is to dwell on its romantic and sentimental side and to ignore the grubby business infrastructure that must be created to keep the relationship going. When some event occurs that is adverse to your original desires, you find yourself entangled with the business end, aware that you have insufficiently planned for the dispute. So one of the great obstacles to either divorce or reconciliation is the want of an explicit understanding of each party's rights and duties. The source of the problem is your initial consensus that love and sentiment could carry you over the rough spots. Yet when the relationship falls apart, its legacy is a classic business dispute. Now the second time people get married, given the tribulations of the first go-round, they often think in more pragmatic terms, and they plan a prenuptial, or antenuptial, agreement to place the business arrangements on a sound footing. Warm sentiments can then flourish after marriage because both parties know that if a shipwreck does occur, a sound plan is in place that allows them to extricate themselves with fewer difficulties than before.

It is with this outlook, I think, that we should approach the relationships between another sentimental field—art—and its peculiar business infrastructure. Most people will not have purchased this volume in order to read lawyers' views on the complexities of unconstitutional conditions or the conflicts of interest that exist between members of a board of directors and the permanent curatorial staff. Instead, what most often draws people to this topic in general and to the Brooklyn Museum controversy in particular is the art itself. The freshness, the freeness, the creativity of the spirit, the imagination, the ability to put images together in unsuspected ways captivate all of us. When things go well, of course, the tendency is to neglect the grubby infrastructure that maintains the engines that power artistic development. But an art museum is sort of like a duck: above the water it looks wonderful, carefree, and gracious; yet below the water it has to paddle furiously to maintain its serenity above the waves. Or art institutions are like an automobile, with its stylish exterior and its piston engine under the hood.

Unfortunately, when I went to graduate school, I opted for the duck's paddles and the piston engine. So I'm the lowly lawyer who could not, and still cannot, put together a string of glorious adjectives to describe a work of art in the way Carol Becker and others are able to. It's hard enough for me to remember the primary colors. Art is just not my business. But then, of course, when the shipwreck comes, matters change. I remember the most important commercial in the history of advertisement, the one for Fram filters. The car mechanic holds his can of Fram and says, "You can pay me now or you can pay me later." His message is that investing in a car before a breakdown is a lot cheaper than repairing it afterward. Like many lawyers, I make a living by being paid later, when a transaction or institution blows up in your face. And that, in a word, is what happened with the Brooklyn Museum and the *Sensation* exhibition.

So the questions that we have to face in the wake of the Brooklyn controversy only start with understanding how to disinter the difficulties associated with the *Sensation* exhibition, and these are of course difficult enough in their own right. In addition, however, we must learn to abstract ourselves from the diversions and from the personalities of so conspicuous an event. The larger question that we have to broach, reluctantly perhaps but necessarily nonetheless, is what kind of institutional structures we can create to preserve the freedom of art while allowing this creative work to continue on a sound, sustainable basis. In this regard, the relationship between art and business is not all that different in kind from the relationships that a university has to its business infrastructure. Similar tensions are found in both arenas. How these should be resolved I cannot say with certainty. But I will at least outline some of the reasons why the dilemma is so difficult.

I think the simplest way in which to analyze the situation is to reveal as a lawyer my enormous preference for what I like to call the clean deal. The clean deal says that if you are going to buy something, then you are going to buy it outright, no strings attached. If you are going to sell something, then don't put a restrictive covenant or clause in the contract of sale. Essentially, the preference is to create transactions in which the legal relations between parties are relatively transparent, so that when disputes arise, the boundaries between individuals will be sharp enough to allow them to go their separate ways. Unfortunately, in business, sometimes if you have only clean deals, you're broke, which is a state of affairs to be avoided. So the problem that faces every kind of public institution, whether it be a university or an art museum, is how to use money donated by people who have narrow agendas so that the institution can continue to achieve its public agenda. More concretely, every institution must decide what kind of strings it can accept on gifts so that it can continue with its independent mission while simultaneously receiving external financial support. In a world in which unrestricted gifts are rare, it is all a matter of compromise, adjustments, and pragmatics of one kind or another. Judgment matters, and it is hard to preserve, especially in the face of temptation.

This volume is not about art as such. It is about how we can answer this question from multiple perspectives. Some contributors, the lawyers, will say that when strings are attached by the government, it may well be that the First Amendment will intrude and limit the way in which the government can pull the strings that possesses under some contract or lease. The government may think that it has a marionette on the opposite end of those strings, but it is a marionette whose strings can be pulled only in certain prescribed ways. But there are two sides of this relationship, and other contributors will describe what it is to be a marionette on the other end of those strings. They will report that they do not enjoy marionette status when the strings are manipulated by people who are ignorant of the profession that they practice. And others of a more academic persuasion will tell how difficult it is to design a marionette that works well for all people on both sides of the strings. And so it is that we are in the fortunate position to have assembled an able cast of authors to reflect on the interactions between art produced at the highest level and the grubby engines of law and business that are necessary to drive it. I believe that in this volume we will learn how difficult it is to structure sound professional, social, and legal relationships even when people with divergent desires act in the best of faith. And of course we must reserve an appropriate degree of umbrage for those who might in bad faith seek to upset whatever delicate balance we can create for the artistic institutions of the United States. With that warning in place, I should like to welcome the reader to what promises to be a stimulating volume on some of the major challenges facing the artistic community.

PART II

Art and the First Amendment

GEOFFREY R. STONE

The Questions of Free Speech

The text of the First Amendment provides in relevant part: "Congress shall make no law abridging the freedom of speech." The first thing you will notice about this text is that the First Amendment applies to the Congress. It says nothing at all about the City of New York. So, you might wonder, how do we get from this text to the Brooklyn Museum of Art controversy, which of course involves not Congress but New York City?

There is a long answer to this question and a short answer. In this context, we will have to settle for the short answer, which is this: Through a complex process of both further constitutional amendment—that is, amendments after the enactment of the First Amendment—and the gloss of judicial interpretation, "Congress" has come to mean "government." For purposes of this discussion, you will just have to trust me on this, and take it as a given.

Thus, we can now restate the text as follows: "Government shall make no law abridging the freedom of speech." Government in this context includes all branches, agencies, and officers of the federal, state, and local governments. It includes not only Congress, but the president, the State of Illinois, the City of New York, the University of Vermont, and police officers in Dubuque.

Note, however, that although this definition includes all branches, agencies, and officers of government at every level, it does not include any institution or individual who is not the "government." Thus, although the University of Illinois can violate the First Amendment, the University of Chicago—a private institution—cannot. Thus, the rights guaranteed by the First Amendment, like the rights guaranteed by the Constitution generally, limit the actions of government but not the actions of private institutions or individuals. I cannot violate the First Amendment, try as hard as I might.

So, the First Amendment effectively provides that "government shall make no law abridging the freedom of speech." Now, as has often been said, this sounds pretty absolute. The amendment doesn't say that government shall make no law "unreasonably" abridging the freedom of speech but that government shall make no law abridging the freedom of speech—period. There are no if's, and's, or but's about it.

That should make life—and the law—simple. For the City of New York to withdraw funds from the Brooklyn Museum of Art because it disapproves of the museum's exhibitions obviously "abridges"—that is, lessens—the museum's freedom of speech, so we can now bring this discussion to an end.

Of course, nothing is that simple. Indeed, this was precisely the point of Justice Oliver Wendell Holmes's famous hypothetical about a man falsely crying fire in a crowded theater. Surely, he argued, the First Amendment can't protect that, nor could it logically give George W. Bush or Al Gore the right to break into my home at two o'clock in the morning to rail at me with a bullhorn about why I should support him for president. The amendment, in other words, can't quite mean what it appears to say. Something is amiss.

The problem is this: What, exactly, is this thing called "the freedom of speech" that may not be "abridged"? Does "the freedom of speech" mean the right to say anything I want at any time in any manner in any place without limitation, or is it a term of art that must be defined? As Justice Holmes's hypothetical suggests, definition is necessary, and that's where it starts to get hard.

Does the "freedom of speech" include the right falsely to cry fire in a crowded theater? The right to threaten a judge? To bribe a voter? To advertise toothpaste? To exhibit billboards with sexually explicit images? To contribute unlimited amounts of money to a political candidate? To burn a flag? To burn someone else's flag? To distribute leaflets? To drop leaflets from a helicopter? To disclose government secrets? And so on.

We know that the government may not abridge the "freedom of speech," but it is far from obvious what "the freedom of speech" is. Of course, we won't answer that question in the essays that follow, but we will touch on at least one facet of the question—specifically, to what extent, if any, does the First Amendment protect not only political expression but artistic expression as well?

Then there's the question of what we mean by the word *abridge.* Suppose we agree that the First Amendment protects the right to exhibit art, in the sense that the government cannot constitutionally make it a crime to exhibit art. But even if the government would "abridge" the freedom of speech by attempting to criminalize art, does it necessarily follow that the government would also abridge the freedom of speech by refusing to subsidize art?

The First Amendment may prohibit the government from banning the distribution of leaflets, but does that mean the government must give people money to pay for the leaflets? And if the government doesn't have to subsidize leaflets, why should it have to subsidize art? Put simply, does the refusal to subsidize speech "abridge" the freedom of speech? That is another question touched on in the following essays.

Finally, there's the problem of partial or unequal subsidies. Even if the government has no constitutional obligation to subsidize speech, may it decide voluntarily to subsidize some speech but not other speech? Does such a "partial" subsidy "abridge" the "freedom of speech"? For example, can the government decide voluntarily to subsidize political speech but not commercial or artistic speech? Can it subsidize only those theaters that perform Shakespeare? Can it subsidize family-oriented movies but not movies that are inappropriate for children? Can it subsidize good art but not bad art? Can it refuse to subsidize art that demeans racial minorities, insults religion, or is inappropriate for children? These, too, are questions confronted in the *Sensation* case.

CASS R. SUNSTEIN

Culture and the Constitution

A Guide for the Perplexed

The government devotes a great deal of money to the promotion of culture. With taxpayer money, the government supports artists, writers, musicians, and private institutions, including museums. But the government must be selective; it cannot support all artists or all museums all the time. With respect to culture, what are the limits on the government's power? When may the government impose criminal or civil restraints or withdraw benefits or refuse to fund?

In this essay I attempt to clarify the First Amendment issues, principally by exploiting two sets of distinctions. The first is the distinction among (1) criminal and civil remedies, (2) penalties, and (3) "mere" failures to fund. The second is the distinction among (1) viewpoint-based rules, (2) viewpoint-neutral but content-based rules, and (3) content-neutral rules. For present purposes, the first set of distinctions should be sufficiently clear. The second set of distinctions is designed to separate rules that aim at the speaker's viewpoint ("No one may receive funding whose work opposes Christian theology") from rules that aim at content but not viewpoint ("No one may receive funding unless their work deals with World War II"), and both from rules that do not turn at all on content ("No museum in New York may receive funding unless private donations are under $100,000 per year"). To get ahead of the story, and to put some qualifications and complexities to one side, the resulting set of constitutional principles looks as outlined in table 1.

This essay comes in four parts. Part I deals briefly with the simplest

Table 1 ***Constitutionality of Various Government Actions and Rules Relating to the Promotion of Culture***

	VIEWPOINT-BASED RULES	VIEWPOINT-NEUTRAL BUT CONTENT-BASED RULES	CONTENT-NEUTRAL RULES
Criminal/civil remedies	Unconstitutional	Unconstitutional	Depends on outcome of a balancing test
Penalties	Unconstitutional (probably the Brooklyn Museum case)	Probably unconstitutional	Depends on outcome of a balancing test
Mere failure to fund	Should be and probably is unconstitutional (?)	Probably constitutional (unless there is hidden-viewpoint discrimination)	Almost certainly constitutional

question, involving criminal and civil remedies imposed on art. Part II explores the topic of "penalties." Part III investigates the idea of a "mere failure to fund." Part IV is a conclusion, with some observations about First Amendment law in this context.

I. Criminal and Civil Remedies

The term *censorship* is loaded and sometimes contested, but it is usually taken to include any effort to impose criminal sanctions on speech. If the government seeks to criminalize private speech, including art, it faces an extremely heavy burden. Here the question is whether the government can fit the speech at issue within the conventional categories of regulable speech, most prominently libel, incitement ("clear and present danger"), commercial speech, and obscenity. These are emphatically narrow categories.[1] To show incitement, for example, the government must demonstrate that the speech at hand is both directed to incite and is likely to incite imminent lawless action.[2] It is hard to imagine artistic works that would be regulable under this standard. Notwithstanding the continuing controversy over whether "obscenity" should be regulable at all, it is clear that museums and artists have little to fear from the Supreme Court's understanding of the constitutional standard. It was clear, for example, that Robert Mapplethorpe's work could not lawfully be counted as obscene, and his ultimate vindication in court was no surprise to informed observers.

Though the law could have gone otherwise, what is true for criminal sanctions is equally true for civil remedies. If the government authorizes a public enforcement official to collect civil fines for objectionable speech or if it grants a right of recovery in tort to private litigants, it must meet the ordinary constitutional standards. It is exceptionally difficult to meet this burden.

There is one qualification to the discussion thus far: content-neutral restrictions on speech meet a lower standard, one that involves a degree of balancing.[3] If, for example, the government says that people may not use loudspeakers on the public streets after midnight or may not engage in protected expression on private property, there is unlikely to be a legitimate constitutional complaint. But, for the most part, this qualification is irrelevant to government control of art and museums: What would a content-neutral restriction look like in this context? We could imagine, perhaps, a performance artist who sought to defy generally applicable prohibitions on nudity in public places, and here there would be a genuine constitutional issue, with reasonable arguments both ways. But, in general, criminal and civil remedies, in this setting, are likely to be based on the content of speech, and as such those remedies are overwhelmingly likely to be unconstitutional.

II. Penalties

The discussion thus far has been straightforward; these are the simplest and most conventional First Amendment cases. Shift now to a somewhat more complicated issue, arising whenever the government attempts to eliminate "benefits" for those who have engaged in expressive activity of which the government disapproves. These are cases involving what the complaining party would like to treat as "penalties" on constitutionally protected activity.

Let us define "penalties" as the *denial of benefits that would have been conferred if not for speech to which the government objects.* In the ordinary refrain, these are penalties on the exercise of what is claimed to be a constitutional right. Consider some easy cases from other contexts. A welfare recipient speaks out against the mayor; welfare benefits are promptly withdrawn. A low-level government employee attends meetings for the Conservative Coalition; she is fired as a result. Someone with a government grant for scientific research turns out to be a member of the Socialist Party; when public officials learn about this fact, they withdraw the grant. In all these cases, the First Amendment has been violated. The government has used its power of "largesse" to punish the exercise of constitutional rights.

What does this mean in the cultural context? It means that the government cannot withdraw from a museum or artist benefits to which either would be entitled if the reason for the withdrawal is expression that is not independently punishable under the First Amendment. Suppose, for example, that the government is leasing public property to a museum, but that, in response to an exhibit to which the government has objections, the government cancels the lease or refuses to renew it (when it otherwise would). This is clearly a penalty and therefore constitutionally unacceptable. This point is largely sufficient to resolve the problems raised by Mayor Rudolph Giuliani's effort to withdraw funds from the Brooklyn Museum as a result of a controversial and perhaps offensive exhibit. The best argument on behalf of the mayor would be that he attempted a "mere" failure to fund (see below). But the facts reveal a penalty (on what would otherwise be the city's course of action), not a mere failure to fund.

A content-neutral penalty would be in a different category. Suppose, for example, that the government finds it necessary to use buildings formerly leased to museums for other purposes, such as military functions or prisons. If so, there is unlikely to be a serious First Amendment question. The best challenge would suggest that there is no good reason for the decision not to use the relevant buildings as an outlet for expression—that the shift from expressive to other purposes fails any sensible "balancing test." This would be an uphill battle for plaintiffs, but the basic analysis is straightforward: it involves an assessment of the strength and legitimacy of the government's purposes, as compared with the burden on expressive activity. This is an analysis that is likely to lead courts to validate content-neutral measures that might otherwise count as objectionable penalties.

III. Failure to Fund

When the government is simply refusing to fund, its power is at the apex. In funding artistic work, the government is inevitably selective, and if it is going to be selective, it is certainly permitted to make distinctions on the basis of content. Indeed, that is what selectivity means in this context. But there are many wrinkles here. They are best explored through distinguishing among a series of cases, actual and imaginable.

1. Discrimination among Artists, without Discrimination on Grounds of Content

Suppose that the government is funding private museums on a per-exhibit basis. Suppose that it decides that for a certain year it will provide funding only to projects by American artists on the ground that it wants to support "domestic art." There should be no constitutional problem with this decision. The government has a legitimate interest in funding American artists, and discrimination of this sort does not favor or disfavor any point of view, or indeed favor or disfavor any subject matter or speech of any particular content. To be sure, there might be some indirect connection between American citizenship and artistic content, and the First Amendment problem would be heightened if the discrimination were conspicuously responsive to speech of a disfavored content.[4] But in the absence of clear evidence of an implicit effort to regulate viewpoints discrimination among artists is entirely acceptable. This view seems to follow from *Regan v. Taxation with Representation of Washington*, where the Court upheld a statute that allowed veterans' organizations, but no other organizations, to deduct political contributions even if a substantial part of their activities were devoted to attempts to influence legislation.[5] The Court emphasized that this distinction was not an effort to suppress ideas and that the government could reasonably reward veterans in this way. The decision suggests that discrimination among artists should be generally acceptable. Note that from this conclusion it does not follow that the government could reserve funding to those who believe in God or who are prepared to vote for the Republican Party. Efforts of this kind should be invalidated on the ground that they amount to a form of implicit viewpoint discrimination against both art (indirectly) and artists (directly).

2. *Subject-Matter Discrimination*

Suppose that the government decides to fund projects, for the year, relating to the subject of American history. Suppose that any museum is permitted to apply for funds, but no proposal will be considered unless it relates to American history. This decision is constitutionally objectionable. The government is not discriminating against any point of view. To be sure, it is favoring material of a certain subject matter, and this step is more controversial than discriminating among artists. But a funding decision limited to a certain topic is unimpeachable.

This answer would be easiest to reach if the funding decision at issue was one of a number of diverse decisions, as, for example, when one funding agency is selective in one way (American history only), another is selective in another way (behavioral economics only), and yet another is selective in still another way (avant-garde art). It would be somewhat harder if the funding restriction were global—if, for example, no government agency could fund art that did not relate to American history. In that case, it would be possible to fear viewpoint discrimination, and here a sense of context should be quite helpful.

3. "Pure" Viewpoint Discrimination

Suppose now that the government engages in unambiguous viewpoint discrimination. Suppose, for example, that it decides to fund projects, for the year, relating to the subject of American history, but it refuses to consider any project that "casts America or its leaders in an unfavorable light." This is a harder case. At first glance, the refusal might seem plainly unconstitutional. Discrimination on the basis of viewpoint is the core concern of the First Amendment,[6] and the policy at issue plainly embodies viewpoint discrimination. However, the government itself is perfectly entitled to speak in a viewpoint-discriminatory way. If government officials decide, during a period of national celebration, only to celebrate and never to criticize, there would be no offense to the Constitution. Might not the government funding be seen as analogous to government speech? If so, might not government be permitted to give funds only to programs whose viewpoint it approves?

The Court's puzzling decision in *Rust v. Sullivan* seems to support this conclusion.[7] There the Court appeared to have held that Congress could discriminate on the basis of viewpoint in the grant of funds to private organizations engaged in family planning. More specifically, the Court said that Congress could require that taxpayer funds be devoted only to "projects" in which those engaged in family planning do not counsel people about abortion and do not engage in lobbying, dissemination of materials, and provision of speakers to increase the availability of abortion. In upholding this funding limitation, the Court said that the government "has merely chosen to fund one activity to the exclusion of the other" and that its regulations were intended "to ensure that the limits of the program are observed." It added that when "Congress established a National Endowment for Democracy to encourage other countries to adopt democratic principles, it was not constitutionally required to fund a program to encourage competing lines of political philosophy such as Communism and Fascism." For the Court, it was crucial that the case involved no penalty but a mere failure to fund. Here the government "is not denying a benefit to anyone, but is simply insisting that public funds be spent for the purposes for which they were authorized."

Taken on its own, *Rust* might seem to stand for the broad principle that the government can allocate its funds however it wishes and hence that the government can give money to the causes that it favors in order to promote governmentally preferred points of view. In subsequent cases, however, the Court has raised serious questions about this reading of *Rust*. In *Rosenberger v. Rector and Visitors of University of Virginia*, the Court struck down a University of Virginia policy authorizing university subsidies of some student publications but forbidding subsidies for student publications that "primarily promote or manifest a particular belief in or about a deity or an ultimate reality."[8] The University cited *Rust*, which appears strongly supportive of the selective subsidy. But the Court distinguished and narrowed its prior decision in such a way as to leave unsettled the status of viewpoint discrimination in government funding.

The Court explained that the government can "regulate the content of what is or is not expressed [1] when it is the speaker or [2] when it enlists private entities to convey its own message." Thus *Rust* was merely a case in which the government "used private speakers to transmit specific information pertaining to its own program." This means that a government appropriation of "public funds to promote a particular policy of its own" can legitimately be accompanied by appropriate "steps to ensure that its message is neither garbled nor distorted by the grantee." But it does not follow that the government may impose "viewpoint-based restrictions" when the government "does not itself speak or subsidize transmittal of a message it favors but instead expends funds to encourage a diversity of views from private speakers." In this case, the University of Virginia did not contend that those who were eligible for university support are the university's agents; student organizations "are not subject to its control and are not its responsibility." Thus when the university has decided to pay private speakers "who convey their own messages," it "may not silence the expression of selected viewpoints."

There is obvious tension between *Rush* and *Rosenberger*; and the implications of the two cases, taken together, are far from clear. The distinction seems to be that in *Rosenberger* the university did not contend that it was attempting to "convey its own message" or implement "its own program." But what if the university said that its funding policies involved "its own program," broadly speaking? What if the university denied that its purpose was "to encourage a diversity of views from private speakers"? What if the university said that it sought to encourage diversity but subject to certain restrictions, on the ground that some funding decisions would create too much entanglement between the state and religion? In any case *Rosenberger* could be understood broadly or very narrowly, and, as the opinion is written, it is not clear that it stands as a barrier to a government decision to refuse to fund art that it deems offensive, even on the basis of viewpoint.

Compare in this regard the Court's most sustained encounter with the question of government funding of the arts, *National Endowment for the Arts v. Finley*.[9] There the Court was asked to assess a statute asking the National Endowment for the Arts (NEA), in establishing procedures to assess the artistic merit of applicants, to "take into consideration general standards of decency and respect for the diverse beliefs and values of the American public." The Court upheld the statute against facial attack; but what is especially important here is what the Court did not say. The Court did not conclude that the government could give out taxpayers' funds however it chose. It did not accept a "strong" reading of *Rust v. Sullivan*, which would allow the government to choose, at its discretion, its preferred candidates for public subsidization. Instead the Court found it necessary to emphasize that the statute at issue was not, in fact, a form of viewpoint discrimination.

Thus the Court said that the considerations listed in the statute are "susceptible to multiple interpretation," and nothing in law was introduced that "in practice, would effectively preclude or punish the expression of particular views." Both the "decency" and the "respect" criteria could be understood in a constitutional fashion, as, for example, by attempting to give special consideration to "projects and productions . . . that reach, or reflect the culture of, a minority, inner city, rural, or tribal community." Because artistic funding was necessarily based on content discrimination, this case was not covered by *Rosenberger*, which was (what the Court called) an indiscriminate effort to encourage a diversity of views from the private sphere. And the Court left open the possibility that in particular cases "the denial of a grant may be shown to be the product of invidious viewpoint discrimination." Thus any "penalty on disfavored viewpoints" would present "a different case." Justice David Souter dissented on the ground that this was in fact a form of viewpoint discrimination; Justice Antonin Scalia, joined by Justice Clarence Thomas, concurred in the result, invoking a strong reading of *Rust* and suggesting that the government may "earmark NEA funds for projects it deems to be in the public interest without thereby abridging speech."

It is not easy to reconstruct the law as constituted by *Rust*, *Rosenberger*, and *Finley*. The strong version of *Rust* appears to have been rejected by the Court; unambiguous viewpoint discrimination appears to be impermissible, even with respect to the allocation of government funds for art. However, the government may itself speak as it wishes, and if the government wants to create a "program" for a proposed point of view and to enlist private speakers in the endeavor, it is permitted to do exactly that. Thus, for example, the government might have a project for democracy or a project for the reduction of smoking among teenagers, and it might pay private speakers to help. It might even be possible for the government to have a special artistic project whose purpose is to encourage (for example) celebration of the nation's natural beauty. In such cases, *Rust* would probably govern. But where the government is engaged in a general funding process for art, it is unlikely to be permitted to discriminate on the basis of viewpoint. Of course the distinction between a specific program and a general funding process is far from transparent.

4. Genre Distinctions and Temporal Distinctions

Suppose that the government is deciding which museums to fund; suppose too that it chooses to fund museums that offer traditional art rather than museums that specialize in avant-garde art. This is a somewhat harder case than those discussed thus far because the line that is being drawn is not based merely on subject matter (which would be acceptable) or purely on viewpoint (which would be unacceptable). Many artistically informed observers would think that a government distinction of this kind—traditional art yes, avant-garde art no—encodes something more like viewpoint discrimination. Probably the best conclusion is that since the government is permitted to fund artistic work of a certain content, it can favor work that fits within aesthetically preferred categories as long as it is not expressly discriminating against any point of view. If the government is refusing to fund art that is perceived to threaten existing government institutions, the argument for invalidation is strengthened. And here too it matters whether the line is local or global.

5. Deference to Taxpayers and Their Sensibilities

In many cases, including *Finley* and *Brooklyn Museum*,[10] the government is likely to be refusing to fund projects out of deference to the sensibilities—moral, aesthetic, and otherwise—of taxpayers. What is the status of this deference?

Here the key question involves the content of the relevant taxpayer sensibilities. If taxpayers are calling for viewpoint discrimination, the case is no different from case 3 above. If the government's decision is based on the judgment that taxpayers would find the relevant work "offensive to traditional morality," the issue is a bit harder because the viewpoint discrimination is less obvious. But it seems reasonable to say that in such a case, the government, acting at the behest of taxpayers, is attempting to entrench traditional morality, and this is a form of viewpoint discrimination. This conclusion shows why *Finley* was such a difficult case; the Court's conclusion that the statutory criteria showed content but not viewpoint discrimination seemed to be rooted in a judgment that they were merely "factors" and did not require the government to accept or reject any particular position.

If the government is deferring to purely aesthetic judgments, it is likely to be on firm ground. Here the analysis would be similar to that in cases 1, 2, and 4 above. If the government chooses not to fund a show consisting of avant-garde art, on the ground that taxpayers would find the show "confusing" and "ugly," it is probably acting constitutionally unless there is reason to suspect that something else is at work.

The upshot of this discussion is that deference to taxpayers should be analyzed similarly to any other form of selective funding. What matters is the ground for the selectivity.

6. *Withdrawal of Funds: A Special Case?*

Thus far all the cases have involved a refusal to fund in the first instance, rather than a withdrawal of funds that have been promised. This case appears to fall between a mere failure to fund and an unambiguous penalty. Suppose, for example, that government withdraws support from an exhibit that turns out to have objectionable content; suppose too that no viewpoint discrimination is involved. If this would be acceptable as a failure to fund in the first instance, would it be objectionable if it is a withdrawal of funds already promised?

For a more concrete illustration, suppose the government has decided to fund a series of museums. It withdraws funding from several shows of avant-garde art. If the government withdraws funding from the museum in general, there is an unambiguous penalty, and the action is unconstitutional. If the government had refused to fund in the first instance, there would be (by hypothesis) no constitutional problem. But suppose that the withdrawal is a genuine withdrawal, and suppose too that it is limited to the shows that were receiving the relevant funding. Is the withdrawal of funds worse than a refusal to fund in the first instance?

It might seem plausible to think that it is. A withdrawal of funds might well offer better evidence of an illicit government motive. When a selective funding agency refuses to give out resources in the first instance, its decision may be based on any number of grounds. And when funds are withdrawn, the case might seem closer to a penalty rather than a refusal to fund. In the case of withdrawn funds, it might seem sensible to say that here the government is deciding to eliminate a benefit that it would otherwise confer merely because of the exercise of a constitutional right. But this seems to be little more than a form of wordplay. Unless there really are grounds to believe an illicit motive is at work and unless there is a penalty in the sense described in Part II, a withdrawal should probably be treated the same as a failure to fund.

IV. Conclusion

My purpose in this essay has been largely descriptive. I have attempted a sympathetic reconstruction of existing law, designed to show some coherence and order and to generate answers to most of the disputed questions. Some serious difficulties remain. Consider just three points:

- It is not clear that the distinction between viewpoint discrimination and content discrimination is always coherent, especially in the area of arts funding. At the very least, many forms of content discrimination might be seen (so to speak) as forms of viewpoint discrimination.
- The line between a penalty and a refusal to fund is far from secure. Whether there is a penalty depends on specification of the normal state of affairs, and when the government is frequently involved in funding the arts, identification of the normal state of affairs may be quite unclear.
- The Court's decisions in *Rust*, *Rosenberger*, and *Finley* do not suggest anything like a straightforward line between permitted and prohibited arts funding. The special problem is in figuring out whether there is a special program (where selective funding is fine, even if based on viewpoint) or a general set of grants (where viewpoint discrimination is banned). Apparently the government is not permitted to make this decision on its own, but it is not clear why, and it is not clear when the government's characterization will be found unacceptable.

These are difficult questions; but it is nonetheless possible to identify principles to resolve the bulk of imaginable problems. The government cannot impose criminal or civil sanctions on speech outside of a few narrow categories of cases. The analysis of "penalties" proceeds in the same way. If people would otherwise have been entitled to government benefits, the benefits cannot be denied on the ground that people have engaged in speech that is not independently regulable under the First Amendment.

The hardest cases involve selective funding decisions, where the government is engaging in what it attempts to categorize as a "mere" failure to fund. If the government is refusing to fund material for content-neutral reasons, there is most unlikely to be a constitutional objection. If the government is refusing to fund material because of a preference for a certain subject matter, there is no constitutional problem unless the subject-matter distinction is suggestive of viewpoint discrimination. Arts funding that involves viewpoint discrimination is forbidden even if there is a "mere" failure to provide resources—at least outside of contexts in which the government explicitly and self-consciously adopts a specific program to encourage a specific point of view. These conclusions leave many open questions, but they create a framework within which to resolve most real-world disputes and to begin inquiries about the most troublesome cases.

NOTES

1. See Geoffrey Stone, Cass Sunstein, Mark Tushnet, and L. Michael Seidman, *Constitutional Law,* 4th ed. (Boston: Little, Brown, 1996).
2. See *Brandenburg v. Ohio*, 395 U.S. 444 (1969).
3. See Stone et al., *Constitutional Law.*
4. Suppose, for example, that government imposed an "Americans only" policy immediately after a general funding program ended up subsidizing art that contained implicit criticisms of American culture.
5. 461 U.S. 540 (1983).
6. See *RAV v. St. Paul*, 505 U.S. 377 (1992).
7. 500 U.S. 173 (1991).
8. 515 U.S. 819 (1995).
9. 118 S. Ct. 2168 (1998).
10. *Brooklyn Institute of Arts and Sciences v. The City of New York,* 64 F. Supp. 2d 184 (1999).

DAVID A. STRAUSS

The False Promise of the First Amendment

Mayor Rudolph Giuliani of New York City tried to cut off funds to the Brooklyn Museum, and sought to revoke its lease, because the Museum's *Sensation* exhibition included paintings that the mayor thought were "sick" and "disgusting" and offensive to people with deeply held religious views. When Judge Nina Gershon ruled that the mayor's threatened actions were unconstitutional, it was natural to think that the First Amendment had proved its value in ensuring that government officials cannot use their control over funding and other resources to restrict speech that they or their constituents find offensive.

It was natural to think this, but it was not right. In fact, the First Amendment is the wrong place to look for protection, if you believe that the government should not withdraw funding from unconventional or unpopular art. The First Amendment cannot reliably prevent government officials from cutting back public funding for that kind of expression. What's worse, if the First Amendment were to be used effectively in this way, the end result might be perverse. That is, the more effective First Amendment arguments are in court, the more government spending on the arts is likely to be cut, and cut in ways that the First Amendment cannot prevent. Decisions like Judge Gershon's, if they became the norm, would end up being Pyrrhic victories.

The battle over government funding of disturbing or unconventional art must ultimately be won in the court of public opinion, not in courts of law enforcing the First Amendment. People who want to resist government efforts to reduce funding of certain kinds of art will have to explain to their fellow citizens why it is important that such funding continue. This is true in the long-run sense that no principle can survive in a democratic society without some level of popular support; it is also true in the short run. Some groups—political dissidents and religious minorities, for example—might consistently be able to count on the courts and the First Amendment to protect them, sometimes even when a popular majority is arrayed against them. But for reasons that lie deep in the structure of First Amendment principles, people who want the government to support unconventional art are not in that position.

The core of the First Amendment is a set of principles designed to prevent the government from punishing people who criticize the government or who express unpopular views. Those principles are relatively easy to design, and, at least in normal times—when public opinion is not too inflamed—they are relatively easy for courts to enforce. The central idea is that the government may not punish people solely because it objects to the views they express. Other legal rules are designed to make sure that the government does not evade this central principle. For example, if the government claims to object not to a view a speaker expresses but to its consequences, the law requires the government to meet an extremely strict standard—a variant of the celebrated "clear and present danger" test—so as to avoid the risk that concern with consequences is a pretext for government hostility to the view itself. That is why the government may not punish people who criticize it for fighting a war, even if the government can plausibly claim that the criticism undermines the morale of the armed forces. Under current law, unless the speech goes beyond criticizing the war to inciting illegal conduct and unless that incitement is likely to be successful—and successful more or less immediately—the speaker cannot be punished.

Government funding of the arts presents a fundamentally different issue from this core First Amendment concern, for two basic reasons. The first is that, as a general matter, the First Amendment permits the government to withdraw from the business of funding art altogether. (This is a slight overstatement—there are certain instances in which the government is required to provide what amounts to a subsidy to speech—but that qualification can be left aside for present purposes.) It definitely does not follow that once the government decides to fund artistic expression, it may be as selective or as discriminatory as it wants. But it does follow that selective funding is on a different footing from criminal punishment, in ways that have important consequences for those who think the First Amendment can be used to prevent the government from withdrawing support from unpopular or controversial art.

The second important difference between a funding decision and the core First Amendment concern with punishing unpopular speech is that the government is entitled to draw distinctions when it funds speech that it would never be allowed to draw when it punishes people. The government can choose to fund theater but not ballet; it can choose to sponsor a troupe that performs only Shakespeare, while refusing to fund other theater companies. But of course the government could never punish someone for staging a ballet or a play by David Mamet. So the First Amendment principles addressed to government funding of the arts have to allow much more selectivity than the core First Amendment principles dealing with criminal punishments.

Mayor Giuliani's effort to evict the Brooklyn Museum was obviously quite different, in several ways, from a government decision to build an opera house instead of an art museum or to fund only a Picasso exhibition. To begin with, Mayor Giuliani was not making a judgment about the funding of a genre of expression; he was making a judgment about a few specific paintings. That alone, however, does not make his judgment suspect. The mayor was also making (in rough terms) an exclusionary, rather than an inclusionary, funding decision. No one could object if a city decided to pay for *Guernica,* and only *Guernica,* to be displayed in a public space. But matters seem quite different if the city offers public support to a Picasso exhibition on the condition that *Guernica* be excluded. Mayor Giuliani's actions are like the latter, not the former, case.

Moreover, Mayor Giuliani objected to the Chris Ofili painting, in particular, because it expressed a point of view that he found disagreeable. Of course he also claimed that the painting lacked artistic value. But he was quite explicit that the painting conveyed an attitude that he did not like. Perhaps judgments about the "viewpoint" or "attitude" expressed by a painting unavoidably coalesce with judgments of artistic merit. But it is certainly easier to make the case that First Amendment values are threatened when a public official is as explicit as Mayor Giuliani was in admitting that his views were based on the message supposedly expressed by the work of art in question. Indeed "admitting" is the wrong word—Mayor Giuliani could hardly have been more eager to tell us his views. That is itself a significant fact, for reasons I will return to. But for First Amendment purposes, the quasi-political and quasi-religious nature of Mayor Giuliani's objections made his lawyers' job much more difficult.

Finally, Mayor Giuliani did not try simply to defund the Ofili painting and a few others. He did not propose just to reduce the city's subvention to the museum by an amount proportionate to those paintings' share of the floor space or some such thing. He tried to eliminate general funds for the museum's maintenance and operational expenses and to evict the museum entirely from its property. It might be possible, theoretically, to distinguish between a simple refusal to fund specific speech—which leaves speakers as free to speak as ever, as long as they pay their own way—and a punitive withdrawal of support from a wide range of activities that seeks to coerce speakers into changing what they say. Mayor Giuliani threatened this coercive kind of action. If he had succeeded, the museum would not have been free to display the Ofili painting even if it had paid for that one display. It would still have lost complete funding for all its other operations, including its lease.

Judge Gershon—with support from Supreme Court precedent—concluded that at least when all these factors occur together, the First Amendment bars a government refusal to fund speech. The city was, of course, entitled not to rent its property or give subsidies to the Brooklyn Museum in the first place. But having already rented the property and offered the subsidies, it could not later cancel the lease and withdraw support in the way that Mayor Giuliani sought to do.

Why can't this case establish a suitable principle that will limit the government's power over funding the arts? In other words, when a government official, acting out of antipathy to the point of view expressed by a specific work, not only withholds funds for the specific work but withdraws a much wider range of government support in an effort to coerce a speaker (in this case, the Brooklyn Museum) not to display the work, the First Amendment draws the line. Why won't that suffice to provide at least a minimal degree of protection to worthwhile artistic expression?

Unfortunately the matter is more complicated than that. In some circumstances the government would be justified in taking actions that seem indistinguishable from what Mayor Giuliani tried to do. Perhaps more important, there are reasons for people who want vigorous government support of the arts to insist that the government have the power to do the kind of thing Mayor Giuliani tried to do, as objectionable as his actions might have been in this case.

Suppose, for example, that a city owns a fairground that it usually rents to private organizations. A few such organizations have activities that the city thinks are especially valuable for young people, so the city allows those organizations to use the fairgrounds for free. One year, one of the organizations that has habitually used the fairground rent-free receives a large contribution from a tobacco company. The organization decides to have, at a central point in the fairground, a display that makes fun of "the nanny state" for trying to discourage people from engaging in risky activities, including smoking, and compares smoking with popular risky sports like snowboarding.

Would the city violate the First Amendment if it decided that this organization could no longer use the fairground rent-free? Suppose the organization offered to pay the pro rata rent for the property on which the objectionable display would stand. Could it then insist that the First Amendment requires the city to continue to supply the rest of the fairground for free? If the city refused to do so, it would, it seems, be acting just as Mayor Giuliani did. It would be withdrawing support from a wide range of activities solely because of its objection to one particular display; and its objection to that display would rest entirely on the viewpoint expressed.

It seems unreasonable to require the city to continue to subsidize this hypothetical fair by providing a large piece of city property rent-free. But it is also hard to see how this hypothetical situation is different from the Brooklyn Museum case. Perhaps the cases can be distinguished on the ground that Mayor Giuliani's objections have more to do with sensitive areas of politics and religion, although the hypothetical fair promoter could certainly claim that it was being punished for its political commentary. Or perhaps the distinction is that the *Sensation* exhibit has a kind of professional artistic integrity that the fair lacks because the judgment of the fair organizers, apparently influenced by the tobacco company's contribution, was affected by financial concerns; but then the integrity of the *Sensation* exhibit was challenged on similar grounds.

Part of the problem—in both the hypothetical case about the fair and the actual Brooklyn Museum case—is that it is difficult, even in theory, to decide when the "subsidy" stops and a "penalty" begins. A prosmoking display would benefit from being included with other activities at a well-known and accessible fairground. The city, in my hypothetical case, could properly say that those benefits, too, were part of the subsidy that the display received from the city and that the firm's offer to pay pro rata rent on the space did not reimburse the city for that part of the subsidy. Similarly, the *Sensation* exhibit benefited from being shown at a museum with the Brooklyn Museum's reputation. No doubt New York City's support of the museum over the years has contributed to the development of that reputation. Mayor Giuliani could claim that his actions were an effort to recoup that element of the subsidy that the exhibit in general, and the specific paintings to which he objected, received.

So it is not clear that Judge Gershon's decision can be generalized into a principle that protects unsettling or controversial art from having its support withdrawn. There is an even deeper problem though. What would happen if a court did rule against the city in the fairground case? One entirely possible response by the city might be that it would never again offer the entire fairground rent-free to any group. Having learned its lesson about the difference between "withdrawing support" and "penalizing," the city might tailor its beneficence much more carefully. It might offer to subsidize only particular displays or activities. Undiscriminating subsidies to fairs would become a thing of the past, because such a subsidy would put the city in a position from which it essentially could not withdraw should it object, on viewpoint-related grounds, to one of the particular activities of the recipient.

The lesson for government funding of the arts is parallel. If Judge Gershon's decision were generalized into an across-the-board principle, government funding agencies would realize that once they fund a museum, an exhibition, a theater company, or a series of performances by an artist, they are essentially stuck with any display or performance that the recipient chooses. The government can defund that one activity, but the courts will require that the rest of the subsidy remain undisturbed. If the funding agency is unwilling to be put in that position, it will simply have to be much more discriminating about its funding decisions. It will fund only the particular things it is certain it likes. For a government funding agency, this is one possible lesson of the Brooklyn Museum litigation.

This perverse outcome—in which a First Amendment victory for arts funding has the long-run effect of producing markedly less arts funding—is attributable to the basic feature of the law of freedom of expression in this area: the government is, speaking generally, always free to refuse funding to the arts altogether. Since the government can refuse to fund art entirely, any legal rule that makes it difficult to withdraw funding sends the message that the government should be more careful about its initial funding decisions. And that will, ineluctably, make the government less willing to fund the arts at all. The Brooklyn Museum case is unusual. But if decisions like Judge Gershon's were more common, it seems reasonable to suppose that funding decisions that currently do not receive much attention from politicians would start to get more attention, and not of a favorable kind. Governments would begin to ask themselves exactly what they are getting themselves in for if they fund this exhibit, this group of performers, or these artists. And funding would become less easily available. This is the sense in which the First Amendment decision in the Brooklyn Museum case could, if it did not remain exceptional, become a Pyrrhic victory.

Of course, the Brooklyn Museum case was exceptional. Mayor Giuliani's actions were unusually blatant. He made no pretense about the basis of his objection to the exhibit. Perhaps we should at least be pleased that the First Amendment provided some protection against this kind of overt attack on unpopular artistic expression. But, once again, I don't think that is the right conclusion to draw.

For one thing, government officials who object to works of art and who want to withdraw funding will not always make things so easy for the lawyers on the other side. As a pretext, a judgment about the point of view evinced by a particular work of art could be couched simply as a judgment about its artistic value, perhaps even with a hypocritical disclaimer to the effect that "of course we respect the First Amendment rights of the artist to express controversial opinions, but no one has a right to public funds, and this art is not what we had in mind when we established this funding program," etc., etc. A court might be able to see through the pretext; but sometimes it might not. A government official who is more concerned than Mayor Giuliani was with winning in court, and less concerned with making a dramatic statement to the public, will have a much greater chance of defeating any First Amendment claim.

Or, even more threatening to government funding of the arts, dislike of a particular painting or performance might masquerade as a judgment about an entire genre or an entire art funding program. Even if the courts can insist that the government not withdraw funding in a particular instance, they cannot police the long-term level of funding. After the immediate controversy has passed—when there are no specific individuals who can claim that their First Amendment rights were violated—the government is free to reduce or eliminate funding to a program. It is certainly plausible that a general reduction in the level of funding for the arts could be the long-term reaction to a series of episodes like the Brooklyn Museum, Robert Mapplethorpe, and Karen Finley controversies. The courts can do essentially nothing to prevent such a result. And a series of victories on First Amendment issues might, for the reasons I have given, make such an outcome even more likely.

Finally, there is a lesson to be drawn from the very fact that Mayor Giuliani was so overt. Undoubtedly Mayor Giuliani did not want to lose in court. But in the end he was surely less concerned with what happened in court than he was with public opinion. The First Amendment is a powerful symbol, as are victories and losses in court, and probably

Judge Gershon's decision made Mayor Giuliani look bad in the eyes of some of the people whose opinion the mayor cares about. But in the end it seems likely that Mayor Giuliani, and other politicians who attack particular government-funded works of art in the way he did, are fully prepared to lose in court because they think they have an opportunity to score points with the wider public. Politicians are in the business of figuring out how to manipulate symbols to appeal to people, and they are likely to be adept at judging when an overt, unapologetic attack on a work of art will be well received by the electorate generally.

In other words, the controversies over art funding that will be easiest for advocates of funding to win on First Amendment grounds—those in which the politicians' attacks are particularly blatant—will be those in which the long-term damage to government support of art is likely to be greatest. Those are the cases in which the politicians really see an opportunity to score points with public opinion. They are the cases in which an outright, ideologically flavored attack on a work of art is especially likely to resonate with the public, so the politician avoids using subterfuge and takes the risk of losing in court. Even if they do lose in court, it is unwise to bet against politicians' assessments of what their constituents think. And, in the long run, popular support for art funding will be eroded.

For all these reasons, the battle for funding controversial or unsettling art cannot be won by invoking the First Amendment in court. Not only can the First Amendment and the courts do relatively little to maintain government support for artistic expression, but much of what they can do will be counterproductive. People who think the government has an important role to play in funding the arts have to make their case to the public, not the courts. When Mayor Giuliani says that the Ofili painting is "sick" and "disgusting"—judgments with which, as he of course knows, many of his constituents will agree—it is not enough to answer with generalities, however true and important, about the First Amendment. People who want to defend government funding of the arts have to explain why the works attacked by politicians are not sick and disgusting, why they are valuable nonetheless, or why the government should not withdraw support from work like this even if it is of limited value. Ringing First Amendment victories, however gratifying, are a sign of underlying weakness in the forum of popular opinion, and that is where the battle for government funding of the arts will be won or lost.

STEPHEN B. PRESSER

Reasons We Shouldn't Be Here

Things We Cannot Say

The most sensational or shocking thing to me about *Sensation* is that experts should be debating the question of what sort of exhibits the Brooklyn Museum should be able to show and that this is not simply a question for resolution by New Yorkers. I find it more than passing strange that a dispute between a popular mayor and a world-class art museum involving the Virgin Mary, elephant dung, and female genitalia is an excuse for bringing together the high-powered intellects in this volume. I find it equally weird that this local dispute was, for all practical purposes, resolved by a federal judge, Nina Gershon,[1] whose name is almost the same as Gina Gershon, a noted star of steamy late-night cable cinema.[2] That coincidence I will not now further pursue, but some sort of explanation for why we're arguing in these pages is called for. Almost one hundred and seventy years ago Alexis de Tocqueville observed that sooner or later virtually every American political dispute winds up in the courts,[3] and now even minor local political disputes end up there, but this is not the way it ought to be. How did this come to pass?

My strategy for trying to understand why *Sensation* ended up in court *will* be first to examine several different perspectives from which we might analyze the Rudolph Giuliani/Brooklyn Museum imbroglio and then to suggest that my particular orientation makes me a somewhat inappropriate commentator on these matters. Nevertheless, I will proceed to argue that the dispute should have been resolved in Mayor Giuliani's favor because he had partnership law and at least some constitutional law on his side. I will then suggest that the dispute between the mayor and the art museum resulted from two different conceptions of the First Amendment and that Judge Gershon's opinion in the Brooklyn Museum's favor embraced one of these conceptions and wrongly employed it to grant an injunction. I will also argue that Judge Gershon was wrong broadly to construe the law of the First Amendment while refusing broadly to construe the partnership arrangement between the city and the museum. I will conclude by asking whether resolving this dispute against the mayor was really in the best interests of art.

Multiple Perspectives; or, Why I'm the Wrong Guy for This Job

Let's tick off the dimensions along which we could analyze our problem. Most obvious is the political dimension. You have Rudy Giuliani, the most effective Republican mayor of New York in recent memory, an Italian American Catholic and former prosecutor, who was widely believed to be about to undertake a Senate campaign against Hillary Clinton, recent witness before federal grand juries, wife of the first elected U.S. president to be impeached, and a champion for the progressive wing of the Democratic party. A defeat by Clinton of Giuliani would be a great victory for that political point of view, which is generally supported by the national media. It is no surprise, then, that the progressive political forces in New York and in the national media were quick to find reasons to criticize the mayor for his intervention to seek to prevent the display of the allegedly offensive works, nor is it any surprise that conservative Republican commentators were quick to praise the mayor and disparage his critics. It was easy for both sides in the dispute (which quickly seemed to resemble both sides in the senatorial race) to rally their supporters and draw attention to it.. That helps explain the prominence of the dispute, but since reason and analysis rarely solve ideological disputes, further discussion of the surface-level politics involved will probably not serve our ends here.

There are somewhat deeper political issues involved, however, that are worth our study and on which I wish to dwell a bit longer. These involve the state and federal dimensions of this battle and the invocation of the First Amendment, to which I will return shortly. For now it should be observed that federalism, our notion of dual state and federal sovereignty, is a bedrock political principle of our republic and that the First Amendment was designed to support it. It is an extraordinary irony that currently, as in the dispute before us, the First Amendment and the Bill of Rights are so often invoked to employ the unelected judges in the federal judiciary in attempts to quash the efforts of elected state and local officials. The political purposes of the First Amendment and of federalism and the manner in which they were thought to promote popular sovereignty are of crucial importance to us, and these purposes supply my principal theme.

There is obviously a cultural dimension to this dispute, as well, which involves aesthetic discretion and the educational aims of art and not just whatever First Amendment freedom the Constitution guarantees to the purveyors of *Sensation.* What is the purpose of art, what kind of art should be displayed to the public? Is slicing and displaying mammals, doing self-portraits in your own blood, or flinging elephant dung "art"? Who ought to be deciding those questions? Should the answers be different if we are talking about private or public displays? Should art be funded by the public? What kind of artistic freedom is necessary for our culture to flourish? It ought to be obvious by now that the First Amendment might have something to say on these questions; at least in contemporary America one can't separate the cultural from the legal any more easily than one can separate the political from the legal. Yet there are limits to the invocation of the First Amendment here, and there are limits to what ought to be permitted in the name of culture.

Culture exists to improve aesthetics, virtue, and morals, and if some art instead encourages decadence and corruption, perhaps those concerned with the preservation of culture, or at least civic virtue, ought to be free from the obligation of supporting that art. It is for this reason, I think, that the First Amendment has never been held to protect obscenity. As we think about public funding for *Sensation,* then, we have to come to grips with these cultural questions and figure out how they inform and circumscribe what ought to be done with the law. I'll return to this notion at the end of this paper.

But I'm just a provincial law professor, and I profess no professional artistic training. We were told, in college, that you needed to discuss the fine arts at cocktail parties if you hoped to succeed as an upper-middle-class professional. Accordingly, I took a course we called "Spots and Dots," or twentieth-century painting, and because I enjoyed it, I also took a survey course on Western art that was taught at the lunch hour and featured endless slide shows. It was called "Darkness at Noon." This doesn't exactly make me Kenneth Clark, or E. H. Gombrich, or Bernard Berenson, but I know what I like, and pig parts in formaldehyde, blood, and elephant dung aren't it. And perhaps this is indicative of my ideological and political and even legal perspective, and the reader of these remarks deserves to have those spelled out in order the better to evaluate and discount the arguments I make.

I am a constitutional fundamentalist and a political paleoconservative. I believe that the English political philosopher Edmund Burke, although he wrote on different topics, did a pretty good job laying out the principles of the founders of the United States and that a little-known classic by neo-Burkean Russell Kirk, his *Conservative Constitution*, captures what that document was designed to do.[4] As I've tried to make clear in my own writing, to boil it down to the essentials, the authors of the Constitution, worried about the activities of shameless demagogues in the state governments and worried about the future of commercial prosperity in the American republics, created a national government and a Bill of Rights designed to promote liberty but to temper liberty with restraint.[5] They believed that liberty couldn't exist without laws, that laws couldn't exist without morality, and that morality couldn't exist without religion. They believed it was wrong to impose a national religious orthodoxy on Americans, but they believed that state and local governments had the responsibility of producing a virtuous citizenry and one that understood the importance of morality and religion to good government.

I am what we call today a "social-issues" conservative and not a free-market conservative. Yet, in politics I like George W. Bush better than Pat Buchanan, and that brings me to the second important element of my professional professorial perspective (social conservatism or, if you like, paleoconservatism is the first). Bush aligned himself with the WWJD school of Americans, those who determine right from wrong by asking, "What would Jesus do?" I have an approach to the First Amendment that's somewhat similar. It is the WWJMD approach. You ask, "What would James Madison do?" I couple my social-issues conservatism, then, with original understanding, and I hold with Judge Learned Hand that if you want to know what the Bill of Rights means, the only legitimate question is what did those who enacted it mean?[6]

Holding these views, I realize I am of limited use in this company to address the issues we are supposed to address because my perspective—social conservatism and original understanding—has little, if anything, to do with current First Amendment jurisprudence. For example, I think I must be in a tiny group of scholars who believe that the First Amendment doesn't apply against the states at all. It isn't just the text of that amendment, which, you may remember, provides restrictions merely on the legislature of the United States—"Congress shall make no law . . . abridging the freedom of speech"[7] —although I do think that text is significant.

Where I am odd here is that I reject the notion that the Fourteenth Amendment, which provides that no state shall deprive any person of the "equal protection of the laws," or of "due process," of the "privileges and immunities of United States Citizenship," was intended selectively to incorporate the Bill of Rights against the state governments or was understood to have that effect. This theory has enabled the Court to read the word "Congress" in the First Amendment as "state legislators and local government officials" in order to apply the restrictions of the First Amendment against the state and local governments, even though this was not what the framers of the First Amendment intended.

The Supreme Court began to accept this "incorporation" doctrine in the early twentieth century because of what the justices appear to have believed about the historical intention of the framers and ratifiers of the Fourteenth Amendment, but I believe that the justices were wrong. Although undeniably a few persons may have believed this was the intention of the Fourteenth Amendment, the evidence is strong that most people did not understand it in that manner. To believe that the Fourteenth Amendment involved such a radical constriction of state and local sovereignty in areas far removed from the slavery controversy, which spawned the Fourteenth Amendment, strains credulity and would have led to much more contemporary discussion on the issue than we can find.[8] Accordingly, I start from the proposition that whatever Rudy Giuliani wants to do with Chris Ofili is not a matter of constitutional law or at least is not one for the federal courts.

But this opinion—that the Fourteenth Amendment did not authorize the incorporation of the First Amendment against the states—cannot be uttered in respectable company in the academy today. This is so even though the Bill of Rights, which was conceived as a protection against a possibly grasping federal government, is perverted when it is treated as a way for federal courts to tell state and local governments what they can and cannot do. Sensible legal historians spend their time trying to come up with historical justifications for incorporation doctrine.[9] So, lest I get drummed out of the profession, I won't say anything further about the dubious nature of incorporation theory. Let's assume the First Amendment does apply to the states, as virtually everyone in the academy does.

I might also quibble with the assertion that pictorial representations of the kind that we are dealing with here are protected by the First Amendment, as I adhere to the minority view once articulated by Robert Bork that the First Amendment was designed simply to protect political speech of a kind familiar to the framers.[10] I am able to draw distinctions between speech and acts, for example, which leads me in directions again different from those of most of my colleagues. Like 80 percent of the people, but like only about one-tenth of one percent of the academy, I believe that flag desecration is not speech. I believe that *Texas v. Johnson*,[11] the Supreme Court case that said it was, is wrong, and thus I don't think the Flag Protection Amendment presents a First Amendment issue. If we asked Madison, I think he'd tell us that bisected animals and dung-splattered, genital-encircled Madonnas were not what he had in mind. As an originalist, I'd be inclined to reject the line of cases that states that the fine arts come within the protection of the First Amendment, but again I'll drop that view because there have been too many Supreme Court cases that have held to the contrary.

Even with all of these concessions from the jurisprudence of original understanding, however, the task is not made dramatically easier as we try to figure out the application of the First Amendment to the matter before us. The Supreme Court's First Amendment cases, particularly where they apply to the activities of local government, are surely one of the most confusing bodies of doctrine since Hammurabi hammered out his stele. I have taken the position that the constitutional jurisprudence of the Supreme Court is so irreconcilable and so incomprehensible that the only way to make sense of it is frankly to admit that the justices decide what result they want to reach in a given case and then simply pick from the rich variety of doctrine now available to support any point of view.[12] I am obviously not alone in advancing this particular theory; it has been a staple of law school teaching for almost a couple of generations now. This notion, that judging is really result-oriented and has little to do with legal doctrine, called "legal realism" in the academy, is secretly or not-so-secretly harbored by virtually all law professors, most lawyers, and perhaps even most judges.[13]

It broke my heart, as a tender young law professor, when I heard a justice of the U.S. Supreme Court admit as much in an after-dinner gathering. But I still refuse to believe it. I've been resisting legal realism since we members of the class of 1971 at Harvard Law School were told to buy the bible of legal realism, Jerome Frank's *Law and the Modern Mind* (1930), as recommended reading the summer before we matriculated. It was part of a long list of selected books, but I remember it as the first on the list and, accordingly, the only one that most of us read. I suspect it fatally tainted a whole cohort of American lawyers. I still believe in the rule of law in spite of all that. The rule of law was what the framers thought separated us from the arbitrary misrule of the British king and Parliament, and it was thought to be a fundamental prop for popular sovereignty. I still believe that, and I will now proceed to assume that, legal realism notwithstanding, the rule of law still exists, and I will try to figure out what the governing law in our case actually is. Thus I will ignore not only the absurdity of the incorporation doctrine but also the inescapeableness of legal realism. Let's be honest. Trying to be a lawyer or legal analyst today is much like living in Alice's wonderland. As the White Queen advised Alice, one ought to be prepared to believe six impossible things before breakfast.[14]

Mayor Giuliani Was Right: Insights from Partnership Law

But let's proceed. Even if the First Amendment applies against state and local governments, and even if we're bound by preexisting legal doctrine, and even if it's being made up as we go along, I still believe that an objective analyst could conclude that Mayor Giuliani was free to demand the removal of art he deemed offensive in the *Sensation* exhibit. The First Amendment, whatever it means, should not have been seen to be implicated in the dispute, and there is Supreme Court doctrine, no less, that leads to this result, as I'll explore in a little while. There is other law that ought to lead us to this conclusion as well, and I'd like to start there.

Most of us might state the question we're addressing as "Should a municipal government be able to ban art it regards as offensive?" Stating the question in this way makes the issue seem like censorship. My chair is in legal history, but I have a secret identity as a professor of business law (at the Kellogg Graduate School of Management, no less), and I regard the issue before us as the interpretation of a partnership agreement between two entities, the City of New York and the Brooklyn Museum. As even Judge Gershon was wont to observe, the arrangement between the museum and the city is actually described as a "joint partnership between the City and a group of private citizens" in the official "Procedures Manual for New York City's Designated Cultural Institutions."[15] Both the city and the museum find it in their interest to join forces. The museum gets some essential funding from the city, and the city is able to perform its traditional function of education and, in particular, of inculcating civic virtue in the citizenry by exposing them to the fine arts in the museum's collection. Just as Plato understood in the *Republic*, not all art is suitable for this purpose,[16] and thus perhaps some artwork is inappropriate.

The Supreme Court has told us, in *Rust v. Sullivan*, that the federal government can, in effect, even fund one side of a controversial issue and forbid those who wish to present the other side from speaking about it as long as they accept federal funds.[17] Thus, family-planning clinics that accept federal aid are barred not only from performing abortions but also from counseling about abortions. It is true that, generally speaking, the government is not supposed to make content discriminations when it finds itself involved with speech, so that, the Supreme Court has told us, it cannot, for example, ban flag burning; but where the government is funding pursuant to a public policy, *Rust* seems to tell us, this rule doesn't apply. This is made clear by the dissent in *Rust*, which protested the majority opinion on just this content-discrimination ground.[18] The fact, then, that the Brooklyn Museum has traditional representations of the Madonna should not bar the New York mayor from seeking to exclude nontraditional offensive representations of her. This should be especially true if he regards his task as mayor as involving the encouragement and protection of religion, which I have already suggested was one aim of our country's founders.

If the mayor and the Brooklyn Museum are jointly engaged in the same endeavor, I don't see any reason why Mayor Giuliani shouldn't be free to threaten to end the partnership, on the theory that the purpose of the joint venture is being jeopardized by the course the museum has chosen to take. It is, after all, hornbook partnership law that any partner can dissolve a partnership, and it is hornbook law as well that partners have an equal vote in controlling the operation of the partnership. The city's corporation counsel, Michael Hess, defended the mayor's actions on a similar theory:

> Well, I think the mayor's view, and to speak for a moment about that one picture, which has been the center of controversy, that picture is a picture entitled "The Virgin Mary" [sic] and it's a picture, as was said before, of the Virgin Mary surrounded by small vaginas and covered with elephant dung. Now the mayor, in seeing that, said that's not appropriate. . . . In the mayor's view, it's totally inappropriate to use taxpayers' money to put that up on the wall. *In addition, we feel that, . . . because there is a contract between the museum and the city, there's an obligation on the museum's part to look at what they're putting up on the wall before they do it. And to limit this kind of painting. The museum's director has said, no, he doesn't feel it's his obligation at all. He takes the show as he received it from London, and just puts everything up on the wall. We think that violates the contract and the lease. And if he won't do it, then it becomes the city's obligation, since we're on the other side of that lease, to look at what's going up on the wall.* And when something as vile as that—because it absolutely does derogate someone's religion, because of that the mayor draws the line and says this isn't controversial or challenging art, this is way over the line, and the taxpayers shouldn't pay for it.[19]

If partners are equally divided with regard to a course of action to be undertaken, that conduct should be deemed unauthorized.[20] If the museum was unwilling to take down *The Holy Virgin Mary*, Mayor Giuliani should have been allowed to pull the plug on the exhibit.

Indeed, it seems to me that the mayor could have even taken the position that the Ofili *Virgin*, given the representations of female genitalia, was pornography. He could have argued that it met the constitutional test of offending community standards and had no redeeming artistic or social qualities, and he could have sought to exclude it on those grounds.[21] However, since Ofili had won some celebrated artistic honors in England, that would have been a difficult tack to take, and if one contemplates the Ofili *Virgin*, a fair-minded observer might take it as an intriguing celebration of virginity or perhaps fecundity, and thus it would be difficult to conclude that it was utterly without redeeming social or cultural importance. Eventually the call would have been one for a Brooklyn jury to make, and it would have been difficult to predict the outcome. If I were advising the mayor, I might have been tempted to play the obscenity card. But he's a better politician than I am, so let's move on from that argument as well.

Let's come back to the partnership analogy, for a moment. As I've indicated, the rule in a partnership is that the partners have equal rights to control the decision-making process. Although the lease, the contract, and the relevant legislation do not contemplate constant ongoing intervention by the mayor, he does have the ultimate power of canceling the lease and withholding payments. He may do this when the museum "shall cease to be maintained according to the true intent" of the legislation that created the partnership between the city and the museum.[22] I see this as a way of guaranteeing his equal participation in the educational endeavor.

No one, not even Judge Gershon, disputed the mayor's right (even under the First Amendment) to pull museum funding and evict the museum if it decided, for example, to become a museum of pornography.[23] So what we're dealing with here, it seems to me, is drawing a line between pornography and the purposes of the lease or determining when the mayor is authorized to act. *Rust* and the general principles of partnership law tell us this is a call for him to make, as the executive voice of the city, and the First Amendment doesn't restrain him. I conclude that he was within his rights to threaten to withhold funding and yank the lease if he felt some items in the *Sensation* exhibit were inappropriate for the museum's educational mission and were, indeed, threatening that mission.[24]

Whether or not you find *Rust* compelling, however, there is at least some Supreme Court authority that suggests that the First Amendment doesn't apply to the state at all when it is funding the arts. This is the clear message of Justice Antonin Scalia's concurrence in *NEA v. Finley*.[25] There, relying in part on *Rust*, he makes the point that every time the legislature makes a funding decision, it, of necessity, excludes the expression of particular viewpoints. The implication is that to regard each and every one of these funding decisions as barred because they implicated the First Amendment would be to paralyze government.[26] Scalia took the position in *Finley* that the federal government was free, in funding the National Endowment for the Arts, to declare that "indecent works" would not be funded.[27] It must be admitted, though, that the majority in *Finley*, waffling, did not go that far, and indicated only its view that Congress could dictate that the decency of a work be a factor to be considered, although not necessarily a determinative one.[28] Scalia's position led Judge Gershon, by the way, to all but ignore *Finley*, as she brushed off the majority's opinion as not only not controlling but essentially empty of content.[29] (This emptiness of the majority opinion was also the burden of Scalia's *Finley* concurrence.)[30]

What's the First Amendment All About? Two Theories

Perhaps it is appropriate at this point to indicate that part of what seems to distinguish the perspective of judges like Gershon or the dissenters in *Rust* or, indeed, the lawyers for the Brooklyn Museum of Art from the thought of Mayor Giuliani or Justice Scalia or the majority in *Rust* is a difference of opinion over what the First Amendment is supposed to do, what might be described as its underlying theory. I'm on shaky ground here, perhaps, but if I can ally myself with Scalia et al., I can say again that I believe I can perceive a theory that grounds the First Amendment for them (as for my fellow contributor to this volume, Cass Sunstein) in the promotion of popular sovereignty.[31] The First Amendment is designed to protect the right of the people to the information they need to accomplish their exercise of civic virtue, their participation in the governance of the Republic.

The First Amendment, then, is about politics and is about promoting the will of the people. Indeed, in its original conception, I suspect it's about promoting a unitary vision of the will of the people, just as I believe we can read Madison's *Federalist* 10 as revealing a general attitude on the part of the framers that there is a unitary vision of the good. Such a vision had something to do with restraining demagoguery, stopping irresponsible printing of currency, frustrating schemes for the redistribution of property, and checking interference with contracts.[32] This might lead me in directions a bit inappropriate for the task at hand, but accept for the moment the idea of a vision of the general will that is unitary in nature or accept at least an objective notion of the good that can be discovered once special interests are brushed aside.[33] That's the mayor's view. If one reads the Constitution and the First Amendment as promoting an objective notion of the good, it is not inconsistent with that notion, say, to suggest that the government can underwrite one way of representing the Madonna in museums but not another way. Indeed, if I'm right about the perspective of the framers, they would have believed that Giuliani was doing the right thing in trying to encourage and not discourage religion since they believed, as I've indicated, that religion and morality were necessary props for good government.[34]

There is, however, a different theory of the First Amendment, which we saw pungently limned by Floyd Abrams, a lawyer hired by the Brooklyn Museum, when he appeared on *The NewsHour with Jim Lehrer.*

> This [the *Sensation* exhibit] is a very interesting, provocative, challenging controversial effort, which the people of Brooklyn, the people of New York, the people of America ought to have a chance to see. . . .
>
> Taxpayers' money ought to go for culture because it's good for taxpayers. . . . [T]he Brooklyn Museum serves the public . . . by having exhibitions of a variety of sorts. One sort is a particularly challenging, controversial sort. It's good for the people of Brooklyn and New York to have a choice for them to decide whether to go to this exhibition. . . . [The mayor's threat to cut off aid to the museum] seems to me contrary to the whole notion of freedom of expression in America.[35]

For Abrams, in other words, the First Amendment isn't about unitary conceptions of the good. For him, the First Amendment is about stretching your mind, about letting a thousand flowers bloom. For him, I think, the First Amendment is designed to promote thinking like that reflected in the notorious "mystery passage" in the Supreme Court's opinion in *Planned Parenthood v. Casey;* the plurality wrote, "At the heart of liberty is the right to define one's own concept of existence, of meaning, of the universe, and of the mystery of human life. Beliefs about these matters could not define the attributes of personhood were they formed under compulsion of the State."[36] To put it slightly differently, this is Justice Oliver Wendell Holmes's idea of the First Amendment protecting the marketplace of ideas,[37] of maintaining a bazaar (or perhaps the "bizarre") from which one can pick and choose, with no view having any more claim to First Amendment validity or legitimacy than any other.

This "different strokes for different folks" idea is, of course, John Stuart Mill's conception expressed in *On Liberty*,[38] and it remains, I think the contemporary orthodoxy of the First Amendment. The First Amendment is about individual self-actualization. Except that it's not. Or at least originally it wasn't. Mill didn't write the First Amendment. Madison didn't either, of course, but he has a better claim to illustrate what it's all about than Mill does, and I'm more comfortable relying on the thought of *Federalist* 10 to illuminate the First Amendment than on Mill's musings with Harriet Taylor.[39]

For me, then, just as for my fellow contributor Sunstein, the First Amendment is about furthering the goal of popular sovereignty, although I would also see it as playing a role in fostering dual sovereignty as expressed in the Constitution, meaning federalism, meaning discretion exercised on the part of local officials in the performance of their political responsibilities. Museums, museum directors, wealthy art owners, or even their lawyers should not be permitted to wrap themselves in the First Amendment and, to mix metaphors badly, to use it as a club to beat back the legitimate exercise of local government. The English translation of all of this, I think, is that the call was Mayor Giuliani's to make. If he objected to some of the objects in the *Sensation* show, they should have been yanked.

Irreparable Injury? Where Judge Gershon Went Wrong

This brings me to another odd legal aspect of this case, the stroke that for all practical purposes decided the dispute against the mayor. I refer to Judge Gershon's granting an injunction to the museum to stop the mayor from withholding funds or taking any other action to threaten the museum. When I was in law school an injunction was supposed to be an extraordinary remedy, granted only when there was no adequate legal redress, available only when there was "irreparable injury" that only a court order—enforceable by the contempt power—could prevent. To be fair to Judge Gershon, she mouthed the words "irreparable injury" and cited some precedent to the effect that any deprivation of First Amendment rights constituted "irreparable injury."[40] But even if we're willing to concede that the First Amendment is relevant here, is the temporary withdrawal of a couple of artworks from the *Sensation* exhibition really "irreparable injury"?

After all, it appears that at any point during this dispute the mayor would have ceased his machinations if the Ofili *Virgin* had been pulled from the show.[41] The withdrawal might well have been temporary, while a state court reviewed the problem, and perhaps there could have been an expedited state court proceeding. I find it difficult to believe how a few New Yorkers' not being able to see the painting at the Brooklyn Museum, while rights in doubt were adjudicated, would have been irreparable injury. Whatever message the Ofili *Virgin* conveyed could certainly have been conveyed by the reproductions of it that had by then become widely available. It would have been possible, I suspect, to have *The Holy Virgin Mary* displayed elsewhere, perhaps even to have erected a separate structure at private expense.

If it later turned out that the museum won its case in state court, money damages could have served as compensation perhaps. Reading through Judge Gershon's opinion, where every single legal doctrine is pushed to the limits to rule against the mayor, especially in light of the malleability of these doctrines, perhaps I can be forgiven for thinking that Judge Gershon shared something of the philosophy of the Brooklyn Museum's director, a philosophy that amounted to near contempt for the mayor's views, at the least, and perhaps even contempt for the views of the public itself. As Abrams almost seemed to suggest, the public, and its representative Mayor Giuliani, couldn't possibly know what was best for it with regard to art—that was a call for its betters to make.[42] Worse, I sense here an attitude I've often seen among some of my law-professor colleagues—that state courts can't be trusted, that they are too narrow and provincial—and when it comes to the First Amendment (or a particular conception of it), only the more cosmopolitan federal courts have access to the necessary wisdom.

In short, then, I can't say that there was any chilling of speech here that was substantial enough to constitute the grounds for an injunction based on the threat of "irreparable injury." What seems to me to have happened is that the museum managed to use an extraordinarily broad conception of the First Amendment in order to trump any claims by the mayor that the museum's public educational mission was being perverted. For me, then, the question boils down, probably, to more the political than the legal one: Who ought to decide how the public funds that are committed to art should be spent?

Broad and Narrow Construction: First Amendment Mania

Judge Gershon, the Brooklyn Museum, its lawyers and academic defenders take the position that once money is committed to art, the First Amendment vests in art administrators complete discretion over how the money is to be spent. They appear to claim that this is true even when express and implicit legal safeguards are built in to maintain public participation in the process. I refer here to the lease and contract with the museum, which I have suggested gave the city the right to pull funds if it believed the contract was being breached and to evict the museum if it was failing to fulfill the terms under which the lease was granted.[43] Perhaps this is a bit of a stretch in construction since this idea is not spelled out with precision in these documents. That this power in the mayor to cancel for misuse in this case was implicit rather than explicit led Judge Gershon to proceed to rule that the lease gave the mayor no such power and that he was in breach of the arrangements by threatening to cut off funds and begin eviction proceedings in order to "punish" the museum for exercising its First Amendment rights.

But if I have broadly construed the lease and contract and narrowly construed the First Amendment rights, surely Judge Gershon has done precisely the opposite. She refuses to extend to the lease the same very loose standards of construction she applies to the First Amendment. For her the First Amendment is paramount, and everything else must bend to accommodate its broadest construction. For me the property and contract rights guaranteed by the Constitution are first in importance, both historically and structurally, and I am reluctant to use the First Amendment as a tail to wag the dog of property rights and dual state and federal sovereignty.

Judge Gershon was quick to find constitutional violations here, but I was trained in law school that when faced with a possible constitutional violation by government officials, one strained first to construe their action in a manner consistent with the Constitution, and only if no other construction was available did one find a constitutional violation. The kind of immediate resort to the First Amendment and the charges of unconstitutional behavior on the part of the mayor by Abrams and others, I suspect, are not what my teachers and orthodox constitutional jurisprudence had in mind. In addition, a string of authorities suggest that when a federal judge is confronted with a dispute that state authorities are perfectly capable of handling, discretion is supposed to be the better part of valor, and the federal court is supposed to leave it to the state court to resolve. Judge Gershon considered these authorities;[44] but having convinced herself that the mayor's arguments regarding the lease were advanced in bad faith[45] (a conclusion with which I disagree), she blithely brushed them aside in order to rush to issue her injunction and protect what she believed to be the First Amendment and its values.

One shouldn't cast too much blame on Judge Gershon here though. While I think she was dead wrong on the federal-versus-state issue—I think she should have let the state courts handle it—and while I think she was wrong in refusing to understand the nature of the "partnership" between the City of New York and the Brooklyn Museum, which was a public-private partnership between equals who had equal power to call the shots, for every call she made there was ample case-law authority. I suspect she would have been eventually reversed on appeal on the state-federal issue and perhaps on the First Amendment issue as well, but this is far from certain.

Current constitutional jurisprudence does contain cases, such as *Rosenberger v. Rector*, which imply that once the government makes the decision to fund First Amendment activities it can't pick and choose which ones to fund based on an ideological preference for one over the other.[46] Thus in *Rosenberger* the court held that once the University of Virginia decided to fund student publications, it could not refuse to fund one that was religious in nature. Even though the establishment clause has been read to mandate a "wall of separation between church and state," the religious group had First Amendment rights of speech which the establishment clause could not trump. It would have been impermissible viewpoint discrimination, said the court in *Rosenberger*, to fund secular speech but refuse to fund religious speech.

Judge Gershon used that analogy in the dispute before her,[47] as did the Brooklyn Museum's defenders. Even more powerful, I thought, was their argument that if Mayor Giuliani was right, the mayor of New York could walk into the New York Public Library, find a book that he didn't like—say Hitler's *Mein Kampf*—and demand that either it be removed from the shelves or he would yank whatever city funding the library received.[48] The logic of my position does require this, I think, unless the New York Public Library does not have a similar statutory, contractual, and leasehold partnership agreement with the city, in which case, of course, the mayor would have no say over the library at all, nor could he claim any. But even if this mayor doesn't participate in the funding of this library, the point is still a powerful one, and if I'm right on the law, any time a public library gets public funding, any public official can threaten to ban particular books. This is, of course, what happens all the time, but there seems to be a consensus among the enlightened elite, at least, that it is a bad thing.

The mayor's lawyers, confronted with this problem, appear to have tried to argue that the case of a library book is different from a painting because a painting has much more expressive power. Judge Gershon quite properly rejected that argument since the dispute really was about the limits of freedom of expression, and if the Ofili painting came within the First Amendment's protection, the fact that it had more expressive power than a book should have entitled it to more rather than less protection.[49] My only way out of this puzzle, apart from using the notion expressed by Scalia in his concurrence in *Finley* that the First Amendment is not ever involved when the question is selective funding of the arts or apart from my partnership analysis (which turns on the "who decides" question), is just to suggest that sometimes in interpretation of the First Amendment lines have to be drawn and libraries are different from art museums. Perhaps libraries and those who maintain them are entitled to greater deference because we all agree that the core of the First Amendment is freedom of the press and in particular freedom of the press exercised in the discussion of ideas about popular sovereignty and government. Surely even *Mein Kampf* deserves protection under this analysis.

Once you stretch the First Amendment from its roots in the protection of political thought to include all forms of expression, you've begun to make it a bit too elastic, and you've begun to create situations like the one before us, where what is essentially a local-government problem (allocation of funding for the arts, the nature of public education) can be decided only by the federal courts. Again, I think that's wrong. This is where the constitutional and legal turn back into the political or the cultural and where I wind up right back where the mayor started out. Perhaps there is something wrong with the use of public funds to display artwork which is perceived (wrongly, I suspect, but that's beside the point) by an official observer as hostile to religion. As the mayor said, "You don't have a right to a government subsidy to desecrate someone else's religion."[50] If First Amendment doctrine suggests otherwise, then perhaps First Amendment doctrine simply makes no sense. If that's the law, as Dickens said, then the law is "a ass, a idiot."[51]

Conclusions: The Separation of Art and State

And that brings me to one of my concluding points, one that I advance with deference because I'm not sure I really believe it, but the question ought to be asked. If a mayor or a city government is told that when it funds the arts, even in an express partnership context, it has no control over what art is funded, what should the rational response be? I think it is to suspend further funding of the arts, and it is clear that there is some interest in doing so at both local and federal levels. Is this what the art community would really like to see happen? As a practical political (if not a cultural) matter, might it not make sense to trade a bit of artistic freedom or license in return for continued support? After all, there will always be private funding available as well, and once an artist has an established reputation, it's even more available.

Or perhaps artists ought to consider whether public funding of the arts, in a rich capitalist nation like ours, is a good idea at all. Even if we put to one side the inevitable pressures toward orthodoxy that public funding will create, some claim that public funding of the arts will lead to mediocrity. Paul Johnson wrote in the *National Review* that "no state in history has ever spent more on the arts per capita, in the years 1960–2000, than France. And what do we find? France now has no outstanding poets, novelists, or playwrights, no painters or sculptors of the slightest consequence, no architects worth employing and no front-rank composers. The immense fertility of the years 1910–50 has vanished as if it had never been."[52]

One of the powerful arguments for the prohibition of a national religion, in the First Amendment's establishment clause, is that a state-supported denomination will inevitably lead to using religion for crass political purposes and perhaps even perverting religion to meet the needs of those in power. To preserve the spiritual aspects of religion, to preserve the purity of its search for truth, to avoid the taint of temporal special interests, so it was said (by Madison, at least), there ought to be separation of church and state.[53]

For the same reasons, perhaps, there should be separation of art and the state. This is worth pondering, but there have been many triumphs of publicly funded artwork, such as Thomas Jefferson's state capitol at Richmond, or Giovanni Bernini's and Michelangelo's work at the Vatican. The Bernini and Michelangelo examples are probably not good ones because they flow from a conception of the state that allows theocracy and might be better viewed as Church patronage rather than state patronage. And honesty compels the conclusion that without public funding the great museums of the world (and the Brooklyn Museum is one) simply could not be maintained. I love many of these museums, and I wouldn't want to lose them, so I'm reluctant to see public funding of the arts disappear.

Still, it is private funding that brought together the *Sensation* exhibit in the first place since the works were from the private collection of Charles Saatchi. I have had nothing yet to say about a major theme of this volume, whether the possibility of appreciation in value of Mr. Saatchi's artworks, once they are exhibited with the use of public funds, raises any ethical or First Amendment problems. I will say nothing on the topic except that Mr. Saatchi may have provided evidence that casts some doubt on whether private funding can be expected to produce great art either. Ofili's *Virgin* poses no threat to the *Mona Lisa*, and *This Little Piggy Went to Market, This Little Piggy Stayed at Home* is not likely to be mistaken for Chartres or even *Les Demoiselles d'Avignon* or *Nude Descending a Staircase*. We have a maxim in the law that "hard cases make bad law." I think I may have learned that bad art makes hard cases.

NOTES

1. See *Brooklyn Institute of Arts and Sciences v. The City of New York*, 64 F. Supp. 2d 184 (1999) (opinion by Nina Gershon, U.S. District Judge for the Eastern District of New York).
2. See, for example, *Showgirls* (1995), *Bound* (1996), and *Black and White* (1998).
3. Alexis de Tocqueville, *Democracy in America*, ed. J. P. Mayer and M. Lerner, trans. George Lawrence (1835; reprint, New York: Harper & Row, 1966), 248.
4. Reprinted as Russell Kirk, *Rights and Duties: Reflections on Our Conservative Constitution* (Dallas, Tex.: Spence, 1997); see also Russell Kirk, *The Conservative Mind: From Burke to Eliot, 7th ed.* (Washington, D.C.: Regnery, 1995).
5. See, for example, Stephen B. Presser, *Recapturing the Constitution: Race, Religion and Abortion Reconsidered* (Washington, D.C.: Regnery, 1994); Stephen B. Presser and Jamil S. Zainaldin, *Law and Jurisprudence in American History*, 4th ed. (St. Paul, Minn.: West, 2000); Douglas W. Kmiec and Stephen B. Presser, *The American Constitutional Order: History, Cases and Philosophy* (Cincinnati, Ohio: Anderson, 1998); Stephen B. Presser, "Some Realism about Atheism: Responses to the Godless Constitution," *Texas Review of Law and Politics 1* (1997): 87.
6. See, generally, Learned Hand, *The Bill of Rights* (Cambridge, Mass.: Harvard University Press, 1958).
7. U.S. Constitution, Amendment I (1791).
8. For the boldest articulation of the view that the Fourteenth Amendment did not incorporate the Bill of Rights and thereby apply the First Amendment against state and local governments, see Raoul Berger, *Government by Judiciary: The Transformation of the Fourteenth Amendment*, 2d ed. (Indianapolis: Liberty Fund, 1997). See also Presser, *Recapturing the Constitution*, 160–170.
9. For two highly praised attempts, see Michael Kent Curtis, *No State Shall Abridge: The Fourteenth Amendment and the Bill of Rights* (Durham, N.C.: Duke University Press, 1986), and Akil Reed Amar, *The Bill of Rights: Creation and Reconstruction* (New Haven, Conn.: Yale University Press, 1998).
10. Robert Bork, "Neutral Principles and Some First Amendment Problems," *Indiana Law Journal* 47 (1971): 27.
11. *Texas v. Johnson*, 491 U.S. 397 (1989), holding that flag desecration is speech protected by the First Amendment.
12. See, generally, Presser, *Recapturing the Constitution*, 3–5.
13. For an introduction to legal realism, see, generally, Presser and Zainaldin, *Law and Jurisprudence in American History*, ch. 6, sec. C.
14. Lewis Carroll, *Alice's Adventures in Wonderland* and *Through the Looking Glass* (1865 and 1871; reprint, New York: Bantam Books, 1981), 157.
15. *Brooklyn Institute v. City of New York*, slip opposite 3–4, quoting the "Procedures Manual," 3.
16. I'm taking some liberties with my citation to Plato here. I refer to Plato's famous barring of Homer and Hesiod from his Republic. See Plato, *The Republic*, Bk. II, trans. B. Jowett, vol. 6 of Great Books (Chicago: University of Chicago Press, 1990), 321, where he suggests that those poets be barred because it is necessary to "establish a censorship of the writers of fiction, and let the censors receive any tale of fiction which is good, and reject the bad." Still, Plato justifies his rejection of Homer and Hesiod because the tales they tell are false; he likens this situation to one "when a painter paints a portrait not having the shadow of a likeness to the original" (321). Plato would have been no fan of Ofili, I suspect.

17. *Rust v. Sullivan*, 500 U.S. 173 (1991).
18. In *Rust*, "the Court, for the first time, upholds viewpoint-based suppression of speech solely because it is imposed on those dependent upon the Government for economic support." *Rust v. Sullivan*, 204 (Blackmun, J., dissenting).
19. Transcript of *The NewsHour with Jim Lehrer*, October 8, 1999 (on Nexis) (emphasis supplied).
20. See, for example, *Summers v. Dooley*, 94 Idaho 87, 481 P.2d 318 (1971); and see, generally, William L. Cary and Melvin Aron Eisenberg, *Cases and Materials on Corporations*, 7th ed. (Westbury, N.Y.: Foundation Press, 1995), 35–39, and sources there cited.
21. For these standards for obscenity, see *Roth v. United States*, 354 U.S. 476 (1957).
22. *Brooklyn Institute v. City of New York*, 187–188 (quoting from the lease and legislation).
23. Ibid., 204. "The City and the Mayor argue that, if the court enjoins the withholding of its subsidy, the Museum will be free, under the protection of the First Amendment, to do anything at all, even transform itself into, for example, a museum of pornography. That, of course is absurd."
24. See also on this point Michael Hess, corporation counsel of the City of New York, explaining the city's position on *The NewsHour with Jim Lehrer* on October 8, 1999 (transcript on Nexis):

    [T]he museum has a contract and a lease going back over 100 years with the city, which gives some obligations to the museum, as well as obligations to the city. For the first time in the course of that lease, the Brooklyn Museum has violated that obligation to put on an exhibit that really is to have open access to the public, to train young people in artistic things, and to really put on an appropriate show for the citizens of the city. . . . [T]he city's view of the art is that it's totally inappropriate, certainly for children, and beyond that, it's really not even for the general public the kind of exhibit that taxpayers should pay for. . . . [B]ecause of the nature of the art itself, the more than controversial, the actual upsetting, violent, disgusting view of some of these paintings, they shouldn't be supported by taxpayer money. . . . [I]t violates the lease that the Brooklyn Museum entered into, which lease talks about shows appropriate for schoolchildren.
25. *NEA v. Finley*, 524 U.S. 569, 590 (Scalia, J., concurring).
26. Ibid., 597–599.
27. Ibid., 590–597.
28. Ibid., 581–587.
29. *Brooklyn Institute v. City of New York*, 202.
30. *NEA v. Finley*, 590. "'The operation was a success, but the patient died.' What such a procedure is to medicine the Court's opinion in this case is to law. It sustains the constitutionality of 20 U.S.C. Sec. 954(d)(1) by gutting it."
31. See, for example, Cass R. Sunstein, *Democracy and the Problem of Free Speech* (New York: Free Press, 1995).
32. James Madison, Alexander Hamilton, and John Jay, *The Federalist Papers* (1787–1788; reprint, New York: Penguin Books, 1987), 128. Madison explains that a large republic, where factions cancel each other out, will have a better chance of avoiding "a rage for paper money, for an abolition of debts, for an equal division of property, or . . . any other improper or wicked project."
33. I develop this notion in Presser, *Recapturing the Constitution*.
34. See text accompanying and surrounding notes 4–5 above.
35. Transcript of *The NewsHour with Jim Lehrer*, October 8, 1999 (on Nexis).
36. *Planned Parenthood v. Casey*, 505 U.S. 833, 851 (1992).

37. *Abrams v. United States*, 250 U.S. 616, 630 (1919) (Holmes, J., dissenting): "[T]he primary goal of the First Amendment is to guarantee a 'marketplace of ideas,' where truth and honest debate emerge from a multiplicity of voices."
38. J. S. Mill, *On Liberty* (1859).
39. For the profound influence of Mill's wife, Harriet Taylor, on *On Liberty*, see, for example, the introduction to the Penguin Books edition (New York, 1974) of *On Liberty* by Gertrude Himmelfarb, 16–20.
40. *Brooklyn Institute v. City of New York*, 197: "The Museum is suffering and will continue to suffer irreparable harm if an injunction is not granted. 'The loss of First Amendment freedoms, for even minimal periods of time, unquestionably constitutes irreparable injury.' *Elrod v. Burns*, 427 U.S. 347, 373 (1976) (plurality opinion); *Bery v. City of New York*, 97 F.3d 689, 693 (2d Cir. 1996), cert. denied 520 U.S. 1251 (1997)."
41. See, for example, ibid., 191, where Judge Gershon quotes the mayor as saying, "You don't have a right to a government subsidy to desecrate someone else's religion. And therefore we will do everything that we can to remove funding from the [Museum] until the director comes to his senses."
42. See text accompanying note 35 above.
43. See text accompanying notes 15–24 above.
44. *Brooklyn Institute v. City of New York*, 193–196, discussing the principles of *Younger v. Harris*, 401 U.S. 37 (1971), and its progeny, which suggest that when an adequate state remedy is available and state proceedings are underway, federal courts should abstain from involvement in the dispute.
45. *Brooklyn Institute v. City of New York*, 192–198 (semble).
46. *Rosenberger v. Rector and Visitors of the University of Virginia*, 515 U.S. 819 (1995).
47. *Brooklyn Institute v. City of New York*, 204–205.
48. For Judge Gershon's use of the *Mein Kampf* point, see ibid., 202–203; for Floyd Abrams's invocation of the "book in the library" argument, see *The NewsHour with Jim Lehrer*, October 8, 1999 (transcript on Nexis).
49. *Brooklyn Institute v. City of New York*, 202–203.
50. Quoted by Judge Gershon, ibid., 191.
51. Charles Dickens, *Oliver Twist*, ed. Peter Fairclough (1837–1838; reprint, New York: Penguin Books, 1966), 461.
52. Paul Johnson, "Toward Recovery," *National Review* 52, no. 1 (January 24, 2000): 41.
53. See, for example, James Madison's "Memorial and Remonstrance against Religious Assessments" (1785), in Robert A. Rutland and William M. E. Rachal, eds., *Papers of James Madison* (Chicago: University of Chicago Press, 1962), 8: 295.

J. MARK SCHUSTER

Who Should Pay (for the Arts and Culture)? Who Should Decide? And What Difference Should It Make?

What can a public-policy analyst add to a debate that has already been framed as a legal debate? That is the challenge presented to me.

The controversy surrounding the *Sensation* exhibit at the Brooklyn Museum inexorably draws our attention to the legal debate as a way of making sense of the unfolding drama. Why? Partly, I suppose, because we like to identify clear winners and losers; we prefer to be right rather than wrong; we would like to see "good"—as defined from our own perspective—prevail; and we are curious to figure out who exactly occupies the legal high ground in this story.[1] But how you perceive the high ground depends almost entirely on where you stand. If that is true, perhaps the law is not the only body of knowledge worth consulting in order to discover why such controversies occur and to predict how they might play out in the future. In any event, what we can generalize from this incident is much more interesting than deciding who is right and who is wrong, or who behaved well and who behaved poorly.

Our attention is also drawn to a legal framing of the controversy because, whether we are museum directors, museum visitors, museum supporters, or simply informed citizens, we desire clarity about the rules within which we are going to have to operate. But suppose that we had such a rule firmly rooted in law and that it provided clear and unambiguous instruction to arts-funding agencies as to how they could and should behave in such circumstances. Would those agencies that we ask to fund the arts and promulgate cultural policy on our behalf then be content with behaving in that way? An answer to this question has to be found, at least in part, in how arts-funding agencies and the institutions and artists that they fund behave in practice rather than in theory.

I will argue that we need to take account of three broad sets of changes in order to understand how museum-funding controversies are likely to play out: changes in the arts-funding system itself, changes in museums themselves, and changes in the attitudes of citizens. Each of these topics deserves at least a chapter in its own right, so I will have to compress a tremendous amount of material into a limited amount of space. I claim to know most about the first, so that is where my focus will lie.

At the heart of the Brooklyn Museum uproar was Mayor Rudolph Giuliani's view that the wishes of those who were funding the exhibit through public support were not being adequately represented and that it was incumbent on him to step in and play that role. In other words, in the mayor's view, there was a mismatch between those who were providing communal funding and those who were ultimately deciding how that communal funding was to be spent. I have avoided using the phrase *state funding* here because it seems that the more general point of a mismatch between those who pay and those who decide is the important one.

What is the American arts-funding system? In the American "model," at least with respect to direct aid, arts funding is supported by general tax revenues but is separated to some degree from the political process by reliance on peer panels to make recommendations about projects, for which the state may not provide more than 50 percent of the cost.[2] Each of these elements is important to the design of the system: a reliance on general tax revenues, which reflects the idea that arts funding is in the common interest; some insulation from day-to-day politics (although not as much insulation, it is often argued, as that provided by the arm's length principle in Great Britain); the involvement of peers in advice giving and, less frequently, in actual decision making; the consideration of specific projects with no presupposition of ongoing support; and the idea that other sources must share the burden of the costs of any particular project. But while this model has been at the center of government support for the arts in the United States, whether it currently is an adequate representation of the entire system (or, indeed, whether it ever was) is doubtful. When we attempt to describe government funding systems we inevitably describe them as though they were both uniform and stable. Neither is actually the case.

First, at any particular moment there is considerable variation in arts-funding systems across levels of government. While many of the state arts agencies originally modeled their decision-making procedures on those of the National Endowment for the Arts (NEA) (whose procedures can, for the moment, be assumed to be those I have described as the American "model"), there is now considerable variation across the state arts agencies in how they make funding decisions. Moreover, little evidence suggests that the hundreds of local arts agencies conduct their funding processes in this manner. It certainly does not seem to be the way that New York City structures its arts funding.

Second, debates concerning the design of an appropriate arts-funding policy, fueled, on the one hand, by various arts-funding controversies such as the one we are considering here and, on the other, by a desire to provide what were thought to be more reliable resources to the arts and culture, have led to a variety of new ways of amassing and distributing communal resources for the arts and culture. These changes become particularly clear if we take an international comparative look at what is happening to arts-funding structures; we are witnessing the implementation of a wide variety of new answers to the question "Who should pay for the arts and culture?"

Finally, and for similar reasons, these same debates have also led to a wide variety of new answers to the question that Stephen Presser rightly identifies as being key: "Who ought to decide how the public funds that are committed to art [and culture] should be spent?"

To make the ecology of funding and decision making even more complicated, one now observes multiple forms of fundraising and fund distributing even within single arts-funding agencies; this development makes it difficult indeed for the manager of an arts institution to figure out how to tap these various spigots and for the public-policy analyst to untangle their separate effects. Nevertheless, it is incumbent on us to attempt to do so if we are to understand the impacts of the system we have designed and if we are to truly understand the implications of arts-funding controversies such as the one at the Brooklyn Museum.

Who Should Pay?

If there is a societal benefit associated with the arts that goes beyond the enjoyment of private individual consumers, then there is an argument for some communal involvement in the provision of those extra benefits, and resources are therefore needed. Where will they come from? The traditional answer is general tax revenues, but it no longer is the only answer. Two movements in government finance have particularly affected the arts and culture. The first is the movement to contract the size of the public sector. Resources are no longer sufficient to pay for those services that have heretofore fallen to public-sector provision, it is claimed, and activities that are deemed to be at the margin are experiencing substantial budget cuts. This move has led to a variety of ways to get the arts off-budget" and to a variety of ways to rearrange communal funding. A second, and not unrelated, idea has been to more nearly match those who benefit and those who pay by implementing more narrowly targeted revenue-raising schemes for each sector. Because audiences for the arts and culture come from particular demographic slices of society, this idea has led some to the conclusion that general tax revenues are an inappropriate source of funds for the arts and culture. Taken together these movements have led to a search for "new," or at least alternative, revenue sources. The theoretical question of who should pay has become translated into two practical questions: How can we find more money, and how can we find more appropriate money?

Accordingly, I will now describe what I see as some of the more significant trends in revenue raising for the arts. Some programs have concentrated on increasing "public" revenue, but public revenue with rather different characteristics than general tax revenues.

Dedicated State Lotteries

An innovation in arts funding is the use of dedicated revenues from government-run or government-licensed lotteries to fund the arts and culture. This approach is becoming common, particularly in English-speaking countries with a tradition of arm's length arts councils. Lottery revenues are (or have been) earmarked for the arts at the state level in the United States, at the provincial level in Canada and Western Australia, and at the national level in Ireland, New Zealand, Finland, and the United Kingdom. State or local lotteries or both are also used to fund the arts in Germany. Note that while dedicated state lotteries may, in fact, provide increased revenues to the arts and culture, they pose an interesting problem of their own when it comes to considering the incidence of payments and benefits; the British tabloid press has been eager to point out that it is the poor working-class bloke who wagers a few quid on occasion who is paying for, among other items, the renovation and expansion of the Royal Opera House.[3]

Dedicated Taxes

In the United States, as well as elsewhere, a variety of dedicated taxes have been implemented in order to help fund the arts and culture: hotel/motel taxes, admissions taxes, entertainment taxes, special taxation districts, to name a few. In the six-county region surrounding Denver, Colorado, for example, a one-tenth of one percent increment in the general sales tax is dedicated to arts and science facilities. In Argentina, an additional tax is collected on movie tickets and deposited into a variety of funds that aid libraries, the motion-picture industry, and the arts more generally. On occasion, special taxes are implemented to create self-financing within a particular subsector. Generally, this tax is later refunded if the revenues are spent within the sector. Take, for example, the French film industry. A supplementary tax is collected on admissions to French films; it can be recouped by the producer but only if it is reinvested in a new French film. These are generally seen as cross-subsidization schemes; some operate within the tourism industry, others operate within particular artistic sectors or particular geographic areas. As such, they are generally seen as a way to bring those who pay into better alignment with those who benefit.

Another category of answers to the question of who should pay focuses on using state action to increase the amount of private money available to the arts and culture.

Required Expenditures

One rather blunt way some governments have increased private resources flowing to the arts and culture is to require such expenditures. In Spain, savings banks are required to reinvest a portion of their profits in their communities. Some, like La Caixa in Barcelona have supported extensive programs in the arts and culture. In Sweden, the way in which corporations were first "encouraged" to get involved in supporting the arts was by requiring them to provide artistic experiences as part of their corporate programs for their employees. Throughout the world, governments have implemented "percent for arts" legislation. Typically, through these laws governments require of themselves that a specified percentage of the construction cost of new facilities must be spent on public art associated with that facility. Such laws have also been used to require private expenditure on artworks. In some places (for example, San Francisco) developers are required to pay into linkage funds to ameliorate the impact of their large-scale real estate projects. These linkage funds may include funds for arts and cultural activities. Required expenditure also seems to be happening across levels of government. In Russia, a law requires municipalities to spend a specified percentage of their budgets on the arts and culture. What effect this law will have remains to be seen.[4]

Incentives

The area of incentives has provided fertile ground for innovations in arts funding. With most incentives, some government resources are provided contingent on the increased deployment of private resources in the arts and culture. Perhaps the most familiar and most widely used incentives are tax-based incentives, but even within this category there is considerable variation.[5]

Matching Grants

Matching grants are another American innovation that has begun to show up in the arts-funding packages of a number of countries. With a matching grant a promise is made to a selected institution: for every additional $X you are able to raise, the funding agency will provide $Y. In this way the recipient is challenged by the funding agency to increase its base of support. Matching grants have come to be widely used in the United States by private donors as well as by government agencies. Ironically, this program, while designed to promote diversity in fundraising and decision making, works in practice, to bring different funding sources in line with one another to fund the same initiative. The matching-grant experience suggests the possibility that plurality of decision making does not necessarily imply diversity of decision making, or, put another way, having more decision makers does not necessarily ensure that different decisions will be made.[6] But this is getting a bit ahead of my story.

Of more importance in the current instance is the move to what I have termed *reverse matching grants*. Reverse matching grants, instead of challenging particular arts institutions, offer a broad invitation to the field and make the promise that within certain limits any arts institution that is able to attract increased private support will automatically qualify for a government match. What is most important to notice about this form of matching grant is that it is based on public money following private decisions rather than the other way around. Its basic underlying principle is that private donors ought to decide on the allocation of public money in proportion to changes in their private decisions.

This move toward reverse matching grants has ideological roots in the turn toward private initiative as a trigger for appropriate public initiative, and it has a practical and pervasive precedent in the tax deduction for charitable contributions, which itself can be seen as a form of reverse matching grant. But reverse matching grants have another attraction: whenever there is an increase in a government's reticence to decide which artistic and cultural activities are worthy of support, particularly when those decisions might involve unusually vague criteria of aesthetics and innovation that easily cross over into the politically contentious issues of censorship, it may be easier to have the decision take place outside of government altogether.[7]

Institutional Innovations

Some governments have experimented with handling components of their arts funding through institutions external to government. One such method is the freestanding endowment, which functions more like a private foundation than a government agency. The Prince Bernhard Foundation, which works alongside the arts ministry in the Netherlands, is a large foundation independent of government that was created as a reaction to the Nazi example of a centralized cultural bureaucracy. Money from football pools (starting in 1960) and from the national lottery (starting in 1970) has kept the foundation from being completely overwhelmed by the influence of the centrally funded ministry. The Canada Council was originally modeled on the large American private foundations, with its endowment coming from death duties levied on the estates of two prominent industrialists—Sir James Dunn and Izaak Walton Killam. The government of Japan has created the Japan Arts Fund, an independent arts-funding endowment, by providing ¥50 billion matched by ¥10 billion in contributions from private corporations. The *Boston Globe* published an editorial in 2000 calling for the transformation of the National Endowments for the Arts and Humanities into true endowments so that they could be buffered from stormy politics.[8] Part of the theory is that these endowments might prove more attractive to other private contributors later than would a government agency.

From time to time, government arts-funding agencies create new institutions and spin them off into the nonprofit sector. The Massachusetts Council on the Arts and Humanities, prohibited by the state legislature from making grants directly to artists, which the legislature felt would be problematic, circumvented the legislature's restrictions by creating the Artists Foundation, a nonprofit agency that would have an annual contract with the state arts agency and would regrant state money to individual artists. The New York State Council on the Arts has used a similar device. Such intermediary institutions are also attractive for running other programs that the funding agency might find desirable because they may be less restricted in hiring and payment practices and they offer the possibility of attracting sources of funding that would not be attracted to a government agency.

Who Should Decide?

Turning now to my second question—Who should decide how these resources are to be allocated?—we will see that the answers are not entirely independent of one's answers to the first question. Answering this question is simplest when it is asked of private resources allocated by private individuals (even though we, as a society, might not particularly like what they choose to fund). It is considerably more problematic when it is asked with respect to the allocation of public funds, particularly when this allocation is hidden within another mechanism, as it is, for example, with incentives. Here, once again, we find a number of competing models.

Professional Staff/Experts

This is the model we most often associate with a ministry of culture. The decision-making body is the ministry's professional staff, and the decisions of the staff are thought to be legitimate because of its presumed expertise. Interestingly, as one travels down the government hierarchy from national to state to local, the influence of the staff may well increase. This increase in influence may in part be due to a sense that local knowledge is sufficient to make local funding decisions, but it may also be due to the administrative costs of implementing an alternative decision-making mechanism, costs that are seen to be more prohibitive at the local level.

Peer-Panel Review

Peer assessment is at the heart of much of American arts funding. It is also typical of arm's length arts-funding agencies operating on the British model, but it is now quite prevalent elsewhere as well. This model of decision making is based on two assumptions: (1) your peers are the individuals who are best able to judge the qualities of your work, and (2) the decisions that your peers make in response to those qualities best reflect the public interest in arts funding.

The first of these assumptions is probably more widely held than the second. In fact, the second is hardly discussed at all in arts-policy debates. But both are necessary as a justification for entrusting the decision-making process concerning the allocation of public resources to peer-panel review. Even with no further information on the actual practice, it would not be difficult to predict the criticism of peer-panel review: it is a "closed system with friends awarding one another according to values that are not shared by the society at large." In most fields in which the government becomes involved, such a situation would be characterized as a textbook case of "regulatory capture"—the agency created to interact with, subsidize, shape, regulate, or control a particular sector of society has been "captured" by that sector. In the arts we are much too polite to one another to suggest such a possibility.[9]

One should not make the mistake, however, of treating peer-panel review as though it were a single, unitary approach to arts funding; within the NEA itself different forms of peer-panel review with different procedures are practiced. Nevertheless, Frank Hodsoll, when he was chair of the NEA, got into considerable difficulty with the art world for suggesting that peer-panel review might be constrained in a way that would enhance its accountability to the American public.[10] (This incident warrants further attention as it is an example of the field branding what a funding agency was doing as controversial as opposed to the other way around.)

Line-Item Budgeting/Earmarking

As the Brooklyn Museum case suggests, our elected officials are not always reticent to get directly involved in deciding who should receive government support, and considerable evidence suggests that legislatures are becoming more involved through legislative earmarking (line-item budgeting, or "mainlining"). This trend has been visible at all three levels of government in the United States and has caused considerable political problems for those arts councils that have taken what they perceived as the high ground and opposed earmarking.

Even as arts institutions have continued their defense of peer-panel review, they have at the same time lobbied for earmarking in an attempt to garner additional public resources. Through this device an arts institution receives a specified amount directly from the government's budget without any intervening decisions by arts councils or peer-panel review. Edward Arian in his book *The Unfulfilled Promise: Public Subsidy of the Arts in America* suggests that lobbying by arts institutions for line items in the budget or in support of an increased budget for the arts-funding agency in exchange for prearranged grants (a less overt form of earmarking) has increased markedly.[11]

Formula Funding

Another solution to the complexity of arts-funding decision making has been the adoption of predetermined formulas for arts funding. These formulas exist in many guises. The NEA currently must distribute a set percentage of its grant money to state arts agencies either through the base grant to which they are entitled or through the normal decisions of the other NEA programs. In New York State, the state legislature passed a per capita minimum to assure grant distribution to each of the state's counties; the Massachusetts Arts Lottery Council used a state revenue-sharing formula to distribute arts-lottery money to local distribution committees;[12] various state arts councils use formula funding in at least some of their programs, perhaps first qualifying a grantee for a particular program by one procedure or another and then determining the amount of the grant through a formula; and the design of some matching grants makes use of an automatic formula to determine the level of government support. Politicians may impose a formula (instead of specifying particular beneficiaries), or the arts-funding agency may adopt a formula internally.

Finally, a number of decision-making models are premised on allowing individuals to decide how communal resources are to be spent in a decentralized, disaggregated fashion that approximates a private market. Here are just a few.

Tax Incentives and Matching Grants

Tax incentives have this property to the extent that individuals get to choose how the forgone taxes involved in the transaction that has benefited from the incentive will be spent. Matching grants, particularly reverse matching grants, behave similarly. Public money follows private money as its behavioral patterns are matched.

Vouchers

Vouchers provide an even more decentralized decision-making scheme for the allocation of public resources. Favored by economists who wish to promote "consumer sovereignty," vouchers provide a demand-side subsidy: an individual is provided with a voucher with a specified face value; that voucher can then be used to purchase artistic goods or services according to the stipulations of the particular voucher program. While the use of vouchers has been considered in the cultural-policy literature as being primarily of theoretical interest, a number of voucher programs have been run in the arts with interesting results.[13]

Citizen Referenda

Finally, at one extreme of decision making by individual citizens is the use of public referenda to approve cultural expenditures. In Switzerland, major expenditures on the arts are often subject to a public referendum. Between 1950 and 1983 there were 108 such referenda in major municipalities. Of them, 82 percent were passed by a majority of the voters (as opposed to 89 percent for other purposes). Over time the percentage of cultural-expenditure referenda being approved has risen, while the corresponding percentage for all other purposes has fallen.[14]

A complete search of cultural policy would reveal many more examples of innovative programs seeking to provide increased communal resources to the arts and culture and to provide alternative decision-making structures that respond more readily to a variety of communal values, but these examples suffice to make the point that arts- and cultural-funding agencies have been quite creative in tapping revenue-raising instruments that might provide not only more communal resources but also a way to circumvent the decision-making difficulties inherent in certain funding mechanisms. Retrenchment is not the only option, nor has it been the most important one; institutional innovation is where the current public-policy action is.

Taken together these examples demonstrate how the questions "Who should pay?" and "Who should decide?" are percolating up into the arts-policy debate. Seen in this way, the debate is less about what sort of artistic initiatives should be publicly supported or about the future of the NEA or any other arts-funding agency or about the future of public funding more generally than it is about how the public interest is to be taken into account in arts funding. Here, the Brooklyn Museum controversy looms less large and ominous; instead it may be a bellwether of changes in arts-funding decision making that are already underway. It may be a ham-fisted bellwether, but it is a bellwether nonetheless. Whether Mayor Giuliani, Director Arnold Lehman of the Brooklyn Museum, the board of the Brooklyn Museum, or Charles Saatchi is vindicated will not matter very much. The arts-funding system is evolving in ways that will fundamentally change the terrain on which these questions will be engaged.

Defensible Arts Funding

Another change in arts funding is worth noting, a change that fits a bit less neatly under the rubrics of "who should pay" and "who should decide" but that is no less important. Arts-funding controversies are not new. They did not begin with Andres Serrano or Robert Mapplethorpe or the rise of the religious right in American politics (nor will they end with the Brooklyn Museum). What is new is that the defense strategy that once worked for arts-funding agencies in the face of such controversies seems to no longer have the power it once did. Michael Straight's biography of Nancy Hanks, chairman of the NEA from

1969 to 1977, contains a candid discussion of a number of such controversies that plagued the NEA through its early years.[15] What is particularly interesting about these accounts is that the NEA chose to pursue a procedural defense rather than a substantive defense in every single case: "Senator, I appreciate your strongly held personal view concerning this work of art, but I can assure you that the NEA strictly followed the procedures that we have agreed on with the Congress in making this grant. I shall investigate, and if I find that our procedures were violated, I will not hesitate to pull the grant." In those few instances in which a lapse in procedure was uncovered, the grant was rescinded; but in most cases the procedural defense won the day.

Recent controversies have made it quite clear that American legislatures (and the public) are becoming less willing to accept a procedural defense on behalf of arts-funding agencies. Questions are being asked about what the agency hopes to accomplish in its programs and how a particular grant furthers those objectives. From a public-policy point of view, this new emphasis seems unexceptional; should we expect any less from our public agencies, whether they are in the field of education, employment, or the arts? But, in the arts, this marks a clear departure from previous practice, and this departure has not been without the pains that come from a reorientation of a public funding program.

Arguably, this trend can be seen most clearly in the public support of museums. Stephen Weil, an acute observer of the museum world, sees a number of pressures that are combining to bring museums that seek public support to reorient themselves toward public service. "The emerging public-service-oriented museum must see itself not as a cause but as an instrument. In some considerable measure, the cost of maintaining that instrument is paid by the community: by direct community support, by the community's forbearance from collecting real estate, water, sewer, and other local taxes, by the considerable portion of every private tax-deductible contribution that constitutes an indirect public subsidy from the community. For that reason alone, it might be argued, the community is legitimately entitled to have some choice—not the only choice, but *some* choice [emphasis in original]—in determining just how that instrument is to be used."[16]

Today's governments are less willing to pass along public resources to the not-for-profit sector without insisting on accountability, transparency, and effectiveness. In Great Britain, the mantra has become "value for money." Elsewhere, including in the United States, there has been a renewed interest in developing a set of performance indicators that adequately measure institutional effectiveness. As one can imagine, this movement has engendered controversy in its own right and a growth industry in conferences, seminars, and consultants' report. Yet, behind all these demands for accountability, again in the words of Weil, is a single, reasonable, hard-nosed question: "Is this institution demonstrably using the resources entrusted to it to achieve what it said it intended to achieve when it requested and was given those resources?"[17]

Arts-funding agencies are beginning to become much more sophisticated in thinking about how their procedures and their decisions reflect the public interest, and they will have to become even more so. As a case in point, the Council of Europe has been conducting a series of evaluations of national cultural policies of its member states with exactly this focus. Similarly, arts organizations will be forced to think more carefully and more clearly about what it means to accept public resources. Presser points us in this direction when he considers the Brooklyn Museum case from the perspective of partnership law. While I leave it to other contributors to this volume to work out whether partnership law is a legally justifiable branch of the law from which to view and within which to adjudicate the Brooklyn Museum case, it is incumbent on me to notice that all the trends I have been describing do work together to redefine the relationship between a funding agency and its grantees into more of a partnership arrangement.

What is the nature of the funding relationship between an arts-funding agency and the recipient of that funding? Is it a gift? An entitlement? A reward? Or is it an agreement to exchange public resources for activities that are deemed to be in the public interest? This question has seldom been addressed directly in the arts, and, as a result, it has bedeviled arts-funding agencies and their relationships with their clients.

In the British model, a relatively small number of institutions are typically qualified as revenue clients of the Arts Council of England, and they are then assured of receiving rather substantial operating support on an annual basis. This model has made it difficult for successive secretaries general of the Arts Council to have any palpable effect on the policy direction of the agency; entitlement overwhelms any attempt to pursue policy. In one of its periodic policy documents, the Arts Council called for reconceptualizing the grants made by funding bodies as contracts, with all the responsibilities and expectations that contracts place on both parties to the transaction.[18] Unfortunately, little evidence suggests that the Arts Council has succeeded in this endeavor, even as many other events have rendered the Arts Council a less important player in British arts funding than it once was.

In the American model, at least in theory, funding is project-based, though a number of commentators point out that that principle is honored in the breach.[19] Hodsoll, for one, publicly lamented the fact that panel recommendations seem to follow the principle of "history plus or minus," rather than the principle of decisions being made *de novo* with respect to each proposed project. One possible result of recent arts-funding controversies in the United States may be the reaffirmation of project-based support as fundamental; this result would force arts-funding agencies to make specific decisions about specific projects in competition with other projects and to retreat from an approximation of entitled, ongoing operating support.

Whatever else is muddied by the current debate, it does seem clear that it will no longer be sufficient for government arts agencies to simply say, "Well, we spent it on the arts, Senator" in explanation (and in defense) of their funding choices.

Hybridization

From the public-policy point of view one other point deserves to be made concerning museums. Part of the key to unlocking the relevance of the Brooklyn Museum controversy to broader considerations of arts-funding policy lies in how we conceptualize our arts institutions. Until relatively recently, it seems to me, we have too easily fallen into the trap of characterizing arts organizations as either "public" or "private." We have spoken of private museums and public museums as though it were clear which museums belonged in which category and what the implications of that characterization were.

Partly this is a question of posture. If I were a museum director, I would certainly emphasize the privateness of my institution if I were trying to defend it against an interventionist funding agency, but I would emphasize its publicness if I were trying to justify the expenditure of public resources on its programs. But the issue of private versus public goes well beyond one's chosen posture toward fundamental aspects of the structure of U.S. museums. It is not at all uncommon for public elements and private elements to be combined within the same museum. Consider, as one example, the American Museum of Natural History, created in 1869: "[T]he city undertook to pay for the building and its maintenance costs while private donors agreed to support the scientific inquiry intended to take place within its walls."[20] Then consider what happens when the trustees of the building (representing the city, whose demographics have changed dramatically since the founding of the museum) and the trustees of the collection (representing the private, nonprofit interests that founded the collection) disagree fundamentally on what the future of the museum should be. The Brooklyn Museum, too, is a case in point. Is it a private museum or a public museum? It is actually both. The building is owned and maintained by the City of New York, but the trustees of the private, nonprofit entity that operates the museum own and make decisions concerning the collection and exhibitions, and in this case the interests of a private collector need to be taken into account as well.

The complexity of arts-funding controversies when they involve museums is in no small part due to the fact that most museums are private-public hybrids. Many of the recent museum controversies that have come to the public's attention can be explained rather easily if we understand that they are hybrids operating in a world that we heretofore have thought of as being occupied by pure types.[21] If identifying where the public interest stops and the private interest begins in a hybrid museum is no small analytical feat, identifying where the private interest should stop can be treacherous indeed. But that is exactly what we will have to do if we wish to bring the public interest more in line with public funding. In the end, is that not what Mayor Giuliani was pursuing, albeit in his own politically provocative way? And is that not what we want our arts-funding agencies to be doing? And is that not what we would prefer our museums to be pursuing, at least to the extent that they are in receipt of public support?[22]

If we reify the Brooklyn Museum case into a battle between good and evil, between right and wrong, or between the educated elite and the uninformed masses, we are unlikely to inform the general debate very much. If we instead consider its component pieces in the context of emerging questions and trends in arts funding and decision making and with the understanding that we are dealing with a complex institutional hybrid, then I believe that it can contribute, like other controversies before and others to come, to the construction of a robust and defensible system of arts support.

In conclusion, one could do worse than to reiterate the closing sentence of David Strauss's essay: "Ringing First Amendment victories, however gratifying, are a sign of underlying weakness in the forum of popular opinion, and that is where the battle for government funding of the arts will be won or lost." On second thought, maybe I cannot resist the temptation to turn it on its head: "Ringing First Amendment victories, however gratifying, are a sign of underlying weakness in the contribution of museums to the public interest, and that is where their claim for government funding will ultimately be won or lost." We should expect no less of public policy, whatever its field of application.

NOTES

1. If I am correct here, it is probably also worth asking ourselves whether there is something peculiarly American about this tendency. Are other cultures

more willing to accept ambiguity in these matters, to live with self-contradictory arts-funding and cultural-policy systems? Anecdotal evidence would suggest they are, it seems to me.

2. One could equally well argue that the American model is actually a tax-incentive model fueled primarily by indirect aid in the form of forgone taxes. Although this model is not being called into question in the current controversy, it does merit attention in a full discussion of decision making and arts funding and is therefore discussed later in this essay. I am aware that my characterization of the American model here is not directly applicable to the Brooklyn Museum case. In this case, we have local support, not made at arm's length from local government, with no role played by peer review.
3. Of course, there are a number of important public-policy questions that one wants to ask about lottery funding: Does earmarked money end up substituting for rather than adding to direct government funding? What are the implications of taking arts-funding agencies off-budget in this way? Does this trend mean that the arts and culture are being viewed increasingly as part of the "entertainment industry" and that a new principle is operating that says any cross-subsidization should happen within this industry? Are different decision-making mechanisms made possible by moving toward dedicated lotteries? If so, what are their implications for arts funding?

   For a further consideration of dedicated state lotteries, see J. Mark Schuster, "Funding the Arts and Culture through Dedicated State Lotteries—Part I: The Twin Issues of Additionality and Substitution," *European Journal of Cultural Policy* 1, no. 1 (1994): 21–41; and J. Mark Schuster, "Funding the Arts and Culture through Dedicated State Lotteries—Part II: Opening the Way for Alternative Decision Making and Funding Structures," *European Journal of Cultural Policy* 1, no. 2 (1994): 329–354.
4. In a similar vein, British law has been revised to explicitly authorize (though not require) local authorities to make expenditures in the field of the arts and culture.
5. For further discussion of tax-based incentive schemes in the arts and culture, see J. Mark Schuster, "The Other Side of the Subsidized Muse: Indirect Aid Revisited," *Journal of Cultural Economics* 23, nos. 1/2 (1999): 51–70.
6. Once again there are a number of interesting public-policy questions. See J. Mark Schuster, "Government Leverage of Private Support: Matching Grants and the Problem with 'New' Money," in Margaret Wyszomirski and Pat Clubb (eds.), *The Cost of Culture: Patterns and Prospects of Private Arts Patronage* (New York: American Council for the Arts, 1989).
7. The most extreme example of a reverse matching grant is the Business Sponsorship Incentive Scheme in Great Britain; it is worth paying attention to because it represents one clear direction in which public arts funding is evolving. Lord Gowrie, former British minister for the arts, felt considerable pressure from the Margaret Thatcher government to encourage new sources of funding for the arts. Deciding to begin where he felt he could demonstrate the greatest direct interest to new funding sources, he turned to corporate sponsorship; through such sponsorship corporations could derive substantial public-relations and advertising benefits by associating themselves with cultural events and institutions. (The British draw a strict legal distinction between sponsorship and contributions; sponsorship has to be nearly entirely to the advantage of the sponsor.) He created the Business Sponsorship Incentive Scheme by offering to match new or increased sponsorship.

   The most telling aspect of this reverse matching grant, though, is the "enhancement" clause. While it was clear that the corporation's sponsorship money would be used primarily for the narrow purposes of the sponsor—

advertising, banners, logos, and the like—there was a question as to how the public match might be used. The enhancement clause urges that the public match be used by the recipient arts institution to enhance the value of the sponsorship to the sponsor. In other words, the arts are expected not to put the money into general operations or other specific initiatives but to buy additional advertising and public relations for the corporate sponsor. The cleverest sponsors now take full advantage of the enhancement clause by spending the expected match up front. When the match is actually received by the arts institution, it is then repaid to the sponsor. Thus, the idea of a reverse matching grant is carried to its logical extreme.

8. "Political Action for the Arts," *Boston Globe*, January 31, 2000, p. A16.
9. Like many such societal processes, though, it is much easier to see how an individual might have this belief than it is to see how one would study the system in order to conclude whether it is indeed true.
10. For a discussion of this controversy, see J. Mark Schuster, "The Formula Funding Controversy at the National Endowment for the Arts," *Nonprofit Management & Leadership* 2, no. 1 (September 1991): 37–57.
11. Edward Arian, *The Unfulfilled Promise: Public Subsidy of the Arts in America* (Philadelphia: Temple University Press, 1989).
12. Interestingly, this style of arts funding has survived the forced merger of the Massachusetts Council on the Arts and Humanities and the Massachusetts Arts Lottery Council into the Massachusetts Cultural Council.
13. Writing elsewhere, I have discussed the success of the Wintario Halfback Program, a voucher program in which losing lottery tickets in a dedicated lottery became vouchers at half their face value. See J. Mark Schuster, "Funding the Arts and Culture through Dedicated State Lotteries—Part II."

    Heilbrun and Gray, in their textbook on the economics of the arts, discuss vouchers briefly and conclude that it is an idea without a constituency. They seem to mean that the strongest constituents for government arts funding—that is, major cultural institutions—believe that because of their relative influence they can do better under a direct funding system than under a voucher system, which is likely to spread subsidy more thinly. James Heilbrun and Charles M. Gray, *The Economics of Art and Culture: An American Perspective* (Cambridge: Cambridge University Press, 1993), 266–268.
14. In one such instance two Pablo Picasso paintings, *Les Deux Frères* and *Arlequin Assis,* were offered for sale for 8.4 million Swiss francs. These paintings were already on loan to the collection of the Basle Art Gallery, and the government of the canton of Basle-City decided it would spend 6.4 million if 2 million additional could be found privately, but the 6.4 million was subject to a public referendum. In October 1967 there was a lively debate about art and the community and the role of modern art. Ultimately 53.9 percent of the voters voted yes. Picasso was so delighted he donated two further paintings and two drawings to the museum. Bruno S. Frey and Werner W. Pommerehne, *Muses & Markets: Explorations in the Economics of the Arts* (Oxford: Blackwell, 1989), 169.
15. Michael Straight, *Nancy Hanks: An Intimate Portrait—The Creation of a National Commitment to the Arts* (Durham, N.C.: Duke University Press, 1988); see particularly ch. 40, "Following the Market: The Visual Arts," and ch. 46, "Four Controversial Grants."
16. Stephen E. Weil, "From Being *about* Something to Being *for* Somebody: The Ongoing Transformation of the American Museum," *Daedalus* 128, no. 3 (Summer 1999): 254. The idea of museums' changing from being about something to being for somebody is picked up and expanded on nicely in Michael Rushton, "Public Funding of Controversial Art," *Journal of Cultural Economics* 24, no. 4 (2000): 267–282.

17. Weil, "From Being *about* Something to Being *for* Somebody," 252.
18. Arts Council of Great Britain, *A Creative Future: The Way Forward for the Arts, Crafts and Media in England* (London: Her Majesty's Stationer's Office, 1993), 47.
19. And the creation of other institutional mechanisms, such as the Institute for Museum and Library Services, to provide ongoing operating support dilutes this effect.
20. Stephen R. Graubard, "Preface to the Issue 'America's Museums,'" *Daedalus* 128, no. 3 (Summer 1999): vii.
21. For a further discussion of hybridization in museums, see J. Mark Schuster, "Neither Public nor Private: The Hybridization of Museums," *Journal of Cultural Economics* 22, nos. 2–3 (1998): 127–150.
22. Of course, once one recognizes indirect aid through forgone taxes as a form of public support, then virtually every museum is seen to be in receipt of public support.

PART III

Art Off-Limits

PUBLIC RESPECT AND THE READING OF ART

HOMI K. BHABHA

The Subjunctive Mood of Art

Whenever we talk about these issues, we become culture bores because we talk about the culture wars. But I want to suggest that crises within the spheres of education and culture more generally or the arts and arts institutions are crises within a peculiar and properly peculiar private and public realm. I wish to talk about hybridization because this particularly highly mediated, overdetermined, contradictory and complex area of the public-cum-private is where, I think, museums and universities fall, where artists arise, and where the questions of curatorship and arts organizations and practice, and deep policy, too, obtain.

I would like briefly to discuss why I think some of these complications arise in this particular public-private sphere, or public-cum-private sphere, in this rather peculiar articulation. On the one hand, we expect and we know that art is representational. It's about images, allegories, symbols, passion, affect, ideas clothed in metaphors, a highly mediated, highly interpretational, passionate, emotional body of work and practice. On the other hand, when these works enter public cultural institutions, we additionally expect them to be representative. We celebrate artists because they are marginal, because they take us where people normally do not go in their daily lives. We celebrate artists because they live on the edge, and yet, at the same time, this experience is not well served by being considered entirely subjective. The mood of art, I believe, is not simply subjective and individual. I would suggest that the mood of art is subjunctive. It expresses wishes, commands, but, more than anything else, it is a contingent hypothetical or indeed perspective event in the fullest historical and cultural sense of those terms.

However, when art enters what I have called the representative domain of the public institution, certain prescriptions, certain limitations are often brought to bear, particularly when we discuss it in crises. And we do increasingly seem to discuss cultural crises, but we also discuss culture in crisis. I almost begin to think that when any concept of culture is being debated, it is somehow an invitation or a response to a certain crisis. It's almost as if you never ponder your identity until or unless somebody challenges it, questions it, asks you about it—only then do you give a narrative about your identity. So, first, the work of art in the representative domain is somehow not expected to be offensive. We must not challenge certain traditional or stereotypical ways of thinking or visualizing religion, sex, issues of public taste.

Second, often when prophecies arise and crises arise, when works are considered to be obscure in their representation and meaning, it is expected that "we the people" should be more or less able to understand the works displayed in the institutions we financially support. It should never be forgotten that a pile of bricks was once as controversial as *Piss Christ.* Let us also not forget that when T. S. Eliot's *Wasteland,* now the most popular poem studied in Japanese schools, was first published, a whole raft of opinion suggested that by ending the poem "shanti, shanti, shanti," which would not be understood by most readers, Eliot was provoking people to think of "panty, panty, panty."

There is a third issue here too, that somehow art should not contradict the idea of a relatively stable and homogenous cultural citizenship. This issue often emerges when museums or institutions of higher learning attend to new constituencies; questions emerge that we might call issues of the minority public interest. The sense is that this minority public interest is an exacerbation of cultural difference and cultural contradiction where instead there should be a much more harmonious homogenization of what I call cultural citizenship.

Now I have been using the word *we* quite a lot. But who is this "we"? Who are "we" as we are spoken of? Am I speaking for the public interest here? There is a capacity, an overwhelming capacity, to consolidate this "we" each time there is a crisis, as if we somehow know it, as if we've forgotten that the "we" is a highly differentiated, mediated, created community—a community often created through the press, through public opinion, through political manipulation. And yet we continue to speak about the public as this "we," as if we somehow know it, and most often we still try to identify through it.

The "we" is frequently constituted in terms of public funding. For example, somebody who has no knowledge of or perhaps never even thought about art or arts funding, phones up the radio and says, "My dollars are being used in this way" as soon as a crisis occurs. And I suggest that this notion of money as a metaphor for a certain kind of public protest needs much greater attention, particularly in this newly emerging public-private sphere.

The crisis in the public-cum-private sphere was brought to a head by the controversy in Brooklyn—a controversy which included a public institution, a private collector, dealers, public money, and subsidies from the collector. I think Brooklyn is an excellent example of what I call the public-cum-private sphere.

I want to conclude by quoting a brief poem by one of my favorite poets, W. H. Auden, not only because he adds music to the issues discussed in this volume but also because he teaches us, through this poem, three important lessons. One, he demonstrates the great necessity in democracies for a catholicity of taste. Two, he shows us how art and culture inevitably raise irresolvable, incommensurable problems and also describe the rifts and precipices of our daily lives, through which we all have to survive. Finally, he suggests that when art hurts us, it can also simultaneously connect us, as indeed we, as a community of discussion and exchange, have been connected by the Brooklyn controversy through a kind of wounding. Here is Auden's poem "The Composer."

All the others translate: the painter sketches
A visible world to love or reject;
Rummaging into his living the poet fetches
The images out that hurt and connect.

From Life to Art by painstaking adaption,
Relying on us to cover the rift;
Only your notes are pure contraption,
Only your song is an absolute gift.

Pour out your presence, O delight, cascading
The falls of the knee and the weirs of the spine,
Our climate of silence and doubt invading;

You alone, alone, O imaginary song,
Are unable to say an existence is wrong,
And pour out your forgiveness like a wine.

DAVID A. ROSS

An All-Too-Predictable Sensation

Why should we be bothering to think about what went on in Brooklyn? Why are we discussing such a sorry episode in the world of art, law, and public policy? What do we expect to learn from the controversy about the nature of American justice or the politics of culture? Why does the liberal community of First Amendment activists react so obviously to the feigned outrage of yet another politician seeking to use art to generate popular support? Why does the religious right seek to use this affair to indict all of our secular society? When repressive regimes around the world still actively deny basic freedoms to their citizenry, when writers and artists around the world still fear the *fatwah,* why are we so exercised by the pathetic attempts of a mayor in the United States to impose his own sense of moral rectitude and propriety on one of the world's great art museums?

Of course the answers to these questions are as troubling as the problem itself. And some questions do not lend themselves to answers. Some might say that the art world relishes martyrdom and thus engages in "felix culpa" to refresh an outmoded sense of avant-gardism. If art ceases to matter for its own sake, then perhaps it should matter for the sake of the democracy itself. Some might recognize in this affair a particularly postmodern character trait—the confusion of *Schadenfreude* with sympathy. We like to look, and from the safe distance of the academy the view is picture perfect. But, as we know, the reason we care deeply about this affair is that we remain aware that the *Sensation* controversy is far from finished; yet we haven't a clue about what can be done about it. What remains most troubling to me, as an art-museum director, is that the questions dogging this highly publicized fight between New York City Mayor Rudolph Giuliani and the Brooklyn Museum of Art (BMA) are so damned predictable. Let me be frank. The purported issues of public propriety and institutional insensitivity to cultural difference are patently bogus. Chris Ofili's fine and strangely beautiful painting of the Virgin Mary is no more incendiary to the sensibilities of devout Catholics than hundreds if not thousands of works of art and literature similarly displayed and supported by public or quasi-public funds. The artist is well and widely respected as serious (the painting is no sophomoric prank), and the exhibition containing the painting was a serious and proper show of a cutting-edge private collection. So the questions remain: Why this painting, why this exhibition, and why now? And why should the offended sensibilities of devout Catholics be a matter of public policy and not the daily offenses of slings and arrows of ordinary and extraordinary speech felt by sensitive souls the world over? Did it not matter when the painting was exhibited in London or in Hamburg?

The idea that the Brooklyn Museum of Art has somehow violated its contract with the city and the people of New York is mere legalism employed to find a plausible rationale for punishing a museum director who refused to bow before a mayor's inflamed political ego. The Brooklyn Museum of Art's administration has not pledged in its contract with the city to present an art-museum program that satisfies the aesthetic disposition of the city's mayor. The trustees and director of the museum serve the public good by running an art museum intended to serve as broad a set of public interests as professionally possible. That they seem to do very well.

For the record, let me state that the BMA has a solid reputation not only for its scholarship and museological standards but also for its pioneering programmatically expressed concerns for the interests and specifically the cultural interests of the enormously diverse communities of Brooklyn. The still somewhat new director of the museum, Arnold Lehman, is by all measures of professionalism deemed to be very good at what he does. He is extremely experienced and highly respected by his peers. As former president of the Association of Art Museum Directors, Lehman developed a strong overview of the profession, its practices, and its challenges. In three years as BMA's director, Lehman made great strides in building the museum's relationship to its many audiences, including young visitors, strengthened its standing (and its reputation in the funding community), and brought a renewed sense of joy along with a certain measure of showmanship to the BMA. Appropriately,

Lehman took seriously his role within the world's most competitive cultural community, and booking the *Sensation* exhibition was part of a strategy to reacquaint New York City's contemporary art audience with the Brooklyn Museum. Did he make some mistakes? A qualified perhaps is the answer. Apparently under enormous pressure, his staff and he may in fact have made several mistakes, but none of them are hanging offenses. Some of the so-called ethical violations alleged by the mayor, like accepting funding from parties who could conceivably stand to benefit directly from the sponsorship, are in fact common at major museums and not-for-profit cultural institutions in New York and throughout the United States. As government funding withers, art museums will be forced to engage in many different kinds of partnerships with underwriters from the world of commerce and industry. But these kinds of issues—especially if they involve real conflicts of interest—are best addressed in procedural refinements, not in a "he said/she said" dispute played out in the pages of the *New York Times*.

Surprising no one, the mass media and the more specialized art press responded to this affair like a broadcast-network programming department during sweeps week. It's as if a script were written by some hack Hollywood writing team and distributed to all participants in the fiasco in advance of the first shot's firing. What's sad is that in the post–Monicagate world of media spectacles, we seem desperate for issues that will allow politicians to run for public office without having to address truly serious issues. Any scandal will do. In fact, a good art scandal is far easier to discuss than the police murder of Amadou Diallo any day. As fate would have it, I was in New York City the night the first shot was fired in this sordid affair. Along with several hundred other art-world dignitaries, I was attending the opening of the second part of the Whitney Museum's *American Century* exhibition, a show I had organized during my tenure as the Whitney's director. The mayor had issued his first condemnation of the Brooklyn exhibition at an afternoon news conference, and at the elite, art-world preview, the crowd was talking about little else. The buzz added an interesting undertone to the evening, though there was a strange sense of déjà vu as the story about the supposedly offending Ofili painting upstaged most discussion of the *Century* show.

As the only member of the Giuliani administration at the opening, the commissioner of cultural affairs, Schuyler Chapin, felt particularly under siege as he struggled to maintain his diplomatic cool yet not appear to be insensitive to the rapidly emerging sense of outrage; this outrage was fueled by the fact that the mayor not only had spoken strongly against a particular work in the *Sensation* exhibition but had even attacked and threatened the future of the entire museum. BMA director

Lehman, who was also at the Whitney, had—like Chapin—been consumed by the developing event all day. (As was later made public, he'd been in private discussions for several days prior.) The cool and detached director of the Metropolitan joined his other art-museum colleagues at the dinner in mouthing supportive platitudes in favor of the Brooklyn Museum, and the patrons in attendance made it clear that their sympathies lay with the soon-to-be-embattled Lehman.

Adding irony to the proceedings was the fact that the *American Century* exhibition included, as a prominent feature of its decade-by-decade survey, a series of didactic cultural-history installations dealing specifically with the social and political context of American art as it evolved in the postwar period. Organized by the art historian and cultural critic Maurice Berger, this particular aspect of the exhibition culminated in a section outlining and exploring the roots and consequences of the "culture wars" that so consumed the nation from the late 1980s through the mid-1990s. As the former director of the Whitney Museum, I had presided over the institution during the latter half of the "culture wars," and I had become strongly identified with the public stance that no art museum could or should make any artistic compromise with government funding agencies. In exhibitions like the now historic 1993 Whitney Biennial Exhibition, the mid-career survey of Mike Kelley's work (entitled *Catholic Tastes*), or the group exhibition *Black Male: Representations of Masculinity in Contemporary Art,* I learned that the public battles in defense of artistic freedom are *never* about art. Like the firestorm that surrounded *The Perfect Moment,* the memorial retrospective of Robert Mapplethorpe's work I presented in 1989 while director of Boston's Institute of Contemporary Art, the political response to the *Sensation* exhibition was nothing more (and nothing less) than an opportunistic political act, undertaken to advance a solely political agenda. Both the Mapplethorpe case and the Andres Serrano affair were attempts by the religious right to find a high-profile platform on which to fight for the government's right to control a moral agenda including abortion rights, gay and lesbian rights, school prayer, and other Christian Coalition–supported items on the conservative agenda.

The particular aesthetic concerns of Mapplethorpe, Serrano (or any of the others who were similarly caught up in this ideological nightmare) were never the issue. The only point made and made again was that these works had some tie (often tenuous and always minuscule in terms of relative government expenditures) to public funding and that, as a result, any offended person or group in the public could and should be able to insist that the offending work be plucked out. The idea that every book in every public library, every course in every university, every moment of public television, every play presented in any theater receiving some form of public subsidy, every film in a festival or noncommercial venue, every subsidized poetry journal or literary magazine (even if it merely receives nonprofit mailing privileges) can and should be subject to the same level of scrutiny and control is absurd. Of course this would leave time for mayors, senators, or Congressional staff to do little else but engage in this critical analysis, and, on a certain level, you have to love the idea of a culture as enormous, open, and diverse as ours engaging the earnest, full-time efforts of so many dedicated men and women—not only a ministry of culture but cultural police to protect us from ourselves. And of course the serious result of this cultural witch-hunt mentality is that the nation now spends far less on art and culture than any advanced industrial democracy, and we find ourselves unable to find the political will to climb out of the hole in which we uncomfortably reside.

In the case of Mayor Giuliani, the charge that Ofili's work was "sick" and "disgusting" was reportedly prompted by campaign advisors who convinced him that an attack on *Sensation* would provide him with an opportunity to score major points in his attempt to woo conservative upstate voters wary of any downstate, big-city candidate. And while this rings true, I do not doubt for a second the sincerity of the mayor's faith, nor do I dispute his right to voice his opinion about a work of art or literature on public view. It would be the beginning of a wonderful moment in the city's cultural life if the mayor felt compelled to participate in an informed and informing public dialogue about art and its specific values, qualities, and meanings. The sad fact is that Mayor Giuliani had not seen the painting in question before his opinion was voiced.

Regarding the offense to the sensibilities of some devout Catholics (and conceivably others as well), I would even go so far as to say that, as a public spokesperson for the people of the City of New York, the mayor should speak out on behalf of those in minority communities whose rights or sensibilities are being abridged or ignored. The mayor's office is a bully pulpit, and with equanimity and consistency the mayor should attempt to engage the public sense and sensibility from a well-reasoned humanitarian perspective. But that does not mean he or any elected official should imagine himself or herself to be a public censor, nor does it mean that a politician should take cheap shots at the integrity of artists or institutions of art and learning merely to score points in a political zero-sum game.

In my tenure at the Whitney, the mayor never once set foot in the museum. An opera lover, he was known to frequent the Metropolitan Opera, but he rarely if ever visits any of the city's art museums. This does not disqualify him from having an opinion but only goes to support my strong feeling that the mayor was acting out a role in a scripted drama with guaranteed ratings appeal, not truly functioning as an informed or thoughtful critical observer. The mayor could have opened a dialogue about the work at hand and asked important questions with the goal of generating a useful discourse not only about this specific work of art but also about the importance of sensitivity to cultural difference within as complex and hybrid a city as New York. The mayor could have expressed his distaste for the work but kept open the door which might have encouraged mutual respect for the work of artists and the role of contemporary art institutions in an intellectual economy as robust as that of New York. The mayor could have even changed his mind after learning more about the serious artistic merits of Ofili's work and, remaining personally opposed to the work, could have made it clear that understanding holds the possibility that complex and often embattled communities can learn to live together. Instead the mayor called the work "sick" and "disgusting," and using metaphors evoking a health crisis, he proceeded to try to destroy the entire BMA.

Contemporary art is often contentious, and on any given day in one or another of the city's art museums (both directly and indirectly subsidized by city, state, and federal funds) some work of art will surely offend the religious or ideological sensibilities of some community. This is a 100 percent certainty. Taste is another matter entirely, and an even more subjective one at that. Again, without a doubt, many (perhaps a majority) would judge works of art on view in every New York art museum to be offensive, tasteless, or at least disturbing enough to wish they would be unavailable to the minds of impressionable youth. (We are not supposed to be discussing literature here, but, as a fact, our public libraries are filled with politically incorrect tracts, blasphemous literature, scandalous and erotic literature, sexually explicit photographs, and all sorts of art books with images of works of art that make Ofili look like Grandma Moses.)

So what does it mean when a mayor, who has over twenty times attacked and lost to individuals and institutions on First Amendment issues, decides on the eve of the U.S. Senate primary season to attack the Brooklyn Museum because a painting offends his sensibilities as a Catholic? In whose interests does he act? What outcome would he likely expect as a result of his misplaced act of paternalism?

It means that art and artists remain endangered as a class and are to be reminded that though their work has great power (why else be so afraid of, or offended by, a painting?), they have contested standing or protection under the First Amendment. When Mayor Giuliani sought to remove artists from selling their works on the sidewalks of the city, he asserted that unlike writers or publishers whose free speech could not be abridged by prohibiting the street vending of books or magazines, visual artists were not covered by the same guarantees. The city lost that case, but, time and again, the current city administration has made it clear that they consider artists a subordinate class in regard to basic freedoms set forth in the Constitution.

It means that the commerce in art has been demonized to the extent that a private collector, who had legally and quite successfully sold works of art he had acquired, is automatically suspected of some form of self-dealing or misuse of the public trust based on an assumption of guilt by prior association with legitimate art dealers and auction houses.

It means that art museums everywhere need to remain aware of the fact that they can and will be manipulated by political forces unless they are managed by strong administrators who are willing to stand up for, and go to battle on behalf of, art and artists. In Chicago, Jim Wood stood up for the authority of the Art Institute of Chicago to make its own decisions about whether works of art are appropriate for public display. We must be willing to make decisions in an informed manner and then back them with our full authority. The charges that BMA director Lehman chose not to exercise his authority as director are false and misleading. He made a decision to include the Ofili work in the show, then made the decision to keep the work in the show. He made efforts to discuss the work with the mayor and his assistants but was rebuffed and simply ordered to remove the work. He had no choice but to maintain his position.

Taking such a stance means that the education of museum trustees needs to include the deep understanding of the need to guard their institutions against political manipulation. And, of course, it means that we who run art museums in the United States must do an even better job of educating young visitors, communicating effectively with as broad a representation of our constituent communities as possible, and recognize that the art museum is a social instrument. I am certain that if its instrumentality is not used thoughtfully and directly by us, it will be abused by others.

In this regard, the BMA affair also points out that a strong and open relationship with the press is essential if an institution is to emerge victorious from this kind of struggle for the hearts and minds of a community. When the *Sensation* story moved from the art pages to the metropolitan section, as in prior politicized art-news happenings, it became appallingly clear that the press lacked an understanding of how art museums work, what they do, and how they are governed. It seems that under pressure, and perhaps out of inexperience, several contradictory statements may have been made to the press by officials at the BMA, and these contradictions made the entire affair seem only more worthy of investigation. These statements are easy to criticize from the outside, but unless you have found yourself on the frontlines of a major public–relations–based political firefight, you may have no idea of how easily a simple misstatement can be compounded into a potential loss of credibility.

On another level entirely, a lesson we must learn from this affair is that we in the United States must work together as a community to insist that a free nation must adequately protect the sources of funding necessary for the health of our centers of learning (including universities, museums, and libraries); this funding must not be short-circuited by those who fail to recognize the value of free speech and a truly open society. I state the obvious here because in undertaking this attack on the BMA, New York's mayor has made it clear that, at the end of the day, he is working in the interests only of those who will enable him to maintain power and that he has confused this goal with the greater public good.

TERI J. EDELSTEIN

Sensational or Status Quo

Museums and Public Perception

Institutions and individuals once considered almost sacrosanct in our society—the presidency, physicians, philanthropic organizations, the courts—have increasingly come under aggressive critical scrutiny. From the perspective of museum professionals, it seems as if museums have also become a more frequently contested arena. The brouhaha over the *Sensation* exhibition at the Brooklyn Museum of Art is yet one more example. Has the sacralized space of the museum been permanently breached? Has the museum's identity become more contested as a broad series of social constituencies create complex and various responses to its collecting practices and exhibitions? Or have these assaults demonstrated the increasing power and prestige of museums in our society? I believe the answer is yes to all the above.

Of course, a puzzled, even hostile response to contemporary art is, in itself, nothing new. Like most forms of combat, the "culture wars" have been with us a long time. Michelangelo Caravaggio, Gustave Courbet, the Impressionists were all attacked in their own day. Even in the age of museums, when the institution itself conveys a validation of the art it displays, there are numerous instances of tangible antagonistic reactions to the art of the day. I will choose one historical example. In 1913, the students of the School of the Art Institute of Chicago burned imitations of two works by Henri Matisse, *Luxe* and the *Blue Nude*, as part of a demonstration on the steps of the Art Institute to protest the show-

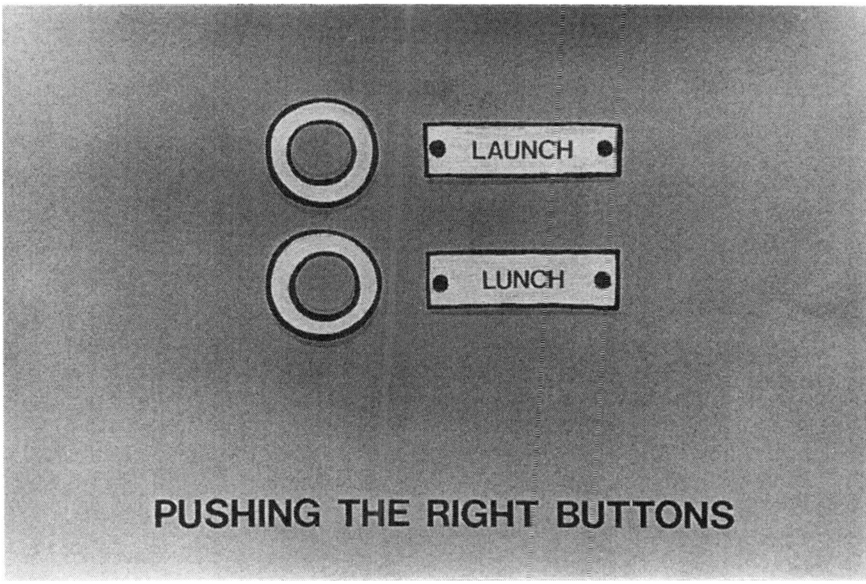

Figure 3. Erika Rothenberg, *Pushing the Right Buttons*, 1982. Acrylic on paper. 18 × 24 in. *Courtesy of P.P.O.W., New York.*

ing of the *International Exhibition of Modern Art,* also known as the *Armory Show.* The exhibition generated other public and critical hostility including protests from the Chicago Law and Order League, which claimed that "this exhibition ought to be suppressed," and an investigation by the state Senatorial Vice Commission. Nevertheless, or perhaps to some degree as a result, it attracted hordes of people—188,650 visitors in only twenty-four days of display, an average of 7,860 people per day. So, in one sense, the battlefield of the "culture wars" has been with us forever.[1]

My first personal experience with controversy came in 1984, when I was directing the Mount Holyoke College Art Museum. We organized an exhibition entitled *The Shadow of the Bomb.*[2] The exhibition explored contemporary artists' responses to the threat of nuclear holocaust and featured works by a number of distinguished artists including Leon Golub, Edward Kienholz, and Robert Morris. We never anticipated any problems with the exhibition, thinking it highly unlikely that anyone in our community was in favor of nuclear annihilation. Some of the pieces, like Erika Rothenberg's *Pushing the Right Buttons* (figure 3), were humorous. But others, such as the *Non War Memorial,* a conceptual piece by Kienholz, which contained cotton army uniforms filled with dirt and displayed on the floor as if they were dead bodies, were more graphic (figure 4). Shortly after the exhibition opened, one of our largest donors

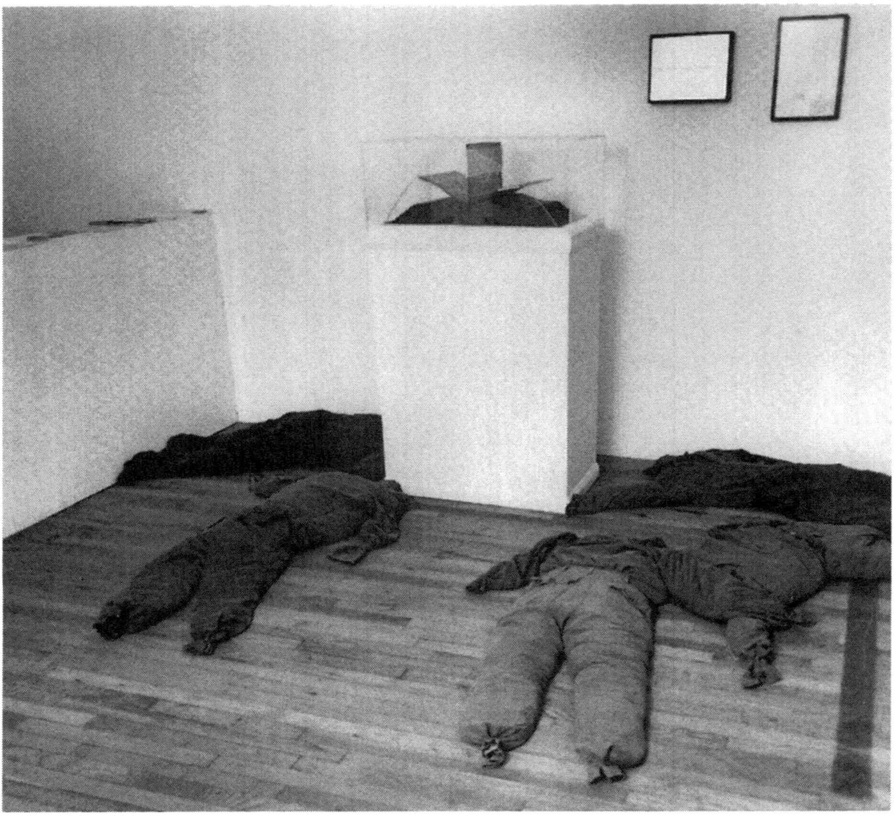

Figure 4. Edward Kienholz, *Non War Memorial*, 1970. American military uniforms from the Vietnam War period, dirt, seeds, book, podium, and Plexiglas box. Dimensions variable. © *Estate of Edward Kienholz, courtesy of L.A. Louver, Venice, Calif.*

(a couple) announced that they were so offended by the exhibition they would never give any more money to the museum. Art was meant only to be uplifting and beautiful, and this exhibition was a dramatic violation of that standard. In vain did I try to give them a crash refresher course in art history, citing numerous conflicting examples of works by artists they admired, such as Francisco de Goya. It was many years later, after much cultivation, that they again made a donation to the museum.

More conventional art is also no guard against controversy. In 1982, when the Tate Gallery in London displayed the Sir Edwin Landseer exhibition, the walls were overrun with paintings of dogs, deer, and other animals. The exhibition featured such well-loved paintings as the portrait from the Royal Collection of Queen Victoria and Prince Albert at

Windsor in which the royal couple are almost invisible in the midst of their numerous pets, and *The Old Shepherd's Chief Mourner*, which depicts a sheep dog with its head on a coffin. Against all expectations, protesters picketed the museum. They were opposed to blood sports, the subject of other exhibited works by Landseer.

Even a consistently controversial show, such as *Sensation*, is not consistently controversial in the same way. When on display in London, the paintings of Chris Ofili caused little or no contention. However, literally violent controversy surrounded the Royal Academy in the fall of 1997 over the inclusion of the portrait of Myra Hindley, a woman convicted of luring young children and murdering them thirty-three years earlier (figure 5). Its offensiveness to segments of the British public was heightened by the technique used to paint it, which was borrowed from Chuck Close's use of his thumbprint to render likenesses in grisaille. For his eleven-foot-high black-and-white-and-gray painting, Marcus Harvey used children's handprints to construct Hindley's features; the likeness was based on a photograph that had appeared repeatedly in the newspapers at the time of the original trial many years earlier and in the intervening years.

Here is an account from the *Independent* of the opening day of the exhibition, September 19, 1997:

> We had shattered glass, megaphones, placards, images of media manipulation, tears, confusion and bewilderment. And that was just in the courtyard. Inside the Royal Academy there was a genuine sensation. A man was apprehended after two canisters of ink were thrown at the much publicised painting of Moors murderer Myra Hindley, made from casts of children's handprints. Minutes later an egg was thrown. . . . It started at 4am when a rock was hurled through a window in Piccadilly next to the Royal Academy banner proclaiming the show. . . .
>
> Outside, the queues were forming, largely students and backpackers. As they queued they were picketed by megaphone by the pressure group Mothers Against Murder and Aggression, urging them not to view the Hindley picture. "They used to hang killers on the gallows. Now they hang them in the gallery," they yelled.
>
> And then they brought in to the courtyard Winnie Johnson, the 64–year-old mother of one [of] the Moor's victims. The distraught Mrs. Johnson was a poignant sideshow, and not a spectacle one would have wished to see at the entrance to an art exhibition. RA secretary David Gordon had invited her to view

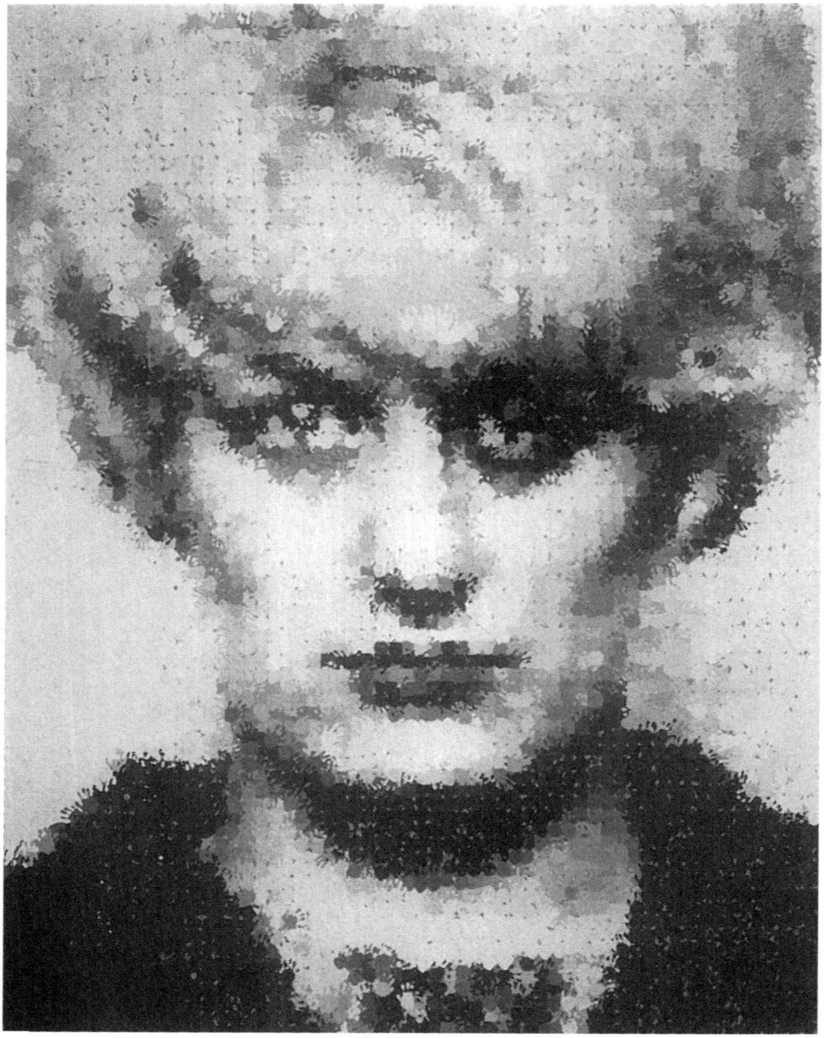

Figure 5. Marcus Harvey, *Myra*, 1995. Acrylic on canvas. 13 × $10^1/_2$ ft. *Courtesy of The Saatchi Gallery and White Cube Gallery, London. Photograph by Stephen White.*

the painting to show her that it did not glamorise Hindley. But she said she would not enter the building.

"Ask the head of the Royal Academy if he would go in and see the portrait of the person who murdered his child," she sobbed. By now the queue was lengthening and the first visitors were emerging from their view of the provocative, ironic, striking mixture of the challenging and the plain silly, a modern-day freak show.[3]

Thus the Royal Academy show involved not only what in this country are First Amendment issues but also the right of privacy and the charge of exploitation of personal loss. The emotional intensity this episode produced makes the Brooklyn situation seem rather trivial. Yet this same painting stirred so little attention in New York that the *New York Times* misprinted the subject's name as Myra Handle.[4]

Of course, newspapers can be counted on to stir up and even to help create controversy. In reading the coverage of *Sensation*, I was struck by how often newspapers described Ofili's *The Holy Virgin Mary* as being "smeared" with elephant dung. As everyone who has even seen a reproduction of the painting can attest, decorated elephant dung is applied to the painting, and it rests on several more pieces at its base. I would venture to say that unless one had been informed by the museum in a label or written description or had read it elsewhere, only a zookeeper would have been able to identify the substance. I wondered why writers for the *Times*, the *Daily News,* and other papers, who had presumably traveled to Brooklyn to see the painting, would use this inflammatory verb, and I also wondered what effect it had on their readers. In its January issue, *ArtNews* interviewed a number of visitors to *Sensation* in Brooklyn. One viewer, Christopher Alexander, a twenty-year-old fine-arts student, commented that he had "heard that Ofili's *Virgin* was 'smeared with elephant dung,' [and] was surprised to see that it was, in fact, a beautiful image."[5]

Some of the problems surrounding *Sensation* at Brooklyn could perhaps have been anticipated. In fact, one might suggest that the ad campaign created by the museum—the warning labels, the statement that the "contents may cause shock, vomiting, confusion, panic, euphoria, and anxiety"—helped to foment the attack. Even without such provocative marketing, it is necessary for each individual museum to have policies in place and communications plans at the ready to handle anticipated or unexpected controversy. Museums spend a great deal of time and a great many staff resources devising disaster plans in the case of a power outage or catastrophic natural event but often little or no time preparing for the possibility of a public outcry against the art on their walls. Brooklyn could have, and perhaps did, plan ahead for a public uproar, but it is not always possible to anticipate such issues. Works of art have always had multivalent meanings, but increasingly their significance is read differently by different groups of stakeholders in the museum. And those interested in the museum as a public institution are increasingly vocal about their opinions.

There is also a necessity for policies that confront complex issues of free speech. I suspect that no one in the arts community would object to the abstract principle of the First Amendment discussed in Part II of this volume. In fact, the professional museum community, represented by such bodies as the Association of Art Museum Directors, did not hesitate to defend the Brooklyn Museum on exactly those grounds. But how do the concepts of the First Amendment relate to a museum's right to choose what to display in its galleries? The situation at the Detroit Institute of Arts when the new director chose to take down an exhibition, *Art until Now*, provides an interesting example. My understanding, from written accounts, is that the agreement with the artist, from several years before, did not specify the art to be displayed. When the exhibition was installed, the director felt that the museum had been unable to plan effectively for the exhibition of such confrontational works, including a piece entitled *Nigger Toe*, which showed a shelled Brazil nut under a magnifying glass. No materials interpreting the pieces for the museum's publics were part of the installation. The artist declined to alter the works, as requested by the museum, and the exhibition was deinstalled after two days. This example suggests the difficult and unresolved tension between an artist's rights and the rights and prerogatives of the museum.[6]

Of significance to the policy issues that the Brooklyn Museum controversy evokes is the fact that the museum itself is less and less immutable as a cultural icon. Once a symbol of almost unquestioned hegemonic social authority, museums, their collections, and their modes of display have come under increasing scrutiny. Hence, the increasing frequency and stridency of protests. Of course, the opposite is also true. Ironically, it is the power of museums as social and cultural institutions, the fact that they are perceived as legitimizing what they display, that creates public anger at the inclusion of works that offend social, political, and aesthetic norms of individuals or groups. The inclusion of a work within a museum, whose history and administrative structures—indeed whose very architecture, which sometimes even echoes a Greek temple—convey power, solidity, and prestige, gives a work of art an aura of sanctity that can be offensive.

Ironically, the Royal Academy in London and the Brooklyn Museum both mounted the *Sensation* exhibition as part of a plan to enlarge and diversify their audiences. These efforts are inspired by a variety of motives. Certainly one is the need to generate increased income, a need born both of cuts in revenue, in certain instances from the government, and of increased expenses. But I believe an even greater motivation is a genuine desire on the part of museums to reach out to and to include more people. *Excellence and Equity*, published by the American Association of Museums in 1992, outlined an audience-based mission for America's museums and provided a template for action.[7] But its drafting was possible only because many museums were exploring just such initiatives. At the time, some of these efforts were only theoretical, many were tentative, and a few were aggressive. Most of them were under the aegis largely of departments of museum education. In the intervening years these audience-development efforts have created a shift in a number of aspects of the museum, from programming to exhibitions, acquisitions, advisory committees, and, in the best instances, to diversity of governance itself. Most of the nation's museums have vigorously sought out acquisitions that mirror the cultural diversity of their communities. They have mounted more exhibitions that supplement or amplify those collections, and even in instances where museums' collections are proscribed by legal mandates, usually put in place by the founders, institutions have actively created programs that attempt to attract larger and more diverse audiences.

Again, these are not new ideas; they reach back, in many cases, to the philosophical structures and founding programs of these institutions. Not many museums were directed by such visionaries as John Cotton Dana of the Newark Museum, but many institutions began with relationships to diverse segments of their communities, at least in the areas of programs and sometimes of exhibitions.[8] However, much of this was, and still is, largely cosmetic. Museums have been increasingly supported, at times prodded, in these efforts by a number of funders who have facilitated museums' outreach initiatives. The Lila Wallace–Reader's Digest Fund Museum Collections Accessibility Initiative and the Pew Charitable Trusts Program for Art Museums and Communities have stimulated innovative programs not only at the museums they have funded but also at those inspired by the efforts of other museums. Many other foundations, including the Nathan Cummings Foundation, the MacArthur Foundation, the Rockefeller Foundation, and the Knight Foundation, have also been active in the funding and encouragement of these kinds of initiatives. The progress of such strategies in making new audiences permanent participants in the life of museums has been slow. It is also not yet clear what the future of these efforts will be without substantial outside financial support.

But, most important, museums must become aware of all the unexpected implications of these initiatives. As museums reach out to and attract larger and more diverse publics, as they invite community groups to actively participate in the life of their institutions, the responses to their permanent collections and particularly to highly publicized special exhibitions are going to be more complex and unpredictable. Works of art that once seemed to transcend any kind of discord are increasingly read differently by individuals or groups that make up museums' audiences. Museums may have to deal with responses from parts of their audiences who object to the implications they see in works of art. Increasingly, the works that are not included in the institution are also problematic to museums. Museums are under widening pressure to demonstrate that their collections, exhibitions, and programs reflect the diversity of their communities. Questions about the representation of gender, race, and geographic and religious origin are familiar and frequent. Undoubtedly museums have always insulted and excluded some members of their community, but now the offended parties are empowered.

Museums need to explore more energetically than they have in the past the implications of their diversification campaigns. It is also especially important that museums diversify all the levels that create and implement policy, most importantly at the trustee level. When the inevitable controversy strikes, informed, supportive, and, needless to say, powerful, well-placed trustees are the museum's most potent advocates.

It is not the museum's goal of being audience-oriented and user-friendly that has weakened and contaminated its authority as a cultural force. Rather, the museum has emerged as a more commanding authorizing agent in a world where authority is so frequently challenged and devalued. However, this aura of the sacred surrounding museums created the real violation of taboos of the *Sensation* exhibition.

The text of the controversies over *Sensation* at its London and New York venues was the freedom of artists to express themselves freely. Annibale Carracci pointed out in the seventeenth century that an artist is no different than a writer; he said, perhaps apocryphally, "An artist 'speaks' with his hands," and I don't think he was referring to the Italian habit of gesticulation. The challenge to First Amendment rights is important and worth defending. But the subtext is the perceived tainting of the hallowed ground with the stigma of money. The *New York Times* wrote in an editorial, "The financing revelations may well do more to jeopardize support for the Brooklyn Museum and its leadership than has exhibiting 'Sensation' itself."[9] The editorial went on to condemn the exhibiting of a private collection, saying that it violated museum practice, a surprising contention firmly reversed by the newspaper's own chief arts writer, Michael Kimmelman, the next day.[10] It seems as if the final title of the story of the Brooklyn Museum controversy is this: *The Money Changers in the Temple.*

What has been revealed by this entire episode is that there is little public understanding of the mechanisms of exhibition organization. In order to accomplish the numerous tasks surrounding this enterprise, which include doing research, acquiring loans, obtaining insurance, creating and distributing catalogues, devising publicity, and securing funding, museums frequently enter into partnerships with many individuals and organizations, and they ask for contributions from many others as well. Some of these relationships are mutually beneficial. That, in itself, should not invalidate them. Exhibitions are not a zero-sum game. And self-interest is not incompatible with public interest. The possibility of their being compatible stands, in fact, at the very heart of the political creation of the United States.

I offer these thoughts to recontextualize the debate about the museum as an educational institution. This is, after all, the basis of its identity from both a charitable and financial point of view since its tax-exempt status derives from it. As educational institutions, museums succeed when they bring thought-provoking art before the public. They also succeed when making available private collections and making visible the role of taste and collecting. But they have failed to educate the public about themselves as institutions. The nature of the sacred is that it contains not only power but mystery. These events have shown us that if museums wish to mitigate the "culture wars," to turn them into skirmishes, they must be more assertive as educational institutions both in explicating the art within their walls to multiple audiences and, just as important, in dispelling the murky clouds that shield their operations from public understanding. They should do this even at the cost of losing some footage in the sacred ground they have traditionally occupied.[11]

NOTES

1. Milton W. Brown, *The Story of the Armory Show* (New York: Abbeville Press, 1988), 206, 210.
2. Sally Yard, *The Shadow of the Bomb*, Mount Holyoke College Art Museum and University Gallery, University of Massachusetts at Amherst, April 1–June 10, 1984.
3. Tamsin Blanchard, "Sensation as Ink and Egg Are Thrown . . . ," *Independent* (London), September 19, 1997, p. 11.
4. *The New York Times*, October 2, 1999; for a discussion of the issues involved, see also Barbara Ellen, "Hindley and the Art of the Cynical," *Observer*, September 14, 1997; Christopher Elliott, "Withdraw Portrait of Me, Urges Hindley," *Guardian*, July 31, 1997.
5. Quoted in Rebecca Spence, "'I'm Not Offended Yet,' Museumgoers Speak Out on 'Sensation,'" *ArtNews*, January 2000, 154–155. This phenomenon was noted in England; see Philip Hensher, "Puritans, Pornography and the Shocking Art of Censorship; 'We Have Been Treated to Wild Fantasies about the Virgin Being "Spattered with Excrement,"'" *Independent* (London), October 1, 1999, p. 5. My favorite description in all the coverage was "dung-festooned" from the *New York Daily News*, which conveyed some idea of the rather happy and festive effect of Ofili's painting; Greg B. Smith, "Brooklyn Museum Must Go, City Tells Judge," *New York Daily News*, January 12, 2000, p. 54.
6. A. J. Dickerson, Associated Press, November 22, 1999; Tim Kiska and Susan Whitall, "Detroit Thrust into Spotlight over Closed DIA Exhibit," *Detroit*

News, November 23, 1999. The Kiska and Whitall article, incidentally, refers to the "Sensations [*sic*]" exhibition, "which included a feces-smeared Virgin Mary."

7. Ellen Cochran Hirzy, ed., *Excellence and Equity: Education and the Public Dimension of Museums: A Report from the American Association of Museums* (Washington, D.C.: American Association of Museums, 1992).
8. For the prescient ideas of Dana, see John Cotton Dana, "Increasing the Usefulness of Museums," *Proceedings of the American Association of Museums* 10 (1916), reprinted with other writings in *The New Museum: Selected Writings by John Cotton Dana* (Newark, N.J.: Newark Museum and American Association of Museums, 1999).
9. "A Verdict on Sensation," *New York Times*, November 2, 1999, p. 26. A similar conclusion had been drawn two years earlier in England. See Lisa Jardine, "How One Man Decides What Is Good Art. The Real Sensation about the Royal Academy's Controversial Exhibition Is the Role of One Private Collector and His Wealth," *Daily Telegraph*, September 18, 1997, p. 28.
10. Michael Kimmelman, "In the End, the 'Sensation' Is Less the Art Than the Money," *New York Times*, November 3, 1999, sec. E, p. 1.
11. Partially in response to *Sensation*, on July 13, 2000, the board of the American Association of Museums adopted "Guidelines on Exhibiting Borrowed Objects." The ethics committee was charged with developing guidelines for corporate funding.

W.J.T. MITCHELL

Offending Images

What is it about images that gives them such remarkable power to offend people? A better question might be, What is it about people that makes them so susceptible to being offended by images? And why is the response to the offensive image so often a reciprocal act of violence, an "offending of the image" by destroying, vandalizing, or banning it from view? Iconoclasm, the defacement or destruction of images, is a good place to start in understanding the nature of offensive images.[1] The psychological forces that lead people to be offended by an image are invisible and unpredictable. But when people set out to offend an image, to censure, denounce, or punish it, their behavior is out in the open where we can look at it. A kind of theatrical excess in the rituals of smashing, burning, mutilating, whitewashing, egg- and excrement-throwing turns the punishment of images into a spectacular image in its own right. When the Soviet Union collapsed, the spectacle of what Laura Mulvey called "disgraced monuments," the toppling and humiliating of statues of Lenin and Stalin, made for wonderful cinema.[2] What makes us think that "offending images" is a good way to deal with them? What assumptions make this kind of behavior intelligible at all?

Two assumptions seem to be in place when people offend images. The first is that the image is transparently and immediately linked to what it represents. Whatever is done to the image is somehow done to what it stands for. The second is that the image possesses a kind of vital, living character that makes it capable of feeling what is done to it. It is not merely a transparent medium for communicating a message but is something like an animated, living thing, an object with feelings, intentions, desires, and agency.[3] Indeed, images are sometimes treated as pseudopersons—not merely as sentient creatures that can feel pain and pleasure but as responsible and responsive social beings. Images of this sort seem to look back at us, to speak to us, even to be capable of suffering harm or of magically transmitting harm when violence is done to them.

This magical view of images is often described as if it were something we have grown out of—a premodern issue, a superstition found only in highly religious societies or in the "primitive" cultures studied by anthropology.[4] My own view is that while there are important historical and cultural differences in the power attributed to images, the tendency to endow them with life and immediacy is fundamental to the ontology of images as such or to a form of life we might call "being with images." Modern, urban cultures may not have many cults of saints or holy icons, but they do have an ample supply of magical images—fetishes, idols, and totems of every description, brought to life both in mass media and in a variety of subcultures. Supposedly obsolete or archaic superstitions about images, moreover, have a way of breaking out in thoroughly modern places like New York City and London. That is why people can still be hung in effigy, why we do not casually throw away or destroy photographs of our loved ones, why we still kiss a crucifix and kneel before an icon or deface it. And when images offend us, we still take revenge by offending them in turn. Far from being defanged in the modern era, images are one of the last bastions of magical thinking and therefore one of the most difficult things to regulate with laws and rationally constructed policies—so difficult, in fact, that the law seems to become infected by magical thinking as well and behaves more like an irrational set of taboos than a set of well-reasoned regulations.

In part, the intractability of offensive images stems from their tendency to take up residence on the front lines of social and political conflicts—from the ancient quarrels of the iconoclasts to the conflicts between Catholics and Protestants to the art scandals of the modernist avant-garde to the culture wars that have degraded American political discourse since the mid-1980s. They make their appearance in these conflicts not only as causes and provocations but as combatants, victims, and provocateurs. To remind you of some notorious offenders that have been centers of controversy and debates over censorship, I offer the following nearly random list of examples both ancient and modern:

Richard Serra's *Tilted Arc*, which offended workers by disrupting the space of the Federal Plaza in New York City, was repeatedly vandalized and was finally removed.

The Vietnam Veteran's Memorial, by Maya Lin, which was initially denounced as an antiwar counter-monument that demeaned the memory of the heroism of American soldiers but has since gone through a remarkable transformation into one of the most revered memorials in the United States.

Robert Mapplethorpe's *Man in Polyester Suit* (1980), which offended conservative viewers who found it obscene and pornographic; it was also seen as an offensive reinforcement of a racist stereotype about black men (figure 6).

Michelangelo's *David*, found offensive for its frank display of the penis, which has sometimes been covered with a fig leaf. As far as I know, it has never been denounced for reinforcing a stereotype about white men.

A 120–foot-high portrait of the Roman emperor Nero on linen that so displeased the gods, according to Pliny the Elder, that they struck it down with lightning.[5]

The swastika, which after a long history as a religious symbol was appropriated as an insignia of National Socialism in Adolf Hitler's Germany and now functions as an almost universal symbol of unredeemable evil.

The Confederate flag, which flew atop the South Carolina state capitol, was the object of protests and legislative initiatives that resulted in its removal.

Jasper Johns's *Flag* (1955), which caused a scandal in Cold War America as a degradation of the flag and is now regarded as one of the great masterpieces of modern painting.

The painting *Myra* (1995), by British artist Marcus Harvey, a ten-foot-high portrait of Myra Hindley, a notorious accessory to serial child murders (see figure 5). This painting, executed with imprints of a child's hand, was regarded as the most offensive image in the *Sensation* show at the Royal Academy in 1997. It was excoriated in the popular press, led to the resignation of senior members of the Royal Academy, and was vandalized. When shown in the Brooklyn Museum in New York in 1999, it attracted relatively little notice and was upstaged by Chris Ofili's painting of the Virgin Mary with dung.[6]

Ofili's *The Holy Virgin Mary*, which became the central focus

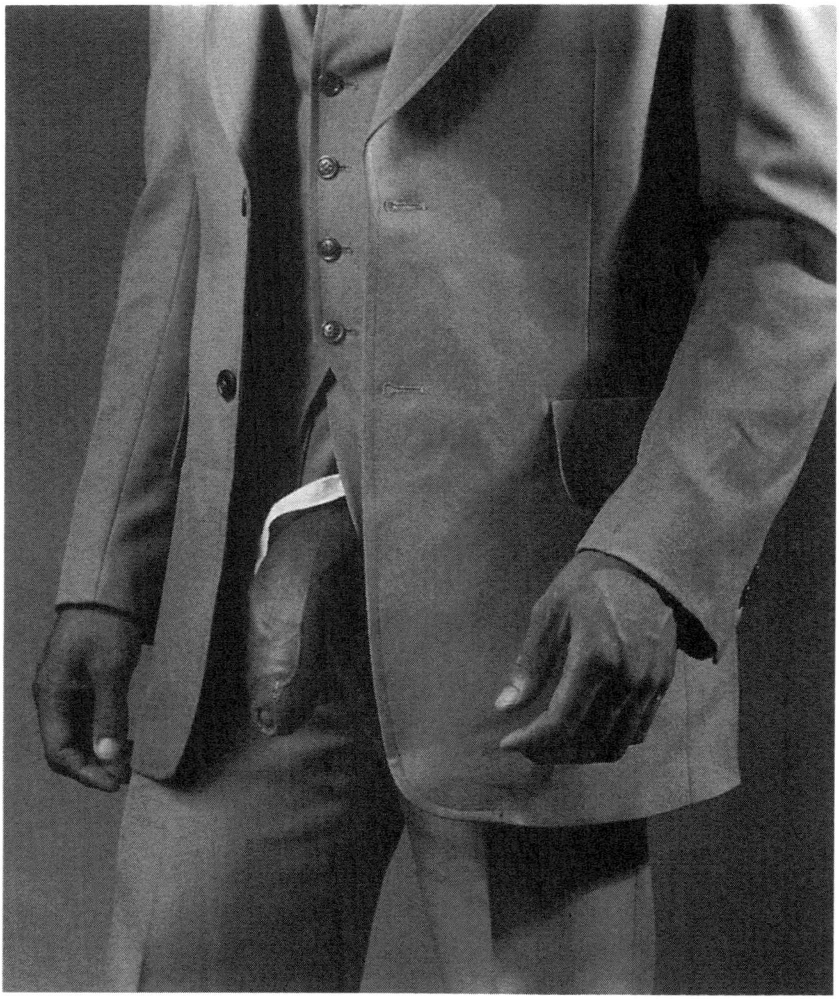

Figure 6. Robert Mapplethorpe, *Man in Polyester Suit*, 1980. *© The Estate of Robert Mapplethorpe. Used by permission.*

of the controversy over the Brooklyn Museum's *Sensation* show, was condemned as obscene and sacrilegious by Mayor Rudolf Giuliani of New York, who attempted to cut off the Brooklyn Museum's city funding. The painting was defaced by a pious Catholic who covered it with white paint.

Damien Hirst, *This little piggy went to market . . .* (1996), which was expected to offend visitors to the Brooklyn Museum but which failed to stir much outrage, even from proponents of animal rights (figure 7).

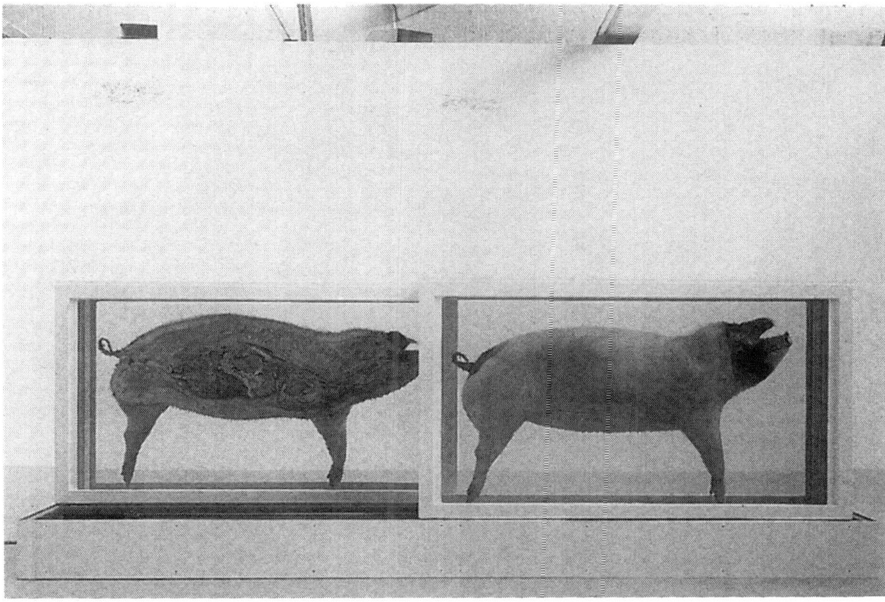

Figure 7. Damien Hirst, *This little piggy went to market, this little piggy stayed at home*, 1996. Steel, GRP composites, glass, pig, formaldehyde solution, electric motor, two tanks. Each tank 120 × 210 × 60 cm. *Courtesy of The Saatchi Gallery and White Cube Gallery, London. Photograph by Stephen White.*

Nicolas Poussin, *The Adoration of the Golden Calf*: the biblical idol, as rendered by Poussin in the early seventeenth century (figure 8). The actual calf so offended God that he ordered Moses to melt it down and force the Israelites to drink it. Then he ordered the massacre of three thousand people, including women and children, for violating a law (the Second Commandment) that he had not yet delivered to them. Poussin's rendering of this scene, however, has never to my knowledge been accused of violating the Second Commandment, although it was the victim of a knife attack in London's National Gallery in 1978.[7]

I cite these images to provide a broad context for thinking about the specific character of the Brooklyn Museum controversy and the kinds of offensive images the exhibit contained. This context may help us recall some obvious points about the complexity and variety of offending images and may suggest some less obvious ways in which those images are treated as if they were persons or animated beings.

First, offending images are radically unstable entities whose capacity for harm depends on complex social contexts. Those contexts can

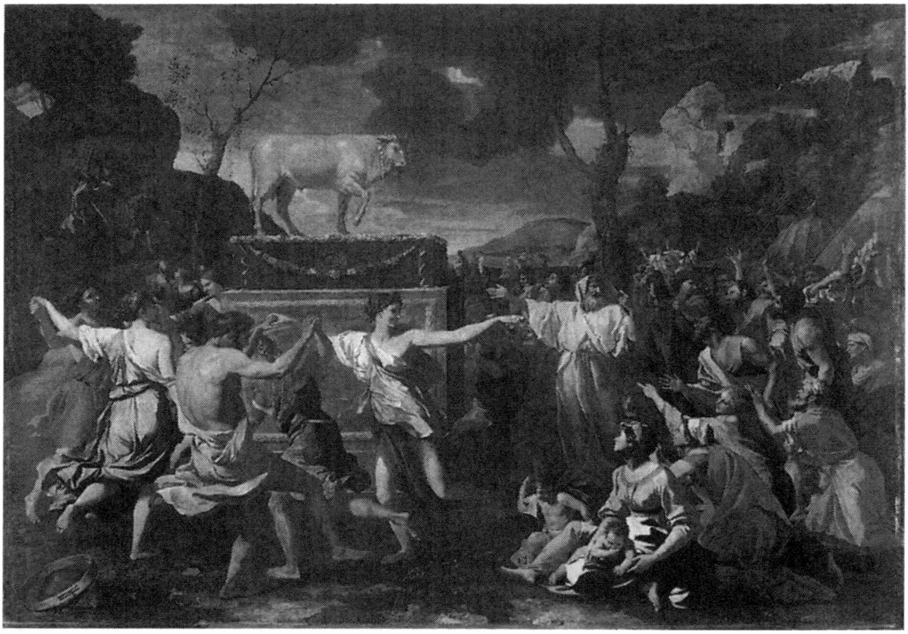

Figure 8. Nicolas Poussin, *The Adoration of the Golden Calf,* 1634. Oil on canvas laid down on board. 154.3 × 214 cm. © *National Gallery, London.*

change, sometimes as a result of the public debate around an image, more often because the initial shock wanes and is replaced by familiarity and even affection. The offensive character of an image is not written in stone but arises out of social interaction between a specific thing and communities that may themselves have varied and divided responses to the object.

Second, offending images do not all offend in the same way. Some offend the beholder, others the object represented. Some offend because they degrade something valuable or desecrate something sacred, others because they glorify something hateful and despised. Some of them violate moral taboos and standards of decency, while some are politically offensive, insults to national honor or unwelcome reminders of an ignoble past. Some offend because of the manner of representation: a caricature or stereotype offends not because of whom but because of how it represents. Like persons, images can be found "guilty by association" with the wrong kinds of people, values, or materials.

Third, if an image offends many people, sooner or later someone will invoke the law and along with it judges, legislators, policymakers, and the police. The cry will go up that "there ought to be a law" about offensive images, and symposia will be convened to formulate policy guidelines. Like a person, the image may even become a "legal subject," a witness or defendant in a legal proceeding, as in cases such as *United States v. 37 Photographs* or *United States v. 12 200–Ft. Reels of Super 8MM Film et al.*[8]

Finally, images are not all offended in the same way. Sometimes the effort is all-out annihilation (as in the melting down of the Golden Calf), to make the image disappear from the world forever, to render it extinct. Sometimes the iconoclastic gesture is only partially destructive, a defacement, disfiguring, dismemberment, decapitation, or other mutilation that doesn't destroy the image but humiliates or "wounds" it in some way.[9] The effect of this tactic is quite different from that of annihilation. The object is not to make the image disappear but to keep it around and to render its appearance in a new way, one that is offensive to the image and what it represents. Caricature is, in this sense, a form of disfigurement and iconoclasm. Most curious of all is a strategy that neither disfigures nor destroys but attempts to "disappear" the image, to hide it away, cover it up, bury it, or conceal it from view. This strategy may or may not be a way of "offending" the image; it is compatible, as we shall see, with a respectful defense of the image against desecration. All in all, then, the three basic strategies of iconoclasm are annihilation, disfigurement, and disappearance.

Images have been offending people since the beginning, since (for instance) God created a human creature in his own "image and likeness" and that creature set about disobeying its creator's orders. Images are not just "like" persons; the relation is much stronger than that.[10] It is common in creation myths for persons to be actually created as images (usually sculpted figures rendered in clay or stone).[11] And in most versions of this story the (human) images "have minds of their own." In the Biblical account, Adam and Eve (the images of God) are tempted by forbidden knowledge and quickly get out of the control of their creator. Offended by the disobedience of his creatures, God expels Adam and Eve from paradise and sentences them to die. Their sin is, in effect, a kind of iconoclasm in that it has disfigured the image of God reflected in them. When God decides to give his chosen people a second chance, if only they will follow his laws, the first law he prescribes is one that forbids the making of images:[12] "You shall not make yourself an image, or any likeness of what is in heaven above, or on earth below, or in the water under the earth. You shall not bow down to them nor serve them; for I, the Lord your God, am a jealous God, visiting the guilt of the fathers upon the children, upon the third and upon the fourth generation of those hating me, but showing steadfast love to the thousandth generation of those who love me and keep my commandments" (Exodus 20: 4–6).

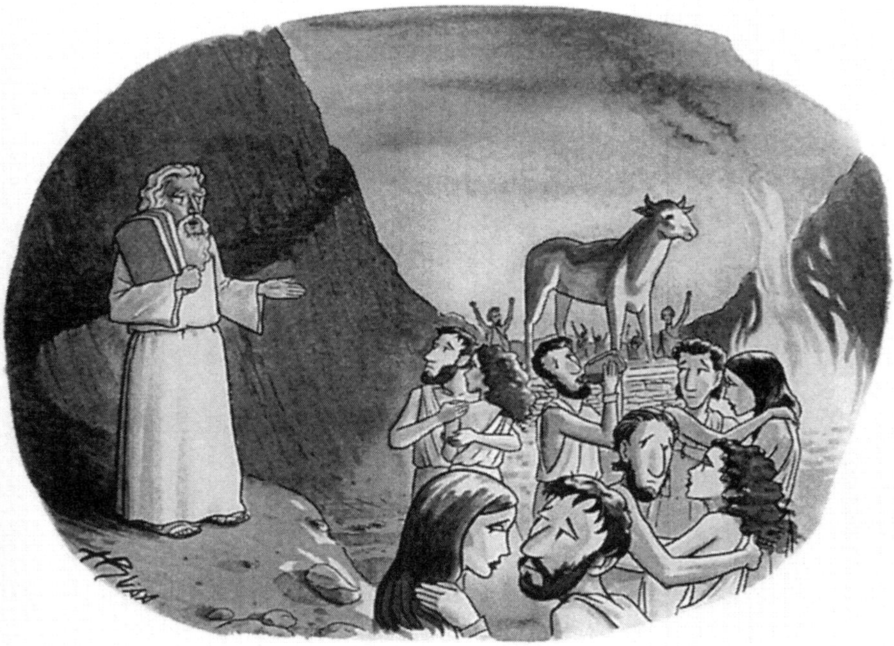

Figure 9. Harry Bliss, "Well, actually they are written in stone," 1999. © *The New Yorker Collection from cartoonbank.com. All rights reserved.*

This commandment, which, as far as I can tell, has never been well understood and certainly never obeyed literally, is clearly the most important law in the Decalogue. God spends more time explaining and defining it than all the other commandments put together. And it seems clear that this is the commandment he takes most seriously, the one that is really "written in stone" (see figure 9). Commandments like "Thou shalt not kill" are not absolute, merely advisory.[13] They are suspended when the situation requires it. Most notably, the commandment against killing is suspended when the murder is done as punishment for an act of idolatry. When the Israelites break the Second Commandment and erect the Golden Calf, God instructs Moses and the Levites to kill all their brethren who have been involved in this most hateful act, the creation of an image that is offensive to God.

Why is God offended by the Golden Calf? The most straightforward answer is, just because it is an image. The Second Commandment forbids making an image of anything. It does not say that only images of God or of rival gods are prohibited, but "any likeness"—presumably in any medium (gold, stone, paint, clay, even words)—of any thing on earth, in the sky, or in the sea.[14] Taken literally, the implication is that there is a "slippery slope" principle at work: if you start making images, inevitably they will, as we say, "take on a life of their own," become idols, and become offensive. The best policy, then, is to stamp out the potential for offense at its origin and prohibit the making of any sort of images. Needless to say, this is an impossible commandment, and neither Judaism nor other aniconic, monotheistic religions have ever followed it literally but have always found ways of getting around it and explaining it away.[15]

Periodically, American politicians propose the posting of the Ten Commandments in public-school rooms (usually after some outbreak of violence). But none of them, to my knowledge, has noticed that if these commandments were followed, art classes would have to be prohibited.

Exactly why, then, is the Golden Calf so offensive? One common reading of the Second Commandment is that images make something material and visible that should be immaterial and invisible. Idolatry, according to this view, is "the worship of wood and stone," a fetishistic obsession with base matter.[16] Even worse is the use of the specific material of gold, suggesting earthly riches, and, even worse, the gold that the Israelites brought out of Egypt and that therefore hearkens back to the Egyptian captivity and the idols of Egyptian religion. The image is offensive, then, both for what it seems to say ("I am god") and for what it is—the crass, vulgar materiality of Egyptian gold. The calf is made out of tainted money—filthy lucre, as it were.

The offensiveness of Ofili's Madonna, similarly, seems based largely in its use of materials, the notorious elephant dung. Like the Golden Calf, it is made of filthy lucre, filth because it is excrement, but lucre because (as Ofili argued) it has great symbolic value in African culture as a sign of fertility and the nurturing of "Mother Earth." Ofili's declaration of intentions, however, was widely disregarded by commentators who were determined to be offended. The artist's respectful use of elephant dung was taken as an insult to the image of the Madonna.[17] The question, however, is, Is it the material that offends, or is it the interpretation of the material as making a statement or (worse) as doing something to the image of the Madonna, defiling her "effigy" as it were? How do we decide whether elephant dung is a symbol of great value and reverence (as the artist insisted) or of filth and degradation? And how do we know what the Madonna does to dung, or dung to her? Does it degrade her, or does she elevate it, redeeming even the most base matter by the appearance of her image?

Ofili's Madonna helps us see the complexly indirect and mediated character of offensiveness in images. One could argue, for instance, that it is not the image that offends us in this work of art. On the contrary, it is the image (of the Madonna) that is being offended. Pious Catholics are offended not by Ofili's image of the Madonna but by the way the image is presented, the materials in which it is rendered. This argument shows us how crucial it is to distinguish between the image or "motif" (the feature of this painting that links it to innumerable other pictures of the Madonna by Peter Paul Rubens, Raphael, Leonardo da Vinci) and the concrete materiality of a specific picture. It is not the species that offends (the class that includes all Madonna pictures) but the specimen, this particular "incarnation" of the species in a monstrous or disgusting version.[18] And the spectator's sense of offensiveness is not direct but vicarious. The logic goes like this: the Madonna's image is offended by being rendered in excremental materials; if her image is offended, then she herself must be offended, and if she is offended, then all who venerate her and her image must be offended as well. If the thing I respect or love is insulted, then I am insulted.

The outrage over Ofili's Madonna, then, is not just a matter of being offended by an image. It is outrage over an act of iconoclasm, or violence to an image, the painting itself seen as an act of desecration, disfigurement, and defacement. When this sort of fantasized perception takes hold, it is amazing how impotent language is to overcome the imagined insult. Ofili's protestations of benign, respectful intentions and the obvious prettiness of his composition were completely ineffectual in countering the outrage. And the most visible expression of this outrage, the defacement of the painting by Dennis Heiner, took a specific form that is worth pondering in its details. Heiner did not attack the painting, slashing it with a knife or throwing eggs or excrement at it. He carefully and deliberately covered Ofili's composition with white paint. Instead of violent defacement or destruction, Heiner chose a strategy that might be called "veiling" or "effacement" of the image, a gesture of protection and modesty. The water-soluble paint was easily removed and did no damage to the composition. Heiner's act was (from his point of view) a defense of the sacred image of the Madonna against its sacrilegious defacement by this painting.

It would be fascinating to ponder what the reaction to Ofili's painting would have been if the artist had declared that it was his intention to insult and degrade the Madonna, instead of denying this intention. One can imagine, for instance, a pious Muslim—or Jew or Christian fundamentalist, for that matter—arguing that the Second Commandment makes it a sacred duty to offend or destroy all images, especially one that depicts the Mother of God and thus is well on its way down the slippery slope to idolatry. One of the strangest moments in the whole scandal was the unwavering solidarity of Jewish organizations with the

Catholic Church against the offensive Madonna. Has everyone forgotten that Mariolatry and the cult of images of the Virgin Mary are a violation of the Second Commandment?[19]

It is somehow fitting that the moral objections to dung Madonnas are paralleled by the hand wringing over filthy lucre in its literal sense—that is, money. The "greater" scandal of the *Sensation* show was that it revealed (oh marvelous revelation!) that art museums are in competition with movies, shopping malls, and theme parks. Art, it turns out, has something to do with wealth and speculative capital. There is nothing so edifying as the moral shock of capitalist cultural institutions when they look at their own faces in the mirror. High-minded people in the museum world (Philippe de Montebello, the director of the Metropolitan Museum of Art, for instance) were shocked by the corruption of aesthetic, curatorial, and institutional autonomy entailed in the relation of the Royal Academy and then the Brooklyn Museum to the Saatchis.[20] Are they modern Medicis? Or hucksters of hype? Was the Brooklyn Museum guilty of unethical and unprofessional conduct in its dealings with the Saatchis? Or was it merely guilty of being indiscreet, flaunting a bit too openly what is a common practice in art museums? Candor and openness about the financial underpinnings of contemporary art have never been welcome in the art world. Hans Haacke managed to offend the Guggenheim Museum by displaying photographic images of the New York tenements owned by some of its principal trustees (figure 10). Haacke's strategy might be seen as the obverse of Ofili's. Instead of bringing a sacred image into too close contact with profane materials, Haacke brought images of profane realities into the sacred space of the museum. The ugly facades of slum properties make visible the filthy lucre that supports the sanitized realm of the aesthetic.

The role of excrement in the realm of offending images is not exhausted by its role as an agent of symbolic desecration and disfigurement or as a sign of the material and monetary foundations of artistic purity. There is also the key question of what is sometimes called "bad art." I take it as a given that most people in and out of the art business think that much of contemporary art is a pile of shit. Despite the art world's timorous and belated defense of the Brooklyn Museum, almost all defenders of the *Sensation* show felt obliged to demonstrate their good taste by declaring that most of the work in that show was just plain "bad art." The mystery is why anyone should be criticized for confirming what everyone already knows, that 90 percent of artistic production is not likely to be remembered long. This is hardly a scandalous revelation; it's just plain common sense. At least half of all the art made must be, as a matter of logic, "below average"; only in Garrison Keillor's Lake Wobegon

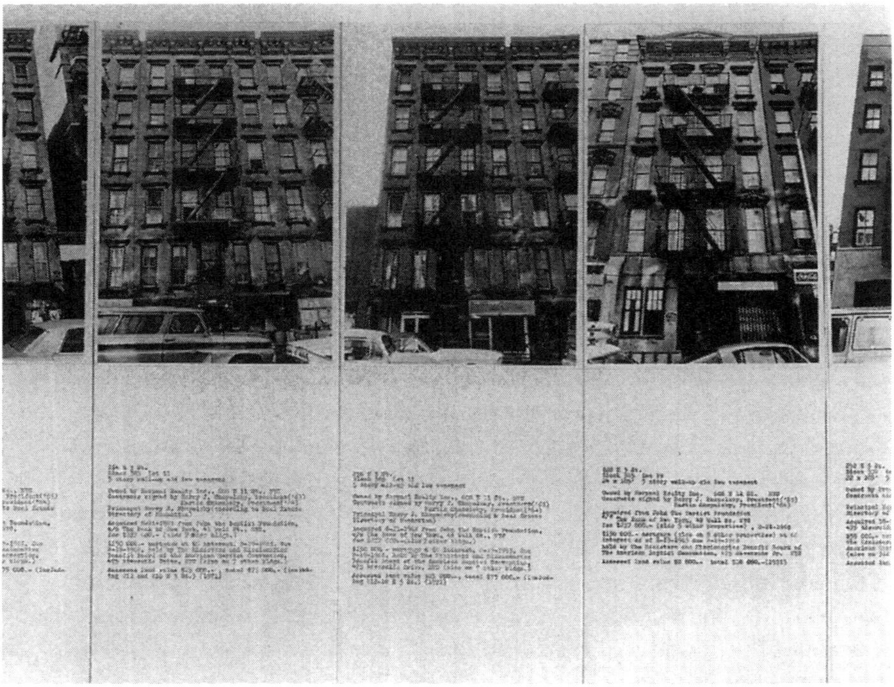

Figure 10. Hans Haacke, *Shapolsky et al Manhattan Real Estate Holdings, a Real-Time Social System, as of May 1, 1971*; first exhibited 1972. Two maps (photo enlargements), one of the Lower East Side and one of Harlem, each 24 × 20 in. (61 × 50.8 cm); 142 photos of building facades and empty lots, each 10 × 8 in. (25.4 × 20.3 cm); 142 typewritten data sheets, attached to the photos and giving the property's address, block and lot number, lot size, building code, the corporation of individual holding title, the corporation's address and its officers, the date of acquisition, prior owner, mortgage, and assessed tax value, each 10 × 8 (25.4 × 20.3 cm); six charts on business transactions (sales mortgages etc.) of the real estate group, each 24 × 20 (61 × 50.8 cm); one explanatory panel, 24 × 20 in. (61 × 50.8 cm). *© 2001 Artists Rights Society (ARS), New York / VG Bildkunst, Bonn.*

can all the children be above average. And there is nothing deplorable or shocking about this fact—no scandal to be uncovered. Vast amounts of second-rate art have to be produced as a kind of mulch or fertilizer for the rare flowering of truly outstanding work. By now, one would think that a jaded, sophisticated crowd like the art world would have come to terms with this as a kind of natural law and given up on the posturing and hand wringing that occur whenever a group show of new, young artists appears. The *Sensation* show, like most group offerings of this sort, was a mixed bag, with a few outstanding and promising works and a fair amount of competent but unmemorable efforts. My own sense of

Sensation was that it was, as these things go, somewhat above average in matters like technical skill, wit, and professionalism of presentation.

As for the display of waste products as art objects, surely this was a moment for art connoisseurs to remind an outraged public that this sort of thing has been going on since the "dirt painters," or rhyparographers, were banned by the laws of Thebes.[21] Excrement, as Jacques Lacan (and every infant) reminds us, is the first medium of artistic expression.[22] For analogues in contemporary art one should see, for instance, Robert Morris's *Scatter Pieces* or Joseph Beuys's corners stuffed with rotting fat. Ofili's tastefully lacquered dung piles are heirs to a long and distinguished art tradition; they are, more precisely, the symbolic pillars of material and spiritual wealth on which the work of art stands—filth and waste transformed into gold by the alchemy of art. Like the Brooklyn Museum, Ofili is guilty only of candor. The great proponent of high modernist "purity," Clement Greenberg, remarked long ago that the avant-garde was linked to the ruling classes by an umbilical cord of gold.[23] Isn't it a bit late, then, to be outraged that museums cater to the rich and must do so in order to survive?

Although I want to invoke the framework of freedom of speech to ensure the utmost latitude for art museums in their exhibition policies, I think it may be important to ponder the difference between speaking and image making, a problem that usually comes up when conservative legal theorists are trying to deny artistic images any protection under the First Amendment because they are not "speech" in any literal sense. What is the difference between offensive images and words? When modern, secular law addresses images, it generally models them on speech—that is, on linguistic, discursive, and rhetorical models—in relation to the First Amendment protection of freedom of speech. Laws regulating speech do not generally address the issue of poetics—that is, of language formally organized to create a mimetic representation or image, a verbal work of art; instead, they deal with language as persuasion, argument, or performance (as in a "speech act" of promising, threatening, or insulting). Most of the attempts to define the offensive character of pornography are based in cases that involve photographic or cinematic images but that treat the images then as if they were conveying speech acts that insult, degrade, and humiliate the (mostly female) subjects of representation and, by extension, all other women as well.

But images are not words. It is not clear that they actually "say" anything. They may show something, but the verbal message or speech act has to be brought to them by the spectator, who projects a voice into the image, reads a story into it, or deciphers a verbal message. Images are dense, iconic, visual symbols; they convey nondiscursive, nonverbal

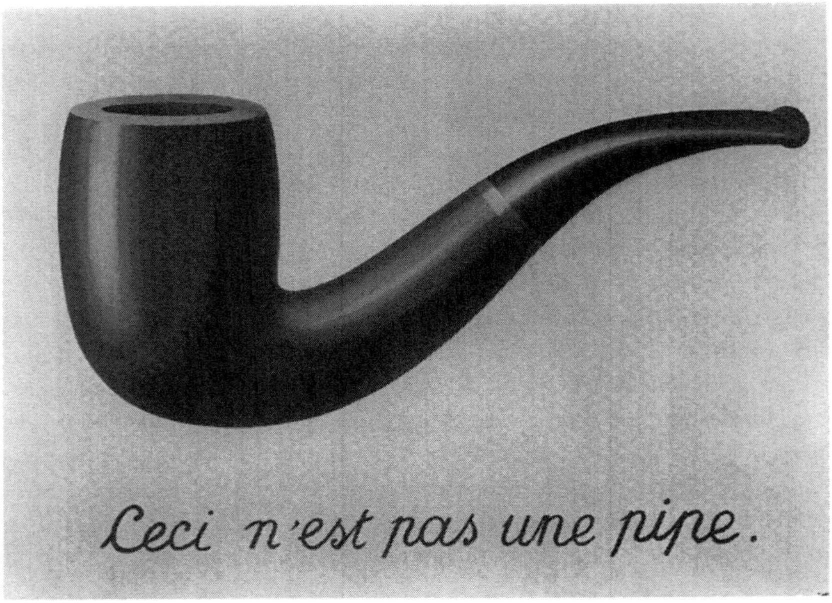

Figure 11. René Magritte, *The Treachery of Images,* c. 1928–1929. Oil on canvas. $25^7/_{16} \times 37^1/_{16}$ in. *© 2001 C. Herscovici, Brussels / Artists Rights Society (ARS), New York. Photograph © Museum Associates / LACMA.*

information that is often quite ambiguous with regard to any statement. Sometimes a picture of a pipe or a cigar is just saying something innocent and straightforward, like "this is a pipe." But it seems to be part of the nature of visual images that they are always saying (or showing) something more than any verbal message can capture—even something directly opposite to what they seem to "say" (for example, "This is not a pipe") (figure 11). That is why a picture is said to be worth a thousand words—precisely because the exact words that can decode or summarize an image are so indeterminate and ambiguous.

A picture is less like a statement or speech act, then, than like a speaker capable of an infinite number of utterances. An image is not a text to be read but a ventriloquist's dummy into which we project our own voice. When we are offended by what an image "says," we are like the ventriloquist insulted by his own dummy. One could decode the dummy's rebellious voice as the discourse of the unconscious, a kind of Tourette syndrome projected into a wooden object. Or one could simply acknowledge that this uncanniness of the dummy, its taking on a "life (and voice) of its own," is fundamental to the game of ventriloquism as such. The voice must not simply be "thrown" into the inanimate object; it must seem to make that object speak with its own voice. The really good ventriloquist doesn't simply impose his voice on the mute thing but expresses in some way the autonomy and specificity of that thing. When Karl Marx in *Capital* asks what commodities would say if they could speak, he understands that what they must say is not simply what he wants them to say. Their speech is not just arbitrary or forced on them but must seem to reflect their inner nature as modern fetish objects. When I claim, then, that the offensive statement made by the image is projected there by the spectator, I don't mean to say that the perception of this statement is merely a mistake or misinterpretation.

That is why it somehow feels both right and futile to punish images, to offend them for the offense that they do to us or "say" to us. Why should we be any smarter than the God who passed a law against images that no one could understand, much less obey? We are always on the slippery slope that leads back from idolatry, offensive images, desecration, and iconoclasm to the mere fact that human beings seem to be inveterate makers of images—images that then seem to have "a mind of their own" and get out of control.

The confusion of images with speech acts is one reason people can be offended by images that they have never seen. Mayor Giuliani and, indeed, a great many of the people who found Ofili's Madonna to be offensive never saw the painting. It was enough for them to hear about it, particularly to hear about the artist's use of elephant dung as a material. Many of those who only heard about the image assumed that the elephant dung must have been smeared on or "flung at" the painting rather than applied carefully, with meticulous ornamentation. The mere verbal report—"image of Madonna with elephant dung"—was enough to convict the image of being offensive. The actual sight of Ofili's Madonna, by contrast, was strangely inoffensive. The picture struck most viewers as sweet and innocuous. It is the verbal label, the naming of the dung, which provokes the perception of offensiveness and the conclusion that the painting must have been transmitting a disrespectful message. As with Andres Serrano's *Piss Christ* (see figure 1), the title and the connotations of the material offend, not the actual visual appearance, the imaginary, fantasized image, not the perceived image. Serrano's urine produces a golden glow around the crucified Christ that reminds one of the golden aureole, or *mandorla*, that is often associated with sacred images. If Serrano had called his image "Christ Bathed in Golden Light," he might have gotten away with it, until some wily critic exposed the connection with the "golden shower" as a perverse sexual practice.

What, then, are the implications for art museums, cultural policy, and the law? My sense is that the *Sensation* scandal is interesting mainly as a relatively benign outbreak of an old malady that we might call the "iconophobia syndrome." People are afraid of images. Images make us anxious. We fight over them, destroy them, and blame them for our own bad behavior, as when we blame "the media" for encouraging moral decay and outbreaks of violence. I'm not saying that we are always wrong to blame or ban images or that the law should take no interest in their control and prohibition. I find it disturbing, for instance, that a New York art gallery would display photographs of lynchings in the United States in the early twentieth century. What purpose, I want to know, is being served by putting these terrible, harrowing images of evil on display for the voyeuristic gratification of the gallery-going public?[24] Still, I would not censor them if I had the power—only protect and veil them from idle curiosity and disrespect. My sense is that the law ought to intervene with offensive images only when they are being forced on the notice of an unwilling public. People have a right not to have offending images thrust in their faces. People also have a right to look at images that others might find offensive.

The questions about the freedom to show offending images are really, then, questions about context more than content—about where and when and to whom an image is displayed. The right of free speech, even political speech, does not allow me to blast you out of your house with a sound truck at four o'clock in the morning. A similar limitation on the display of images—perhaps we could call it the "in your face" principle—can be invoked to regulate the exhibition of images like the Confederate flag, the swastika, or graffiti when they are imposed on unwilling spectators in public spaces, especially spaces like the South Carolina statehouse that claim a publicly representative function. Art museums, however, are special places that ought to enjoy the broadest protections from government interference in exhibitions. Their institutional autonomy needs to be safeguarded from transitory political pressures and the moral outrage of both vocal minorities and moral majorities. Demonstrations in front of museums are a sign of a healthy state of affairs, not a regrettable anomaly that should be averted by fine-tuned policies. Only by preserving a free space of artistic license where offending images are tolerated can we hope to understand what it is that gives images so much power over people and what it is about people that brings this power into the world.

I conclude, therefore, with a proposal for a blockbuster exhibition called "Offending Images," one that would gather all the most egregious offenders into one place. This would be an attempt to describe and analyze the multifarious modes of offensiveness and to diagnose the social forces that give rise to them. It might aim at tracing the long history of offending images across many cultural boundaries, exploring the outbreaks of iconoclasm and iconophobia in the worlds of art and popular media. It would be an occasion for educating people about the histories of human degradation, exploitation, and dehumanization that are so often lurking in the background of the offending images. It would ask who is offended, by whom, what, and how? It would explore the very nature of offensiveness, of the shock, trauma, or injury that images can produce, and try to identify the ways in which an image passes from being merely offensive to being harmful, the graphic equivalent of yelling "fire" in a crowded theater. And it would, finally, include a special gallery of virtual simulations of all the offending images in the exhibition, in which visitors would be provided with all the materials necessary for offending the offenders. Stones, hammers, excrement, paint, blood, dirt, and eggs would be supplied, and visitors would be invited to hurl, smear, and smash away to their hearts' content. This would provide a benign form of therapy and allow lawyers and policymakers to focus their attention on more tractable issues.

NOTES

1. See W.J.T. Mitchell, "The Rhetoric of Iconoclasm," in *Iconology* (Chicago: University of Chicago Press, 1986), for reflections and further references to the enormous literature on this matter. I have also found useful Bruno Latour's "A Few Steps toward an Anthropology of the Iconoclastic Gesture," in *Science in Context* 10 (1997): 63–83, and Michael Taussig's *Defacement* (Stanford, Calif.: Stanford University Press, 1999).
2. *Disgraced Monuments* is also the title of Mulvey's marvelous documentary film on the destruction of Soviet monuments in the early 1990s. Scenes of revelers urinating on the faces of the fallen leaders or of the leaders' sullen countenances languishing in warehouses were especially poignant.
3. For more on this subject, see "What Do Pictures *Really* Want?" *October* 77 (Summer 1996): 71–82 .
4. See Hans Belting, *Likeness and Presence: A History of the Image before the Era of Art* (Chicago: University of Chicago Press, 1994), who argues that the cultic "era of images" (from antiquity to the Middle Ages) has been replaced by an "era of art," in which "subjects seize power over the image" in collections and aesthetic experiences (16). A similar argument is made by David Freedberg in *The Power of Images* (Chicago: University of Chicago Press, 1989), although Belting regards Freedberg's position as unhistorical (see xxi). My sense is that there can be no history of images without some notion of what is abiding about them. The question is not whether images "come alive" but where and how they do so, what kind of life they take on and how people respond to that life.
5. Pliny, *Natural History*, 10 vols., trans. H. Rackham (Cambridge: Harvard University Press, 1952), 9: 277. See also the discussion in my *Picture Theory* (Chicago: University of Chicago Press, 1994), 337–338.
6. It would be worth pondering the contrast between the Royal Academy and the Brooklyn Museum scandals as a tale of two cities—and of two "moms." In London, the scandal was the elevation of an evil mother into a popular icon and a focus of liberal sympathy in the context of widespread hysteria

about pederasty and child abuse. In New York, the scandal was both the degradation of a good mother by an inappropriate pictorial rendering and an offense to Christianity and organized religion more generally. Offending images are clearly not just individual matters but are lightning rods for the energies of large social formations and local cultures.

7. Freedberg discusses this event in *The Power of Images,* 421ff., noting that the attacker never gave any reason for his actions.
8. *United States v. 37 Photographs,* 400 U.S. 817 (1970); *United States v. 12 200–Ft. Reels of Super 8MM Film et al.,* 413 U.S. 123 (1972). My thanks to Geoff Stone for calling these cases to my attention.
9. Belting notes that "'injured' images" react to desecration "like living people by weeping or bleeding"; *Likeness and Presence,* 1.
10. As Belting notes, "The image . . . not only represented a person but also was treated like a person." Ibid., xxi.
11. See W.J.T. Mitchell, "What Sculpture Wants: Placing Antony Gormley," in *Antony Gormley* (London: Phaidon Press, 2000), for more on this matter.
12. I call this the "first law" even though it is the "second commandment" because the First Commandment is not really a prohibition of any sort, merely a declaration by God that he is who he is and no one else. This declaration leads to the prohibition on worshipping other gods, especially in the form of images.
13. See Walter Benjamin on the contingent character of the commandment against murder in his "Critique of Violence," in Peter Demetz, ed., *Reflections* (New York: Harcourt Brace Jovanovich, 1978): "Those who base a condemnation of all violent killing of one person by another on the commandment are therefore mistaken. It exists, not as a criterion of judgment, but as a guideline for the actions of persons or communities who have . . . to take on themselves the responsibility of ignoring it" (298).
14. The commandment refers to the making of a *pesel,* an image carved from wood or stone, but it is generally agreed that the prohibition includes the making of metal figures as well. "To the prohibition of an image is attached a further specification [the ban on "likeness"] which broadens the prohibition to include every representation. The term *temunah* designates the form or outward shape of an object." Brevard Childs, *The Book of Exodus: A Critical, Theological Commentary* (Louisville, Ky.: Westminster Press, 1974), 404–405.
15. Even more striking is the tendency of commentators to ignore the literal meaning completely and to assume that the offensiveness of images is not "built in" to them but must be added to them by wrong usage (adoration of the image), wrong representation (no image of any sort can represent the invisible Jehovah), or wrong referent (this image represents the wrong god, a "strange" God). See Kelman Bland, *The Artless Jew* (Princeton, N.J.: Princeton University Press, 2000), for a decisive refutation of the characterization of Judaism as a culture of aniconism and iconoclasm and for a comprehensive inventory of ways that Jews have evaded any literal reading of the ban on images.
16. Moshe Halbertal and Avishai Margalit, *Idolatry* (Cambridge, Mass.: Harvard University Press, 1992), 39. There could be other reasons for offense besides degraded materiality, of course. The offense could come from the use of the wrong image—a calf, for example, which degrades God to the level of a brute—or it could derive from the adoration of any image at all, regardless of what it represents.
17. Whether elephant dung really is a sacred substance in African religions is somewhat in doubt. Ofili's use of the same substance in what are unques-

tionably respectful paintings of African American heroes, however, seems to support his declaration of intentions, no matter what the facts about African values turn out to be.

18. For further discussion of this distinction between images and pictures as "species" and "specimens," respectively, see W.J.T. Mitchell, "The Surplus Value of Images," forthcoming in *Critical Inquiry*. The concept of the image as "motif" comes from Erwin Panofsky, "Iconography and Iconology," in *Meaning in the Visual Arts* (Garden City, N.Y.: Doubleday, 1955).
19. It did occur to some commentators at the time that the real offense might have been the blackness of the Madonna, an affront to those who are accustomed to blond, blue-eyed images of the virgin. In this case, Heiner's whitening of the image takes on a racial overtone. As far as I know, no one had the effrontery to say this publicly. See Belting's excellent analysis of Mariolatry in *Likeness and Presence.*
20. See also the essay in this book by James Cuno, who implies that a moral distinction could be made between respectable, clean money (the Mellons and the Astors?) and the contaminated money (earned in advertising?) of the Saatchis. Gilbert Edelson's essay on the financial arrangements that underlie museums' relations with wealthy collectors and the art market sheds considerable light on this whole matter.
21. See G. E. Lessing, *Laocoon*, trans. Ellen Frothingham (New York: Farrar, Straus & Giroux, 1969), 18, and Mitchell, *Iconology*, 108, on the control of the arts by civil law in antiquity.
22. Jacques Lacan, *The Four Fundamental Concepts of Psychoanalysis,* trans. Jacques-Alain Miller (New York: Norton, 1981). See specifically the thematic of feces and "the domain of oblativity, of the gift," which is the "drive" of the painter: "He gives something for the eye to feed on" (104, 101).
23. Clement Greenberg, "Avant Garde and Kitsch," in John O'Brian, ed., *Clement Greenberg: The Collected Essays and Criticism* (Chicago: University of Chicago Press, 1986), 1: 11; this article first appeared in the *Partisan Review* in Fall 1939.
24. Since writing these words, I have seen this exhibition at the New-York Historical Society, and I'm fully convinced that the presentation of these photographs is anything but exploitative or voyeuristic. On the contrary, the exhibition is respectful and intelligent, with a quiet and modest presentation that encourages an intensity of attention that is almost devotional. I find nothing in this to offend but a great to deal to mortify, astonish, and shame anyone who thinks that the American "race problem" has been resolved.

DAVID HALLE
ELISABETH TISO
GIHONG YI

The Attitude of the Audience for "Sensation" and of the General Public toward Controversial Works of Art

In his contribution to this volume, David Strauss cautions that the First Amendment is not a reliable protection against government attempts to cut funding to the arts. Strauss concludes that public opinion, not the First Amendment, is the key to warding off government attacks on controversial works of art: "The battle over government funding of disturbing or unconventional art must ultimately be won in the court of public opinion, not in courts of law enforcing the First Amendment. People who want to resist government efforts to reduce funding of certain kinds of art will have to explain to their fellow citizens why it is important that such funding continue."

This chapter deals with two aspects of public opinion. First, what is the audience like for such a show and what do they think of it? The data for examining this question come from an "exit poll" of a sample of those who visited *Sensation*. Second, what does the public think should be done in these circumstances? Does the public favor government funding of the arts? Does the public favor government censorship in general and in particular when publicly funded institutions display material that might be offensive to certain groups? The data for examining these questions come from a national survey undertaken in response to the *Sensation* controversy.

The Show and the Audience at the Brooklyn Museum

To obtain a representative sample, attendees were solicited at random as they exited the gift shop that exhibition-goers had to pass through after seeing the show.[1] The survey was conducted by the UCLA LeRoy Neiman Center for the Study of American Society and Culture. The total sample was 860. The acceptance/response rate for the survey was high—over 85 percent of those asked. Most people were glad to express their opinions on so controversial an exhibition, especially right after seeing it.

What Kind of People Came?

Analysis of the audience for *Sensation* suggests an obvious but important point about such shows: people self-select. On the whole, if they do not think they will like the show, they are unlikely to attend. Thus there were two striking characteristics of the audience. First, few Republicans came. Only 6.1 percent of the sample identified their political-party affiliation as Republican (see table 1). By contrast, 53.9 percent of the sample identified themselves as Democrats, and 17.8 percent as independents. One should, of course, expect a lower percentage of Republican attendees on purely demographic grounds: Republicans are not a large proportion of New York City residents—just 19 percent of those who voted in the 1997 New York City mayoral election identified themselves as Republicans (61 percent identified themselves as Democrats). Even nationwide only 26 percent of eligible voters identified themselves as Republicans in 1998 (38 percent as Democrats, and 34 percent as independents).[2] Still, the proportion of Republicans attending *Sensation* was markedly lower than the proportion of Republicans in New York City or the nation.

Second, the audience was notable for the high proportion with no religious affiliation. Asked to choose a religious preference, 36.7 percent of the sample selected "none." By contrast, national survey data suggest that only around 14 percent of Americans have no religious preference.[3] Charges by Republican politicians that the show was anti-Catholic likely discouraged attendance by Republicans, while the same charges may have suggested to those without religious preference that they might enjoy this show.[4]

Did They Like It?

The audience, by and large, really liked *Sensation*. The first survey question asked: "What did you think of the exhibition overall?" Almost all respondents took this open-ended question as an

***Table 1. The Audience for* Sensation**

RELIGIOUS PREFERENCE	AGE	RACE
Catholicism (16.2%)	10–16 (2.9%)	White (77.5%)
Judaism (19.7%)	17–19 (4.1 %)	Black (5.7%)
Protestantism (10.3%)	20–30 (36.3%)	Asian (6.9%)
Other Christianity (6.3%)	31–50 (38.9%)	Native American (0.3%)
Muslim/Islam (0.6%)	51–65 (13.5%)	Other (9.5%)
Something else (10.3%)	66–88 (4.3%)	
None (36.7%)		
POLITICAL-PARTY PREFERENCE	**SEX**	**LATINO/HISPANIC**
Republican (6.1%)	Male (50.2%)	Latino/Hispanic (10%)
Democrat (53.9%)	Female (49.8%)	Non-Latino/Hispanic (90%)
Independent (17.8%)		
None of the above (22.2%)		

FIRST TIME AT THE BROOKLYN MUSEUM	SEXUAL PREFERENCE
Yes (49.9%)	Heterosexual (87.3%)
No (50.1%)	Homosexual (9.6%)
	Bisexual (3.1%)
PRIMARY RESIDENCE	**EDUCATION**
New York City (52.8%)	11 years or less (3.3%)
Manhattan (24.2%)	12 years, (high school diploma) (3%)
Brooklyn (21.3%)	13–15years (13.8%)
Queens (4.8%)	16 years (college graduate) (27.4%)
Bronx (2.1%)	Some beyond college (17.3%)
Staten Island (0.4%)	Postgraduate degree (35.2%)
Elsewhere in the United States (36.3%)	
Abroad (10.9%)	

Source: Leroy Neiman Center Survey.

invitation to say whether they were positive or negative about the show. The vast majority (74 percent) expressed views that ranged from positive to very positive (see table 2). The extent to which people liked the show was surprising. True, this was a self-selected audience that came to a show about which they had heard an enormous amount. Still, the media discussion had focused on Chris Ofili's *The Holy Virgin Mary,* which was just one of over a hundred works on display. When people said they liked or disliked the show, they were almost all thinking of the entire display, not just a single piece. They were viewing and hearing about most of the works in the show for the first time. A small group (6.2 percent) was very negative, saying they were shocked or disgusted or otherwise hostile. On the surface this group echoed the mayor's reaction, but in fact there were major differences in their reactions to spe-

Table 2. Responses to the Question "What Did You Think of the Exhibition Overall?"

	PERCENT
Positive/very positive	
Interesting/thought-provoking/meaningful	35.5
Very good/wonderful/liked it a lot/nice/beautiful	32.8
Cutting-edge/avant-garde/unique/different	5.6
Neutral	
Acceptable/ok/uncontroversial/nothing offensive	4.2
Somewhat negative	
Unsurprising/boring/banal/derivative	6.1
Do not understand it/too complicated	1.3
Very negative	
Shocking/offensive/sickening/disquieting/unacceptable/ manipulative	4.5
Did not like it	1.7
Other	
Mixed feelings/nonevaluative comments/no response	9.3

Source: Same as for table 1.

cific works, as we will see below. Another group (7.4 percent) was somewhat negative. They were not outraged, just by and large disappointed; they said that the show was dull and boring or that they did not understand it or it was too complicated.

Why did people like the show? One legitimate goal of contemporary art is to unsettle and disturb the audience, to push the limits of what is morally, politically, and socially acceptable. How far did the reactions of the audience for *Sensation* measure up to this standard? The answer is that they came quite close. The largest group (35.5 percent of all respondents) gave the kinds of reasons for liking the show that much contemporary art theory suggests they should have given. They found the works "interesting," "thought-provoking " "meaningful." The following comments are illustrative:

> "The exhibition was an amazing display of work with similar ideas and concepts. It brought up many questions."
>
> "One of the most interesting art exhibits in a long time—this is perhaps because it's mostly figurative, instead of abstract."
>
> "It was very interesting, something different and shocking. I loved it."
>
> "Excellent. Thought provoking, with a tinge of 'Pop Art' theory. Stronger in some areas, while weak in others."

The second largest group (32.8 percent) said that they liked *Sensation* because it had been pleasurable—they enjoyed it, thought it was nice, wonderful, beautiful, and so on. Unlike the first group, they did not explicitly mention being stimulated to thought or provoked, although it is reasonable to suppose some of them were.

Overall, 74 percent of the audience said they liked the show. What about variations by subgroup? Despite the claim that Ofili's piece was anti-Catholic, there is no indication that the Catholics who attended were especially disapproving or upset. Jews, Catholics, and Muslims liked it about as much as everyone. However, Protestants liked it quite a bit less than the average (66.7 percent liked it), while people without any religious preference liked it somewhat more (78 percent liked it). Republicans liked it quite a bit less than most of the audience. Only 63.6 percent liked it, while 13.6 percent were very negative, more than twice as many as the average of all those who attended. Democrats, however, liked the show more than the average (79 percent liked it). Independents liked the show about as much as everyone (74 percent liked it). These figures confirm the earlier findings about political preference. Not only did Republicans tend not to come to *Sensation*, but those who did come tended to be somewhat more negative than the rest of the audience. Heterosexuals liked the show about as much as everyone, but homosexuals and bisexuals liked it slightly more (78.6 and 79.1 percent, respectively, liked it).

Whites liked it about as much as the average, but Asians liked it a lot less (only 59.6 percent liked it), while blacks liked it quite a bit more than the average (83 percent liked it). The reaction of blacks is of special interest given that Ofili and his *Virgin* are black. In part, African American enthusiasm did stem from the fact that Ofili's Virgin was black. When we asked specifically about that work (see below), a fifth of the black respondents made specific reference to this fact (although none referred to the fact that Ofili is black). The following comments are illustrative:

> "I loved it! The hip-hop version of the Virgin Mary is great."
> "I like the fact that the Virgin was depicted with Afro-centric features."
> "Not too many people depict the Virgin Mary as [of] African descent. It's different."
> "Interesting how he blended African and European ideology. It's not often that you see culture depicted in that way."
> "He showed that the Virgin Mary does not always have to be depicted as white but can be a black female."

At the same time, a few African Americans read the image in the opposite way, finding the placing of elephant dung on a black Mary offensive to blacks. As one put it, "This was very offensive on a black Mary. I can't understand the artist. The Virgin Mary represents holiness, god-

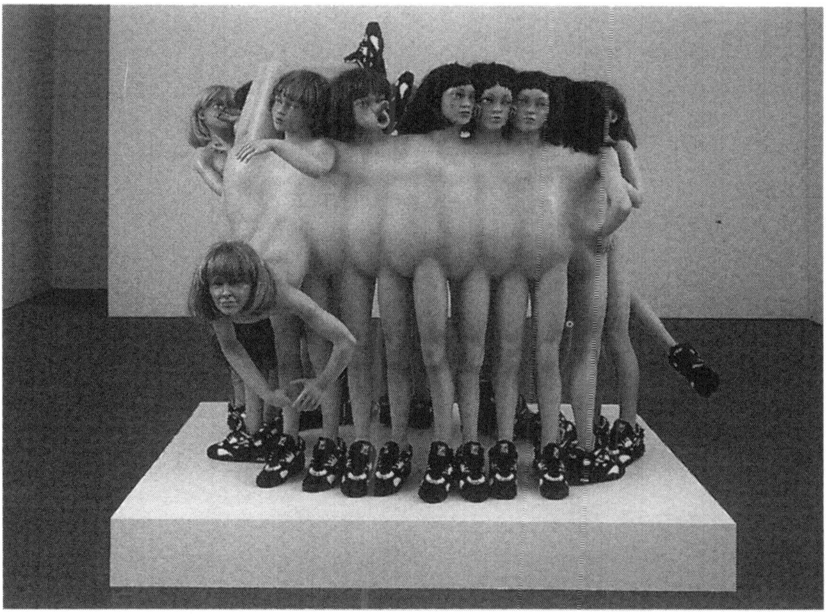

Figure 12. Jake and Dinos Chapman, *Zygotic acceleration, biogenetic d-sublimated libidinal model*, 1995. Mixed media. Dimensions unknown. *Courtesy of The Saatchi Gallery and White Cube Gallery, London.*

liness, cleanliness, not elephant dung and porno clips. This is an abomination to me."

Did They Find the Show Offensive?

Mayor Rudolph Giuliani claimed that some of the works in the show were "offensive." So respondents were asked whether they found the exhibition offensive overall. In addition, they were asked how offensive they found each of five specific works. They were asked about Ofili's *Virgin* because it was the center of the controversy in New York and about Marcus Harvey's portrait of the British child murderer Myra Hindley because that was the center of the controversy when *Sensation* was shown in London in 1997. One of Damien Hirst's dissected animals, *This little piggy went to market . . .* (see figure 7), was selected because Hirst is acknowledged as the leader of the group whose work formed the core of *Sensation*. Further, the September 16, 1999, *Daily News* article that brought Ofili's *Virgin* to the mayor's attention mentioned Hirst's works—the shark in an enclosed glass tank, the smaller animals sliced into sections and preserved in formaldehyde—before Ofili's. The fourth work viewers were asked about was *Zygotic acceleration, biogenetic d-sublimated libidinal model* by Jake and Dinos Chapman (figure 12). It

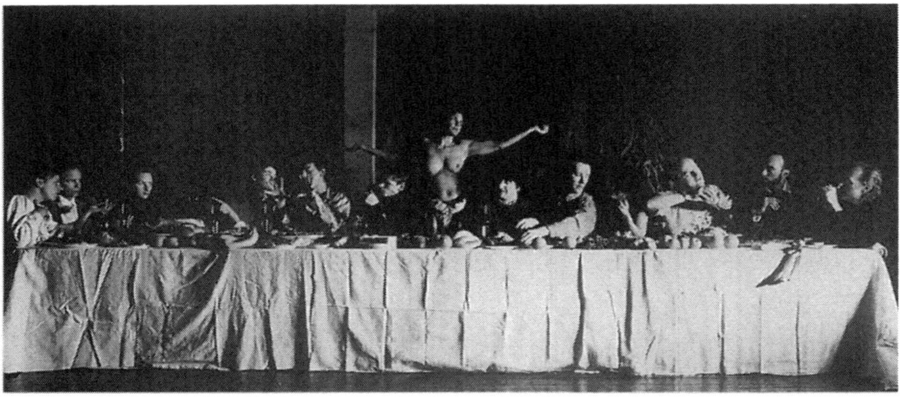

Figure 13. Sam Taylor-Wood, *Wrecked*, 1996. C-type color print. 5 × 13 ft. *Courtesy of The Saatchi Gallery and White Cube Gallery, London.*

was selected partly because it too was highlighted in the *Daily News* article—the second sentence of the article ("graphic paintings and sculptures of corpses and sexually mutilated bodies") refers to this work. More important, the sexually explicit depictions of children echoed some of the child-pornography issues raised in the furor a decade previously over Robert Mapplethorpe's work. Finally, respondents were asked about Sam Taylor-Wood's painting *Wrecked* because it seemed objectively as anti-Catholic as Ofili's piece but raised some different issues (figure 13). The work imitates *The Last Supper,* with the artist, naked from the waist up, depicting Jesus, and her drunken friends depicting the disciples. The fact that the artist was female and had painted herself, bare-breasted, as Jesus raised feminist issues.

The audience, as a whole, was hardly offended by the show. Sixty-three percent found it not at all offensive, and 21 percent found it only slightly offensive. Only 4 percent found the exhibition overall "very offensive."

Respondents were shown pictures of each of the five works, with the following results.

Ofili's work caused less offense than any of the others except *Wrecked* (see table 3). Indeed, the two possibly anti-Catholic pieces—*The Holy Virgin Mary* and *Wrecked*—were the least likely to cause offense. Over 80 percent of the audience found neither of these works "at all offensive." The adjective that people most often used to describe Ofili's *Virgin* was "beautiful." This response is understandable. The Virgin is set in a cheerful yellow and light orange background freely painted in oil; drops of gold glitter on the surface and give the work a Byzantine, jewel-like aura overall. Also, from the distance to which viewers were con-

Table 3. Percentage Finding the Exhibition Overall and Particular Works Offensive

	1 (NOT AT ALL OFFENSIVE)	2	3	4	5 (VERY OFFENSIVE)
Exhibition overall	63.3	21.3	8.2	3.2	3.9
Taylor-Wood, *Wrecked*	86.9	3.9	3.9	0.5	4.8
Ofili, *The Holy Virgin Mary*	81.2	8.3	4.3	1.6	4.6
Ofili, *The Holy Virgin Mary* if painted as a traditional Madonna	75.3	10.3	5.3	4.1	5.0
Harvey, *Myra*	75.1	10.3	5.5	3.2	5.5
Hirst, *This little piggy went to market . . .*	70.6	13.1	6.8	4.6	4.9
Chapman brothers, *Zygotic Acceleration, biogenetic d-sublimated libidinal model*	56.6	15 6	10.5	6.6	10.8

Source: Same as for table 1.

fined, the pornographic cutouts look as much like colorful butterflies as like female buttocks. The elephant-dung breast and supports too are coated in resin, painted with a bluish sheen, and covered in glitter. The following comments give the flavor of the responses and an idea of the variation in attitude:

> "I was actually surprised by how beautiful it was."
>
> "Ofili is obviously talking about his personal experience of Catholicism and how Blacks are ignored and ill considered."
>
> "It wasn't that bad at all."
>
> "Painstakingly beautiful. If he had titled it something else secular, no one would have even really looked."
>
> "Colors were pretty."
>
> "I'm glad the paint came off [reference to Dennis Heiner's vandalism]. It was ethnic and nonoffensive "
>
> "High school quality."
>
> "This painting I felt was thoroughly respectful of the Virgin Mary, except for the pornographic images."
>
> "Unites two cultures, the African and the Christian culture."
>
> "A very sublime, beautiful painting. It should not be in a show with work like Hirst's. The media and Giuliani really don't get what the elephant dung is about—fertility. It is also about making sublime that which is abject (shit and porno)."

Reactions to Sam Taylor-Wood's *Wrecked*, which objectively could be seen as just as anti-Catholic as Ofili's piece, were also quite mild.

Some people liked it; some thought it was derivative and dull; but the largest group commented that they had hardly noticed it at all when going though the exhibition. Outrage, it is clear, typically needs to be channeled and stimulated. *Wrecked* was not the subject of a public attack by the mayor (although in private conversations during the period when the museum and the mayor were trying to negotiate a compromise, he had said he wanted this painting too secluded in a special room).

What about the small group (6.2 percent) who hated the show or the much larger group who, while liking the show, did find some of the works offensive? It was the Chapman brothers' depictions of naked, sexually mutated children that gave the most offense. Only 56.6 percent of the audience saw nothing offensive at all in this work. Eleven percent found them "very offensive," twice the proportion of those who found any of the other four works offensive. This result is ironic: although the Chapman brothers' work was mentioned in the *Daily News* article, after that it scarcely figured in the public debate over *Sensation*.

On the whole, those who found the Chapman brothers' work offensive rejected the artists' idea that these naked and distorted child mannequins were a warning of the dangers inherent in modern biogenetics. Instead, they saw the work as child pornography. The following are comments from the 28 percent of the sample who rated the Chapman brothers' piece at least fairly offensive (score of 3, 4, or 5):

> "Offensive, not beautiful, not artful. Pedophilic, disturbing."
> "Sick."
> "Really disgusting."
> "Most offensive. . . . I don't really agree with the need in our society to sexualize children."
> "Gross, but strangely intriguing."
> "Why are there only girls?!"

Still, not all those who saw the works through the lens of child pornography disliked the art or found it offensive. The following are comments from people who saw the work in this way but did not rate it as offensive:

> "Amazing! A revelation. Goes beyond anything I've seen in challenging attitudes on sex, childhood, and cult of beauty and physicality."
> "Addresses issues that people would rather not discuss or be exposed to . . . sexuality, death, pornography, 'the perfect female.'"
> "I could see what they were getting at (the fixed sexualization

of children and our desire to see children as nonsexual although they *are* very sexual), but I didn't like the work visually."

The artist who caused the second most offense was Hirst. This is not to say that, as a group, the audience found his work offensive. Seventy percent found it not at all offensive, and another 13 percent found it only slightly offensive. The 16 percent of the sample who rated the Hirst piece at least fairly offensive (score of 3, 4, or 5) tended to see it as cruel to animals, perverse, childish, or silly. The following comments are illustrative of those who found Hirst's work at least fairly offensive:

"Very cruel to animals. Very disgusting, not art "
"I don't believe in using dead animals in art."
"Revolting."
"It made me not want to eat pork chops."
"Seeing animals dissected was offensive."

Those not offended by Hirst's work, the vast majority, tended to see it as making a point about our carnivorous appetites, as pro-animal rights, as reminding us of the origins of the packaged and processed meats that we consume, as an interesting biological display, as a commentary on the nature of death, as just very creative. These comments are illustrative:

"I once worked on a pig farm; . . . every Saturday we would round up a sow and pigs and march them to the butcher. Pigs are smart and they *did not want* to go. Now I am a vegetarian, most of the time."
"I thought it was yucky . . . yet effective, and people should see that side."
"A further expression of this Anglo-Saxon meat problem."
"The split cow and pig made me fascinated with anatomy and made me think of a butcher shop. Dead flies made me think of the poor and bad sanitation."
"This was a shocker. . . . I want to buy food at a health food store."
"A good argument for vegetarianism."

Some of the most interesting lessons to be gained from what the audience for *Sensation* said and thought about it revolve around the question of meaning and how hard it is to determine properly. For one thing, the "meaning" of works, which Mayor Giuliani and others are so sure about, is actually quite variable and difficult to predict. Hardly any of the audience took Ofili's *Virgin* as "meaning" an insult to Catholicism. The Chapman brothers' images of naked mutant children disturbed more people. But even here there was much variability in the meaning that people assigned to the work. Most of the audience saw it as a legitimate commentary on the dangers of modern biogenetics rather than as child pornography. Likewise, Hirst's sliced animals were viewed favorably by the vast majority of the audience. Many saw them as, for example, legitimate reminders of the natural origins of processed food. Still, those who disliked Hirst's works—again a group larger than those who disliked Ofili's *Virgin*—tended to see them as cruel and sadistic. The variability of meaning is clear, as is the inadvisability of a single person's determining a work's "meaning."

A further point follows. Methodologically, to adequately determine the "meaning" of a work to an audience is extremely difficult and time-consuming. In this study, the audience was asked about the works right after they had seen them. They were also given photographs of the works to jog their memories. This procedure was the minimum necessary to get even a reasonable idea of what the works "meant" to the audience. Asking people who had not seen the works in the show about their opinions of the works would have been inadequate and crude. For one thing, it is almost impossible to describe pieces like Ofili's *Virgin* in a neutral manner. Does one start with the elephant dung or with the pleasing gold sparkles that give the piece a Byzantine effect? Even after the audience saw a work, many needed a photograph to help them recall the entire work. This methodological point also underlines how problematic it is for a single individual to determine meaning for a hypothetical audience.

Public Opinion Nationwide

The American public turns out to have a coherent, and rather sensible, majority set of views on the central policy issues raised by the debate over *Sensation*.[5] These views are so reasonable that they might well serve as a policy guide for such situations. The structure of public opinion on these issues also goes far to explain both why such controversies break out at regular intervals and why their impact is typically limited.

For data, we relied primarily on a nationwide survey conducted on the *Sensation* debate by the Center for Survey Research and Analysis at the University of Connecticut. This phone survey of a scientifically chosen sample of 1,005 adults was conducted from September 29, 1999, through October 3, 1999.[6]

Should Government Fund the Arts?

Overall the American public clearly supports government funding of the arts. Sixty percent of the national sample are in fa-

Table 4. *Public Attitudes toward Government Funding of the Arts, by Political-Party Identification and Strength of Belief*

	STRONGLY SUPPORT, %	MILDLY SUPPORT, %	MILDLY OPPOSE, %	STRONGLY OPPOSE, %	DON'T KNOW/ UNSURE/ NO ANSWER, %
Total survey	29.7	31.1	15.2	16.7	7.2
Democrat	40.6	29.6	10.5	9.9	9.4
Republican	17.1	31.2	21.1	25.9	5.1
Independent	31.0	34.5	14.6	15.9	4.0
Something else	30.4	32.1	19.6	14.2	3.7
Don't know/no answer	22.0	24.3	10.7	17.9	25.1

Source: Center for Survey Research and Analysis at the University of Connecticut, September 29–October 3, 1999.

vor (strongly or mildly), only 32 percent are against (see table 4). Moreover, almost twice as many people "strongly favor" as "strongly oppose" such government spending. These figures explain why government funding of the arts, despite periodic assaults, survives: it is popular. New York City residents, it should be noted, favored government funding of the arts even more strongly, with 77 percent in favor and only 19 percent opposed. (The data on New York City residents are from an October 20, 1999, poll by Quinnipiac College's Polling Institute.)

This picture should be nuanced. Changes in question wording make a difference. For example, some surveys ask people whether there should be more or less arts funding (as opposed to whether they favor government funding of the arts). The largest group is still in favor of the status quo—of keeping spending at its current levels. But, as Paul DiMaggio and Becky Pettit have pointed out, of the rest substantially more favor reducing than increasing spending on the arts.[7]

Also, support for government funding of the arts varies considerably by demographic and political group. Political-party identification makes by far the largest difference. Democrats and independents are more likely to favor government spending on the arts than are Republicans. Seventy percent of Democrats favor ("strongly" or "mildly") government funding of the arts, as do 65 percent of independents; Republicans are split about evenly on the question. (See table 4.) Multivariate statistical analysis confirms the significance of political-party identification and reveals that the odds of a Democrat's supporting government funding of the arts are 3.9 times the odds of a Republican's supporting such funding.[8] This greater enthusiasm among Democrats, compared with Republicans, for government arts funding mirrors the history of such funding in the United States. Government funding of the arts has occurred in two main steps, both taken by liberal Democratic presidents. The first step, in the 1930s, was the Works Project Administration (WPA), set up by Franklin Roosevelt as a general employment scheme. After the WPA ended in 1943 there was no federal funding of the arts until the National Endowment for the Arts was set up under President Lyndon Johnson.[9] The fact that a significant minority of the public favors decreased funding of the arts explains why from time to time Republican politicians, especially those seeking support from the right wing of the party (in primary elections in New York State, endorsements from the Conservative Party) or those with large Republican majorities in conservative sections of the country (such as Jesse Helms in North Carolina), attack certain publicly funded arts projects.

Should Government Regulate the Content of the Arts in Museums, Public Libraries, or Theaters?

Yet the public—both Democrats and Republicans alike—are clearly against government attempts to regulate the content of works in public museums, libraries, or theaters. Sixty-eight percent think the government should not be able to "ban art in public museums that contains content that might be offensive to others" (table 5). Only 29 percent are in favor of this kind of government intervention. The public is even more strongly against government attempts to regulate possibly offensive material in other key areas such as libraries and theaters. Seventy-seven percent oppose the government's banning "books from public libraries that contain content that might be offensive to others," and 76 percent oppose the government's banning "performances or plays from public auditoriums that contain content that might be offensive to others."

Republicans are just as opposed to the government's banning art in public museums as are Democrats, a finding that has not been stressed in previous studies. Both Republicans (68 percent against) and Democrats (66 percent against) are against such government intervention. Multivariate statistical analysis also confirms this finding.[10] This result is crucial. As was seen before, Republicans are less enthusiastic about government funding of the arts than are Democrats. But driving this relative lack of enthusiasm may be Republican antipathy to government rather than any Republican antipathy to the arts. That Republicans, like Democrats, do not want the government deciding what arts should and should not be seen is crucial. It helps to explain why Republican politicians' attacks on the arts often recede, albeit after having caused sometimes considerable harm.

Table 5. Public Attitude toward Allowing the Government to Ban Possibly Offensive Works in Public Museums, Libraries, and Theaters, by Political-Party Identification and Strength of Belief

	STRONGLY AGREE, %	MILDLY AGREE, %	MILDLY DISAGREE, %	STRONGLY DISAGREE, %
Public museums				
Total survey	17.2	12.2	17.2	50.5
Democrat	20.9	9.8	17.3	48.2
Republican	17.7	11.8	21.3	46.4
Independent	15.9	11.4	13.9	58.1
Something else	10.2	10.1	16.2	60.7
Don't know/no answer	12.6	27.8	13.4	37.9
Public libraries				
Total survey	13.6	7.8	16.3	60.5
Democrat	15	6.5	14.7	62.4
Republican	15.9	8.1	19.7	54.5
Independent	9.7	9.0	15.0	63.7
Something else	9.1	6.5	12.6	69.8
Don't know/no answer	19.9	10.7	21.0	47.5
Public auditoriums				
Total survey	12.7	9.9	22.2	53.8
Democrat	14.8	10.0	22.3	51.6
Republican	13.5	9.4	25.4	50.3
Independent	10.7	9.8	17.9	59.7
Something else	4.7	8.8	17.7	67.4
Don't know/no answer	22.9	14.4	32.5	30.1

Source: Same as for table 4.

Should Cultural Products That Might Be Offensive to Particular Groups Be Displayed in Public Spaces?

The poll just discussed asked people what should be available for display in a bounded institution such as a museum or a library or a theater. But the public seems to draw a reasonable distinction between what can be said in such institutions and what can be said in far more open public settings such as streets and billboards along highways. Museums, libraries, and theaters are institutions with specific, cultural purposes. In order to access their cultural products and displays, the public must make an effort to attend them. There is no chance that the message will go out to passersby who have not made this specific effort.

Public opinion is not in favor of offending groups in broad public spaces that are not limited to people who make a special effort to enter. Respondents were asked whether "people should be allowed to display in a *public place* [our emphasis] art that has content that might be offensive to others." A majority (54 percent) said no ("definitely not" or "probably not"); 43 percent said yes ("definitely" or "probably"). (See table 6.) Further, when the question specifies the groups that might be offended in open public spaces, the public becomes even more cautious and protective of the sensibilities of others. When asked about displaying art in public places that might be offensive to religious groups, 59 percent say no, 39 percent say yes. When "minority groups" are specified, the proportion saying no rises still further, to 64 percent, with 35 percent saying yes. Thus the public tolerance for what is displayed in museums, libraries, or theaters does not carry over into the open public sphere.

Conclusion

Although the controversy over *Sensation* was quite ferocious, raised many serious issues, and even jeopardized individual careers, in one sense it was also normal. Contemporary artists can legitimately attempt to push the boundaries of what is morally, aesthetically, and politically acceptable. This study suggests that the center of gravity of public opinion—both the opinion of those who attend such a show and the opinion of the U.S. public in general on the relevant issues—points to sensible and reasonable ways of handling such controversies. These kinds of disputes are likely to recur because one legitimate goal of contemporary artists is to unsettle and even shock the audience.[11] In the 1980s, Andres Serrano dunked a variety of sculptural objects in a Plexiglas vat of his own urine. The objects were mostly secular (for example, a discus thrower titled *Piss Discus,* a fashion model titled *Piss Elegance*), but some were religious (for example, the Pope titled *Piss Pope*, a crucifix titled *Piss Christ*). The religious sculptures were the object of controversy. Likewise, Ofili applied elephant dung to many of his works but was criticized for applying the material to *The Holy Virgin Mary*. Ofili denied any intent to shock or offend, but his work was packaged in a show labeled *Sensation*, which was clearly intended to stir things up. *Sensation* was an exhibition in search of controversy, a search that is a valid goal of contemporary art.

That a Republican mayor running for election in a state with a large number of Catholic voters would take up the challenge was no surprise. Nor was it a surprise that the focus would be government funding of the arts. Indeed, those who wish to suppress a particular work or show are likely to focus on government funding of the work in question not only because it is an area that the government can control but also because public-opinion data show that about half of those who identify

Table 6. Public Attitudes toward Displaying Possibly Offensive Material in Public Places

	PERCENT
Content that is possibly offensive	
Definitely	20.1
Probably	23.5
Probably not	16.7
Definitely not	37.2
Don't know/unsure/no answer	3
Content that is possibly offensive to religious groups	
Definitely	18
Probably	21
Probably not	16
Definitely not	43
Don't know/unsure/no answer	3
Content that is possibly offensive to minority groups?	
Definitely	15
Probably	20
Probably not	19
Definitely not	45
Don't know/unsure/no answer	2

Source: Same as for table 4.

themselves as Republicans do not care for government funding of the arts anyway.

Yet the mayor's efforts to close the show down were not especially helpful to his popularity, most likely because neither Republicans nor Democrats nor independents at this point in U.S. history favor the government's deciding what should be displayed or performed in artistic and cultural institutions. The public has an enormous mistrust of government in general, and this mistrust probably translates into dislike of the government's deciding what cultural products we will see in our museums and theaters and other cultural venues. This dislike limits how far attacks on particular works displayed in bounded institutions can go.

Finally, the results of the survey of the audience for *Sensation* further undermine the desirability of a single figure, politician or otherwise, acting *in loco parentis* to determine what the public should and should not see. Giuliani picked an item that few in the audience found offensive. Ofili's *Virgin* was taken by the vast majority of the audience as a rather beautiful piece that caused no offense. If any work offended, it was the Chapman brothers' depictions of naked children with grotesque sexual and other organs. Still, even here almost no one thought these works should not be displayed.

It will, of course, be said that the publicity given to *Sensation* caused those who might have been offended by Ofili's *Virgin* to stay away. But this is precisely the point of showing such works in bounded institutions such as museums, which people must make a special effort to attend. Those who are likely to be offended tend to stay away, while those who attend are not likely to be offended. Displaying items in a bounded institution is a reasonable compromise between allowing the freedom that culture needs to flourish and requiring the courtesy that certain groups—ethnic, racial, or religious—should not feel openly insulted in full public view.

NOTES

The UCLA LeRoy Neiman Center for the Study of American Society and Culture provided part of the funding for this study. We are extremely grateful to Janet and LeRoy Neiman for their support. The Luce Foundation initiated this study and funded the survey of those who attended *Sensation*. We are extremely grateful to Ellen Holtzman and Alberta Arthurs from the Luce Foundation. We also thank Paul DiMaggio, who suggested to the Luce Foundation that we could do the study. Frank Romo helped with the survey design, and Vincent Fu, with the data analysis. Jon Marontate, Kurt and Gladys Lang, Albert Berges, and John Evans gave us helpful comments on the essay.

1. If a person declined, the interviewer approached the next person to exit, and so on. On obtaining agreement to an interview, the interviewer escorted the respondent(s) to a table in a next-door alcove set aside for this use by the museum, explained the process of filling out the survey, and then returned to the gift-shop exit. The interviewer then selected the next person to exit the gift shop, asked for an interview, and the cycle continued. Actually, the sampling process was a little more complicated because attending a museum show is a social event—most visitors to *Sensation* came in groups of two or more. The sampling method had to take account of this. When people exited in groups, we requested an interview from everyone in the group, and we administered the survey to all in the group who agreed to take part. A survey of visitors to the Metropolitan Museum of Art conducted in 1994 found that 74 percent came in groups of two or more. See Jeffrey Smith, "Museum Visitor Preferences and Intentions in Constructing Aesthetic Experience," *Poetics* 24 (1996): 219–238.

   We interviewed over a range of days of the week—both weekdays and weekends—since the composition of the audience for museums is probably affected by the day of the week. For example, the audience during the weekend tends to be younger than during the week (Jeffrey Smith, reporting at a January 1999 meeting of the Social Science Research Council's Program on the Arts, on research undertaken for the Office of Research and Evaluation at the Metropolitan Museum of Art).

   Despite our efforts, in one respect the sample is not representative of those who saw *Sensation*. Non-English-speaking people are underrepresented since respondents whose English was weak usually declined to be interviewed. This was unavoidable.
2. The New York City data on party identification are from the 1997 mayoral-election exit poll conducted by Voter News Service. The national data on party identification are from the American National Election Study, 1998, conducted by the Center for Political Studies at the Institute for Social Research, University of Michigan.

3. The national survey data on religious identification are from the 1998 General Social Survey; James Allan Davis and Tom W. Smith, *General Social Surveys, 1972–1998*, machine-readable data file (Chicago: National Opinion Research Center, producer; Storrs: Roper Center for Public Opinion Research, University of Connecticut, distributor). That survey asked: "What is your religious preference? Is it Protestant, Catholic, Jewish, some other religion or no religion?" Our question was very similar.
4. Several other features of the audience are worth noting. This was their first visit to the Brooklyn Museum for about half the sample. They were, presumably, drawn there by *Sensation*. Just over half the sample were from New York City, with almost all of these coming from just two of the five boroughs—Manhattan and Brooklyn. The museum staff said this breakdown was typical of the audiences for most of their shows. Residents of Manhattan, perhaps having attended most of the museums there, will travel to the Brooklyn Museum, as will residents of Brooklyn, presumably in support of, and drawn to, their neighborhood. But residents of the other boroughs who desire to attend art museums seems to believe that they are better off going to Manhattan rather than visiting Brooklyn.
5. For a discussion of the many sociopolitical issues on which public opinion is "reasonable," see Benjamin Page and Robert Shapiro, *The Rational Public: Fifty Years of Trends in Americans' Policy Preferences* (Chicago: University of Chicago Press, 1992). By "reasonable" the authors mean the following: the opinions are coherent and mutually consistent, are fairly stable and do not fluctuate wildly, make sense according to people's values and the information they have, and when they change do so in ways that appear to be sensibly related to new conditions or new information.
6. Sampling error is +/–3 percent at the 95 percent confidence interval. The survey was commissioned by the First Amendment Center. We are grateful to Larry McGill, director of research for the First Amendment Center, and Ken Dautrich, director, Center for Survey Research and Analysis, University of Connecticut, for making their data set available for us to analyze.
7. For an excellent analysis of the survey data on public attitudes toward funding the arts, see Paul DiMaggio and Becky Pettit, *Public Opinion and Political Vulnerability: Why Has the National Endowment for the Arts Been Such an Attractive Target?* Working Paper 7 (Princeton, N.J.: Center for Arts and Cultural Policy Studies, Princeton University, January 1999). Among the issues they discuss are the effect of question wording and the fact that although a majority tend to support government funding of the arts, the minority opposed are more vehement in their opposition than the majority are vehement in their support.
8. The analysis is based on a logistic regression model. Political-party identification is highly significant ($p < 0.001$). Other demographic variables that are significantly related to attitude toward government spending on the arts are age (younger people are more likely to favor it than older people), education (college graduates are more likely to favor it than those with just a high school diploma), and religion (Jews and Catholics are more likely to favor it than Protestants).
9. On the history of the National Endowment for the Arts, see Gary Larson, *The Reluctant Patron: The United States Government and the Arts, 1943–1965* (Philadelphia: University of Pennsylvania Press, 1983). See also on this topic Stephen Benedict, ed., *Public Money and the Muse: Essays on Government Funding for the Arts* (New York: Norton, 1991).
10. Analysis using logistic regression finds that political-party identification is not significantly related to whether people believe that the government should

be able to censor what is displayed in museums. Indeed, in a model that also includes age, religion, education, sex, and income, the only variable that is significant is region, with the South favoring government censorship in comparison with the western, northeastern, and north-central regions.

11. On previous controversies, see Steven Dubin, *Displays of Power: Memory and Amnesia in the American Museum* (New York: New York University Press, 1999); Steven Dubin, *Arresting Images: Impolitic Art and Uncivil Actions* (New York: Routledge, 1992); David Gamboni, *The Destruction of Art. Iconoclasm and Vandalism since the French Revolution* (London: Reaktion, 1997); Nathalie Heinich, *L'Art contemporain: Exposé aux rejets. Études de cas* (Paris: Éditions Jacqueline Cambon, 1998).

PART IV

Shock Value

MARKET-MAKING FOR CONTROVERSIAL ART

JOHN BREWER

Shop Value

Part IV consists of three essays that represent the views of different constituencies in the art and museum world. James Cuno, director of the Harvard University Art Museums, discusses the response of museum professionals—the curator or the boss, the director—to the worrying pressures and controversies that the *Sensation* show exemplifies. Gilbert Edelson, administrative vice president and counsel of the Art Dealers Association of America, looks at the *Sensation* controversy from the perspective of an art-market insider who has represented the interests of one of the most powerful groups in the art world, professional art dealers, and who is intimately acquainted with the complex relations between public museums and private dealers and collectors. Finally, András Szántó, a sociologist of art and culture who is deputy director of the National Arts Journalism Program at Columbia University, examines the role of the press in the controversy.

The three essays are concerned not with freedom of speech, obscenity, or offensiveness, but with the issue of proper professional conduct in the museum world. New York Mayor Rudolph Giuliani accused the Brooklyn Museum not only of displaying sacrilegious and obscene art but also of professional malpractice—the violation of its public mandate because of its complicity with the private and pecuniary interests of Charles Saatchi, other dealers in contemporary art, and Christie's auction house. The three contributors are less concerned with the precise nature and validity of these accusations (although they have their views on them) than with stepping back from the *Sensation* fray to examine the professional and press environment that made them possible.

Cuno's essay eloquently enunciates the anxieties and apprehensions of museum directors and curators who feel themselves under extraordinary "pressure" (a term he uses on more than one occasion) in the contemporary art world. Growing financial pressures, argues Cuno, push directors into turning to a variety of potential donors to raise the funds without which most museums cannot continue their day-to-day activities, much less mount the highly visible exhibitions that feed a museum and its staff's reputation.

The context for this anxiety (also discussed in Teri Edelstein's essay) is the one so lucidly outlined in Mark Schuster's contribution to this book: the collapse of a traditional system of funding characterized by general taxation, peer review, and a ceiling of 50 percent public support. The demise of this system means that less money, perhaps absolutely and certainly proportionately, is coming from public funds. The reasons for this change lie partly in the political controversies that have surrounded the public support of visual art (the "culture wars"), and they are also bound up with the triumph of liberal, free-market ideology in the 1980s and 1990s. The fall of the old system has prompted a proliferation of new ways of raising money for the arts, stimulating innovation among funding agencies and leading to increased collaboration between public and private sectors.

The techniques involved in this new funding regime vary: some, such as line-item budgeting, increase political control of the arts; others, such as formula funding, confer greater artistic license. But all these mechanisms represent a struggle not only to raise or obtain funds but also for control—the determination of how such funds should be used or deployed. And, as Schuster points out, partly because of these pressures, because of the liberalization, in both the good and the bad sense, of arts administration, demands for accountability, transparency, and effectiveness have grown. New funding mechanisms have increased the degree of scrutiny to which museum professionals are subjected.

As Cuno explains, this development is one that some curators and directors regard with apprehension, even while they may have more funds to dispose of than ever before. They fear what Cuno, taking a term from Robert Brustein, calls "coercive philanthropy"—the power of donors and sponsors, whether corporate or individual, like Saatchi, to shape scholarly work in the museum: the content, display, and purpose of exhibitions; their educational agenda; and even their marketing. Cuno frames this fear as the incursion of the interested (self-aggrandizing, profit-minded) donor/collector/sponsor bent on compromising the integrity of a museum staff professionally committed to standards of objectivity and disinterestedness. But more fears may be at work here: an apprehension that the financial power wielded by donors and sponsors can be used to justify greater accountability of museum professionals, to open up their work to greater scrutiny. In such circumstances it is perhaps understandable that museum directors and curators want to assert their control and reassert their right to determine what is in the public interest and to stigmatize donating bodies as interested parties because they are monied.

Another pressure that worries Cuno is the push for popularity and publicity. This desire to boost attendance and enhance publicity stems of course from a contemporary sense of what a public cultural institution should do—reach out to and enhance the quality of life of a large and diverse public. Cuno accepts this goal, but he points to a growing danger that the mutually reinforcing need for more publicity and more funds will put the museum and its staff into situations that will be seen to compromise the institution's public integrity.

Cuno's account makes the *Sensation* affair into a cautionary tale for museum professionals, a "Director's Progress," in which the temptations on the path to institutional success turn out to be moral pitfalls that can be avoided only by an abiding faith in the creed of scholarly objectivity and integrity.

The number of traps and temptations that lie in the museum professional's path is fully revealed in Edelson's essay. Edelson's story is not, however, a moral tale but a candid exposure of the degree to which public museums and private interests are inextricably intertwined. And although he is prepared to defend the principle of curatorial independence so central to Cuno's account, the thrust of his essay is that collaboration between public institutions and private interests is not only inevitable but, by and large, healthy.

Edelson's list of collaborative ventures is a long one. Museums habitually exhibit private collections; include works in exhibitions that they know are for sale; take commissions for works sold as a result of their public exhibition; accept financial support from interested parties, including dealers; accept works of art as gifts and loans from dealers; and deal, via the museum shop, not only in gifts and reproductions but even in works of art themselves.

This collaboration is about the exchange of money, but it is also, Edelson emphasizes, an exchange in which museum professionals benefit from the knowledge and expertise of dealers and collectors. Profit making and a flourishing art world (inevitably a mix of public and private bodies) are not mutually exclusive, as the old snobbery about dealers implies, but create an inevitable and valuable union. In Edelson's robust account, museum professionals are just one group of many in the art community, which includes artists, collectors, critics, auction houses, and dealers, all of whom are complicit in a system in which art and money go hand in hand. In his eyes these groups are no different from any other interest within the arts world. Hence his conclusion, in which he suggests, not entirely tongue in cheek, that museums join the Art Dealers Association of America. Edelson has little time for such vague notions as "the mere appearance of impropriety" or "conflict of interest." If Cuno tells a cautionary moral tale, Edelson's account is shaped in the tough school of American realism. It is time, he seems to be saying, to show and tell.

Like Edelson's essay, Szántó's account of the press coverage of *Sensation* contains some material as shocking as the show itself. He paints a bleak picture of the news media's inadequate and shoddy coverage of the arts, especially visual art, exposing an enclave of American journalism that seems to have abandoned the "objective" and professional standards by which good reporting is normally evaluated. He shows how easily the arts are hijacked for political purposes; how pressures within newspaper publishing help transform art news into scandal and "sensation"; and how inaccurate reporting, of a sort that would be impossible in other kinds of coverage, is both prevalent and unrestrained. The gratuitous editorializing and sententious posturing he describes come not, as one might expect, from experts in the arts but from journalists who usually cover politics and city hall. Such, concludes Szántó, is the low status of arts reporting, a situation he blames partly on the unwillingness of journalists to believe that readers care about culture. Can we imagine an editor sending an arts reporter to cover city hall?

But Szántó, as his title, "Don't Shoot the Messenger," makes clear, does not confine blame for the problems the art world has with the press to unprofessional reporting. It was easy, he points out, for Giuliani to accuse the Brooklyn Museum of professional misconduct because the public had no "preexisting sense of what counts as normal and acceptable conduct for such institutions." The press, even if it had wished to, could not explain this normal behavior to its readers because the workings of museums remain shrouded in mystery. Museums, says Szántó, "are astonishingly inscrutable," not least because of the unwillingness of those who run them to expose their workings to public view. He cites Glenn Lowry, the director of the Museum of Modern Art in New York, as saying, "Any time museums come under the scrutiny that occurred in Brooklyn, it inevitably frays the public trust that museums enjoy." A skeptical reader might see this comment as a public admission that museums do not perhaps act according to their own (obscure) high standards and that they fear scrutiny because of the possible exposure of the contradictory position they occupy. In this context, the response of many museum directors to the Brooklyn crisis was revealing: they were reluctant either to support or to condemn the museum, although they were happy, like Cuno and Edelson, to reiterate their support for curatorial autonomy.

Curators and museum directors fearful for their autonomy, shifting patterns of funding, the interpenetration of public and private interests, poor reporting, secrecy, and obscurity: clearly the problems of the contemporary museum, although they may be encapsulated in the saga of *Sensation* and the Brooklyn Museum, go well beyond it. What then should be done?

None of the contributors suggest a return to the old funding mechanisms, although Cuno betrays a certain nostalgia for a system that made the life of museum professionals much simpler. The new ways of mounting, funding, and organizing exhibits and funding the museum are here to stay. In the face of this pressure, Cuno pleads for curatorial integrity and control, limited by certain procedures and protocols (such as securing funding for an exhibition only after it has been planned) but also based on establishing relations of trust between museums, collectors, and donors.

Cuno's account contains a number of assumptions. Perhaps the most important is that curators and directors know what is in the public interest; this knowledge then entitles them to determine the museum practices that will secure the public good. Cuno himself repeatedly tells us what is in the public interest or for the public good in his capacity as a museum director. This is a claim to power and authority, albeit one made in a situation in which curatorial control seems to be eroding. One of the questions that the Brooklyn controversy highlights is not just what is for the public good—that is, what is good museum practice—but who should determine what that good is. Who speaks for the public?

The authority of the museum professional to decide what is good for the museum and its public has in the past been connected to the custodial, almost sacerdotal power he or she derives from the care of objects and images that bear the sacred labels of heritage or art and are therefore seen as more than private commodities. In consequence it has always been important for museum directors and curators to be (and to appear to be) untainted by commercial considerations, with their public institutions to a large degree cut off from the marketplace. While this separation has always been little more than a polite (though powerful) fiction, changes in arts funding and museum management as well as increased scrutiny make it seem less and less plausible because these changes have had the effect of undermining curatorial authority.

The temptation is to respond by reasserting the old verities—treating curatorial objectivity and commercial involvement as antithetical, depicting the museum as a semisacred space, a temple threatened by moneychangers. These are clearly views that many museum professionals share and that resonate with some sections of the public, but, as we have seen, they are a double-edged weapon when used by museums that can be shown to mix art and mammon and to engage with commercial interests or adopt commercial practices. Moreover, as Edelson points out, compromising curatorial "integrity" may be the only way in which certain (artistically valuable) exhibitions can be mounted. Without the accommodation/negotiation, the exhibit may be of less scholarly value. The notion that monetary transactions may corrupt art is not untenable, but art and mammon are not necessary antitheses.

All of this is not to deny that museum professionals face real difficulties in their dealings with donors, sponsors, and collectors and that they bear a responsibility to museums and their aims, however defined. But it is, in my view, not helpful if they continue to claim a special position as public arbiters on the grounds of their autonomy or "integrity." If special claims are to be made—and no one can doubt that in some situations curators not only wish to but should control exhibits—they should be framed in terms of the knowledge and expertise of curators and staff, as part of a public discussion about the nature and quality of the art they display. Museum professionals, in other words, need to rethink or redefine the grounds of their authority.

Speaking for the public is easy only when the public is assumed to be a distant and unitary body. But the political pressures since the beginning of the 1970s have all been in the opposite direction—toward seeing the public as diverse and heterogeneous, made up of ever-changing constituents who have sought participation not passivity, closeness not distance, and direct representation rather than "trust." Hence Szántó's eloquent appeal for a different relationship between the museum and its public brokered through the press. Museum professionals, Szántó argues, should end their secrecy, reveal to the public the ways in which museums work, and develop a constructive partnership with the media, encouraging attention rather than avoiding it. Only then will museums be sure of commanding public confidence. (Interestingly, in August 2000, when asked by journalists what they liked about the London art scene, a group of visiting Brooklyn artists singled out the mainstream press's tremendous interest in contemporary art. This newspaper item was itself an instance of the skilled press management they applauded.)[1]

We should however be cautious of the liberal assumption that transparency will necessarily help museums. Michael Waldman's 1996 documentary for the BBC about London's Royal Opera House in Covent Garden was made with the management's cooperation. But the insider's view of "The House" proved a public-relations disaster; it led to the resignation of the opera's chief executive and the demise of its administration. Museums have to have their houses in order if they are to benefit from a new policy of transparency.

Szántó's advice to museums that they should present a clearer, more coherent message about art seems equally optimistic. No sword is available to cut the Gordian knot of tangled and conflicting values that define the contemporary art scene. Nor will this situation change unless prevailing notions of multiculturalism, hybridization, and the like are replaced by a new social imaginary. The sources of aesthetic pluralism lie outside the art world, not within it, and if and when they are changed or rejected, the shift will come from elsewhere.

The problems for museums and the art world that the *Sensation* controversy highlights are intractable; they do not lend themselves to an easy solution. No doubt the clearer professional protocols advocated by Cuno, Edelson's more realistic view of museum ethics and practices, and the transparency and partnership proposed by Szántó will all improve the present situation. But we also need to think through the full implications of the shift in power between public institutions and private bodies or individuals that has taken place since the mid-1980s. This issue cannot simply be resolved procedurally, is only identified but not tackled by realism, and is evaded by talk of partnership, which erroneously implies that all parties are equals. Relations between the Brooklyn Museum and Saatchi clearly reveal the radical and growing asymmetry of power, the weakness of public bodies like museums in the face of private wealth. From this all else follows.

NOTE

1. Alison Roberts, "A Brooklyn Cheer for the Brit Art Scene," *Evening Standard,* August 1, 2000, p. 52.

JAMES CUNO

"Sensation" and the Ethics of Funding Exhibitions

Art museums are popular, that has to be said. More than eight hundred thousand people saw the van Gogh exhibition at the Los Angeles County Museum of Art.[1] And some of those were among the thousands who attended the exhibition in the middle of the night, when the museum was open nonstop for thirty-six hours just to accommodate and, yes, *attract* a last-minute surge in attendance. What makes art museums so popular? Well, the art for one thing. People like to look at pretty things. They like to look at things that move, inspire, and sometimes even shock them. They like to look at old things and things they think are difficult to make and cost a lot of money. But people also just like being there, in the museum. It's cool in the summer, warm in the winter, and dry when it rains. There are places to eat and things to buy. You can watch a movie, hear a concert, or go to a class, and often with your whole family. All in all, going to a museum at the turn of the twenty-first century is a fun thing to do. And sometimes it's instructive and inspiring, too.[2]

If museums are so popular, why are so many museums trying so hard to attract even more people? Because high attendance confers legitimacy on the museum enterprise itself. Museums are public institutions, even if they are privately funded. They stand for a public good—easy if not equal access to culture and learning—and the more people who come to museums, the more it can be demonstrated that a public good is being served.

The director of the Brooklyn Museum of Art (BMA) wrote of this goal in a letter to his museum's supporters: "We want to establish the BMA as a primary art destination for every tourist and every resident in New York City, reflecting the ethnic, racial, national, religious, economic, and lifestyle diversity of our population. We want to see our galleries filled with young people, students, artists, families, and scholars whose eyes light up at the prospect of learning through looking. And we want the BMA recognized for what it has always been—one of America's great museums and centers of learning."[3] This is a laudable ambition and one shared by all public-spirited museums. But sometimes the desire to become more popular outpaces the desire to remain a center of learning, especially when, like the Brooklyn Museum, one is trying to jump-start a turnaround in attendance and public profile.[4] Learning and popularity often run at different speeds, the one slow and deliberate and the other fast and opportunistic. The challenge for a museum is to find the right balance between the two—between, on the one hand, acquiring works of art, conducting research, and writing publications on the permanent collection and for temporary exhibitions, and, on the other, programming events and presenting exhibitions, lectures, classes, film series, concerts, and various social events, all geared to attracting and retaining new members and larger audiences.

Larger audiences attract greater funding, not only increased admissions and other forms of earned income but increased support from private and public foundations. And one can't underestimate museums' need to raise funds from an ever-widening range of sources, especially with declining, previously dependable sources of funding from federal, state, and local government agencies. More and more, museums are turning to private individuals and corporations for support, and more and more of these sources are restricting their gifts to certain purposes. In an influential op-ed piece in the *New York Times*, the theater director Robert Brustein called this type of funding "coercive philanthropy."[5]

When a museum is faced with an opportunity to present an exhibition that it believes could help it reach out and expand its audience (in keeping with its mission) and has to decide in a matter of weeks whether it can afford to, the pace of fundraising quickens to a sometimes desperate level. Under such pressure, one can be tempted to consider funding offers that resemble commercial transactions, with the giver expecting tangible benefits in return for philanthropic donations. This type of support is not limited to museums, of course. In 2000, the *Atlantic Monthly* magazine published an article on the insidious influence of corporate support on scientific research in universities.[6] It tells the story of a controversial agreement between the University of California, Berkeley, and

Norvatis, a Swiss pharmaceutical firm and producer of genetically engineered crops, which agreed to give the university $25 million to fund basic research in the university's Department of Plant and Microbial Biology. In exchange, the article tells us, the university gave Norvatis "first right to negotiate license[s] on roughly one-third of the department's discoveries—including the results of research funded by state and federal sources as well as by Norvatis . . . [and granted] the company unprecedented representation—two of the five seats—on the department's research committee, which determines how the money is spent."[7]

This kind of funding threatens the principle of disinterested inquiry, or the unbiased pursuit of knowledge, on which the public trust in universities and museums is built. The public, which subsidizes such institutions, either directly or indirectly through admission fees, gifts, taxes, or museums' tax-free status as not-for-profit institutions, expects them to carry out their duties professionally on its behalf. If, say, in the course of its work the museum's professional staff determines that a particular painting is not by the artist it was originally attributed to, they change the attribution, even if it means "demoting" a popular painting and angering the generous benefactor who gave it. The exercise of taste and discernment free of compromising external influences is the work of a museum, work that cannot be done under the pressure of time or in the midst of an aggressive campaign to increase a museum's attendance and to raise its popular, public profile. Too often such a campaign threatens to throw a museum's basic work off course, as appears to have happened at the Brooklyn Museum during the run up to and the presentation of the *Sensation* exhibition.[8]

According to published remarks by the museum's director, the exhibition was brought to Brooklyn after he saw how popular it was at the Royal Academy in London, where it originated (popular in the sense of both how many people attended the exhibition and how diverse they were in terms of age, class, and race). Further, he thought the exhibition would engage the museum's public on the terms it set for a modern museum. In a letter to the museum's supporters, he wrote of how the museum's "plan to revitalize the very concept of how art—whether the traditional or the most challenging—can speak to people in their own language." "Among other responsibilities," he continued, "our Museum must be central to the topical sociocultural issues, expressed through art, that drive our daily lives."[9] And, by all reports, *Sensation* was a big success: more than 175,000 attended the exhibition (when the director assumed his position in 1997, the museum's annual attendance was only about 300,000), and those who did saw challenging work by

British artists thought by many experts to be among the leaders of their generation.[10]

But at what cost to the museum's public standing was the pursuit of this success? Almost immediately after its opening, the museum was heavily criticized by the mayor of New York, the local and national press, and some museum professionals and academics for letting the private collector whose works constituted the exhibition both determine much of its content and installation and seek funding on behalf of the museum from sources with which he had commercial ties. In other words, the museum's aggressive attempt to reach a larger audience and attract public attention threatened its very standing as a public-spirited institution. Just how did this happen? Let's rehearse the facts of the case as reported in numerous articles.[11]

The exhibition was drawn exclusively from one person's private collection and organized by London's Royal Academy of Arts. Encouraged by the staff of the Royal Academy but warned of how expensive it would be to transport and install the exhibition, the museum director agreed to pursue bringing it to Brooklyn. Soon thereafter, the collector agreed to cover the cost of insuring the works in the exhibition and approached Christie's, the auction house, as a potential corporate sponsor. Having sold through Christie's 130 works by artists represented in the exhibition soon after the exhibition's showing in London, the collector is said to have mentioned that he planned a major sale from his collection later in the year, perhaps again through Christie's.

Meanwhile, the museum director was convinced that he couldn't raise the money to mount the exhibition from other people. When asked why, he is reported to have said, "Almost no private individual wants to put money into [his] pockets. . . . Their response was, 'We are a private collector; he is a private collector. Why would I give my money to show his exhibition?'"[12] He asked the collector himself to underwrite the exhibition, which he agreed to do to the tune of $160,000. The collector also agreed to pay his own expenses when visiting New York to work with the staff on the exhibition's installation. Already known to be a demanding patron, the collector quickly began to influence the content and installation of the exhibition. Indeed, the museum staff member who functioned as chief contact with the collector is on record as having wondered out loud, "Who is doing this exhibition?" the museum or the collector and as hoping that the museum would soon get "a bit closer to the driver's seat—or at least [that] we can all have a hand on the steering wheel."[13]

The collector has often been criticized for benefiting financially from his dealings with artists, dealers, auction houses, and museums. He is known to buy large quantities of works by individual artists, show them in his gallery-sized space (which is open to the public for a fee and which he was planning to expand with the help of a corporate sponsor excited by the success of the *Sensation* showing in London), publish them in book-length, illustrated catalogues, and then sell some (sometimes, a single artist's work in great numbers, thereby affecting the artist's market and reputation for some time to come). Even more to the point, as mentioned, he was known to have sold 130 works by artists in the *Sensation* exhibition just after it was shown at London's Royal Academy and just before he was in discussions with the Brooklyn Museum over its showing there. In addition, a year after the London showing, he announced his intention to open a restaurant called Sensation in London that would display works from his collection and that would be the first of a chain of restaurants to open in the cities where the exhibition was intended to be shown. (The restaurants never opened.)

At the same time as the museum was asking the collector to help secure funding from Christie's for the exhibition's showing in Brooklyn, the museum's director was meeting with the president of Christie's America, where evidently he mentioned that he was undertaking a significant program to deaccession works from "all collecting categories" of the museum and jokingly suggested that if the auction house underwrote the exhibition, the museum's future art sales would be directed to the auction house on an exclusive basis. The president wrote in a memo, "There might be something here worth exploring." Weeks later, the museum sold $21,000 worth of art through the auction house; this was a tiny amount (less than one-thousandth of the house's business that year), but still the chief executive of Christie's International told the *Sensation* collector that Christie's had decided to donate to the Brooklyn exhibition of works from his collection, "given that we were given a lot of property from the Brooklyn Museum for sale."[14]

Ultimately, the auction house donated $50,000 to the Brooklyn showing. This amount represented, in Christie's terms, its "most significant financial commitment to an external exhibition to date." Its director of museum services wrote in a memo, "I would like to see us capitalize on it as much as possible."[15] This commitment, as it was proposed, would result in acknowledgements as a sponsor of the exhibition on the museum's walls and in its monthly bulletin, invitations, and advertisements. So now the museum was working with a sponsor with which it had commercial interests and with which the exhibition's lender had even larger commercial interest. Needless to say, the whole affair got only more complicated, and quickly so. (It didn't help, of course, that at the time Christie's and Sotheby's were the subject of a high-profile, federal antitrust investigation for allegedly fixing the prices they charged to buyers and sellers.)[16]

Soon thereafter, the pop star David Bowie approached the museum through his representatives and offered to give funding to the exhibition. The museum then asked whether he would consider recording the audio tour of the exhibition, and he agreed. Bowie was also interested in promoting the exhibition on his website and ultimately was given permission to do so. There, on davidbowie.com, to which the museum's website provided a link, one could buy art, clothing, and memberships in the pop star's fan club and see an image of a "spin" painting he had made in collaboration with Damien Hirst, one of the most celebrated *Sensation* artists. This "spin" painting was reproduced on the site just below a section on BowieBanc, Bowie's online banking service, which offers customers "credit cards and cheques bearing David's image," and a bit above a notice stating that in late 1998, or just when the *Sensation* exhibition was being negotiated for Brooklyn, Sotheby's and Christie's had record contemporary art sales; the notice was just above another reporting that the readers of the London magazine *Time Out* voted the *Sensation* show the very best art event of the decade. (*Time Out* was a sponsor of *Sensation* in London, and *Time Out New York* was the media sponsor for the exhibition in New York.)

So now the museum was involved with four parties with interlocking commercial interests in the success of the exhibition. The mounting pressure on the director was considerable. The museum was committed to the exhibition, and its costs were soaring: estimated to be $625,000 in March, they were $1.2 million by June and almost $2 million a few months later, in great part because of increasing demands by the collector. When the exhibition opened and the city's mayor launched his attack on the museum, press scrutiny was intense. Unfortunately, the museum did not always respond to press inquiries with full candor. When asked whether the collector had given money to support the exhibition, the director said no. When it was pointed out later that in fact the collector had given money, the museum replied that it was only honoring the collector's request to keep his contribution confidential.

The combination of the museum's acceptance of the collector's active (and some would say extensive) participation in the organization and installation of the exhibition, its involvement with parties with commercial interests in each other and in the exhibition, and its lack of candor in reporting all of this involvement in response to questions from the press led to the suspicion that the museum had abdicated its professional responsibilities to its public and was letting other parties do its business. It began to look as though the museum was a "hired hand" for private interests if not an "interested party" itself, and its reputation suffered accordingly.

In pursuing this exhibition and its funding as it did, the Brooklyn Museum took chances not many museum directors would take, even though many museums in the United States do exhibit private collections and even have the exhibitions underwritten in part by the collector and an auction house with whom the collector has done business (the Harvard University museums certainly have). But there are ways of working with such interested parties without risking the reputation of one's museum. For example, one should wait to seek financial support from a collector until after the curatorial thesis is set and the exhibition checklist is determined. Then one might even secure a gift of a portion of the works in the exhibition so that the museum and its public are permanently enriched by the exhibition. One might even have the collector agree not to sell works in the exhibition for a significant period of time after the exhibition so as to limit the extent of the direct effect of the exhibition on the value of its constituent works. But these things take time to work out, and the rush to bring the *Sensation* exhibition to Brooklyn did not afford the museum such time.[17]

In the end, relations between museums (representing the public's interest) and private collectors and funders are all about trust. Does one trust that the collector or funder has the best interests of the museum in mind? And will relations with the funder or collector enhance or detract from the museum's mission as a public-spirited institution? What are the risks and are they worth taking? With the help of hindsight, one can see that the Brooklyn Museum should not have presented *Sensation* under the pressure of time and on the terms it did.

A museum's reputation is built on trust. And however popular museums are or are becoming, they risk losing that trust if they appear to be serving their own interests or that of their patrons rather than the interests of the public with which, as public institutions, they have a compact that confers legitimacy on their enterprise. This is the lesson of the *Sensation* exhibition at the Brooklyn Museum, a cautionary tale for all of us.[18]

NOTES

1. *Van Gogh's Van Goghs: Masterpieces from the Van Gogh Museum*, organized by the National Gallery of Art, Washington, D.C., 1998.
2. See Judith H. Dobrzynski, "Blockbuster Shows Lure Record Crowds into U.S. Museums," *New York Times*, February 3, 2000, p. E5, in which she notes,

"The number of shows in the United States that attract more than 200,000 people has grown from 14 in 1996, to 18 in 1997, to 21 in 1998, to 31 in 1999."

3. Arnold L. Lehman, a letter to supporters of the Brooklyn Museum of Art, November, 10, 1999. The letter is also posted on the museum's website, http://www.brooklynart.org.
4. See Douglas Martin, "Not Your Father's Art Museum," *New York Times*, October 2, 1997, p. B1.
5. Robert Brustein, "Culture and Coercion," *New York Times*, November 29, 1994, p. A25.
6. Eyal Press and Jennifer Washburn, "The Kept University," *Atlantic Monthly*, March 2000, 39–54. Also see Michelle Falkenstein, "And Now a Word about the Sponsors," *ArtNews*, May 2000, 218–222, and Carol Vogel, "Armani Gift to the Guggenheim Revives Issue of Art and Commerce," *New York Times*, December 15, 1999, pp. B1, B3.
7. Press and Washburn, "The Kept University," 40.
8. The names of individuals are not important here. I am more interested in these events as a case study for museums.
9. Letter to supporters of the Brooklyn Museum of Art, November 10, 1999.
10. The exhibition's attendance is cited in the *Art Newspaper*, February 2000, 6. The director's commitment to broadening the museum's audience had been central to his administration since he arrived at the museum almost three years previously.
11. David Barstow, "Brooklyn Museum Recruited Donors Who Stood to Gain," *New York Times*, October 31, 1999, pp. A1, A40; David Barstow, "Art, Money, and Control: A Portrait of 'Sensation,'" *New York Times*, December 6, 1999, pp. A1, A32; Lee Rosenbaum, "Brooklyn Hangs Tough," *Art in America*, January 2000, 59–63, 143; and Lee Rosenbaum, "The Battle of Brooklyn Ends, the Controversy Continues," *Art in America*, June 2000, 39–43.
12. Barstow, "Brooklyn Museum Recruited Donors Who Stood to Gain," p. A40.
13. David Barstow, "Artistic Differences: A Special Report; Art, Money and Control: Elements of an Exhibition," *New York Times*, December 6, 1999, p. A32.
14. Ibid.
15. Barstow, "Brooklyn Museum Recruited Donors Who Stood to Gain," A46.
16. The investigation had been going on for three years at the time, but it became especially public at this time. See Carol Vogel, "Christie's Is Changing Its Fees in Face of Suits and U.S. Investigation," *New York Times*, February 8, 2000, p. C1, and Carol Vogel, "Top Executives Quit Sotheby's as Art World Inquiry Widens," *New York Times* February 22, 2000, p. C1.
17. The Metropolitan Museum of Art cancelled an exhibition of Coco Chanel designs because of what it thought to be an attempt by the head of the fashion house, which was to substantially fund the exhibition, to influence the content of the exhibition. In explanation, the museum's director said, "I need to be able to assure people that what they see on the walls is not inflected by the money we receive to do an exhibition . . . and if I can't make that assurance, then I'm not doing it." Michael Kimmelman, "At the Met, a Necessary Retreat," *New York Times*, May 28, 2000, sec. 2, p. 31.
18. On the Pyrrhic nature of Brooklyn's legal victory over the mayor of New York's threat to withdraw funding from the museum, see David Strauss's essay in this volume. Strauss concludes that "people who want to defend government funding of the arts either have to explain why the works attacked by politicians are not sick and disgusting or why they are valuable nonetheless or why the government should not withdraw support from work like this even if it is of limited value. Ringing First Amendment victories, however

gratifying, are a sign of underlying weakness in the forum of popular opinion, and that is where the battle for government funding of the arts will be won or lost." The museum's battle for respect and authority as a public institution will also be won or lost in the "forum of popular opinion." And, in this respect, the museum's victory in court may turn out also to have been Pyrrhic.

GILBERT S. EDELSON

Some Sensational Reflections

Sensation created an uproar, albeit not quite the sensation that its sponsors desired. A new art critic arose, proclaiming that while he didn't know much about art and while he hadn't actually seen any of the works in the exhibition, he knew enough to be offended. Mayor Rudolph Giuliani first denounced the exhibition as "sick" and "disgusting." Then he focused his attack on one work, *The Holy Virgin Mary*, by Chris Ofili, a practicing Catholic artist. Claiming that this painting offended the Catholic religion, the mayor threatened to close down the museum if it did not cancel the exhibition. When the museum refused, the mayor caused the city to withhold funds appropriated to pay the museum's general operating expenses.

The museum brought in federal court an action, based in the First Amendment, that sought to enjoin the city from withholding funds or taking any other adverse action against the museum because of *Sensation*. The city, in turn, sued the museum in state court seeking to terminate the lease of the building that houses the museum and to evict the museum and its collection.

The District Court granted the preliminary injunction sought by the museum and castigated the mayor for attempting to censor an art exhibition because it offended him. Both actions were settled. The city dropped its lawsuit and agreed to fund the museum; the museum dropped its lawsuit and any claim for legal fees.

Among the claims made by the city against the museum was that

Sensation improperly furthered the commercial interests of private parties. It was claimed that the purpose of the exhibition was to enhance the value of the exhibited works for their owner, the collector Charles Saatchi; the works could then be sold at auction at Christie's, which had provided financial support for the exhibition. Although this claim was dropped by the city, it continued to resonate. Mayor Giuliani and others, including the *New York Times*, criticized the exhibition on the grounds that it was wrong for the museum to have an exhibition of a private art collection when the exhibition was financed by companies and individuals with a direct commercial interest in the works of the artists in the show.

Some of the facts lent plausibility to the criticism. Although Christie's contribution of $50,000 was disclosed, Saatchi's contribution of $160,000 to cover the cost of the exhibition was not disclosed because, according to the museum, Saatchi requested that his contribution be kept anonymous. Christie's had previously auctioned works from the Saatchi collection, including works by artists in the exhibition, for about $2.7 million dollars.[1] Christie's had also recently auctioned works from the museum's collection in a sale that grossed $21,000.

In addition, the museum sought and obtained modest financial support from some dealers who represented artists included in the show. They purchased tickets for a dinner sponsored by the museum, the proceeds of which benefited the exhibition.

The debate about the exhibition has raised questions and concerns about the somewhat complex relationships among museums, their exhibitions, collectors, dealers, and those who provide financial support for exhibitions, especially exhibitions involving contemporary works of art. Questions have been raised about the propriety of museums' exhibiting privately owned works when the exhibition is perceived to enhance the market value of those works and thereby to confer a financial benefit to the lender.

A number of questions can be asked, among them: Should a museum exhibit a private collection under any circumstances? Should a museum exhibit privately owned works when it has reason to believe that those works will shortly be offered for sale? Should a museum be involved to any extent in the sales of works of art, and if so, to what extent?

Should a Museum Exhibit Private Collections?

An editorial in the *New York Times* of November 2, 1999, states in part: "The exhibition [Sensation] looks like [an] aesthetic enterprise, the method of paying for it like an ethically dubious enterprise. Museums have usually drawn the line at displaying privately owned collections. It is a simple standard and an effective one, even if it is not foolproof. There is no clearer evidence of its value as a standard than the questions raised by the funding of *Sensation*."[2]

The *Times* was wrong; museums certainly have not "drawn the line at displaying privately owned collections." On the contrary, the exhibition of private collections has been a common museum practice for many years. And many of these exhibitions have drawn critical praise from the *Times*.

In an article in the January 2000 issue of *ArtNews*, Patricia Failing listed more than a dozen exhibitions of works from private collections that were currently being shown at museums across the country.[3] Among the more notable private collections that have been exhibited at museums in the United States in recent years have been those of Paul Mellon at the National Gallery of Art, of Walter Annenberg at four major museums, and of Raymond Nasher at museums in New York, Washington, D.C., and Dallas.

Whether a museum should exhibit a private collection depends on whether the collection is important enough to merit a museum show—whether the collection has such quality and importance that there is a public interest in making it available for viewing by a wide audience that might not otherwise see it. The overwhelming majority of private collections that have been exhibited in museums meet this criterion.

Should a Museum Exhibit Works That It Has Reason to Believe Will Be Sold Shortly?

Saatchi was known to sell works from his collection. After disposing of an extensive collection of works by American artists that he had formed in the 1980s, he acquired works by young British artists. Prior to the *Sensation* exhibition he had sold more than a hundred of those British works at auction. Surely there was a risk that he would sell additional works by the artists included in *Sensation* and that the show would enhance their prices.[4]

Should a museum, then, take into account the collector's previous sales activities before mounting an exhibition of a private collection? Of course it should. A museum must have the public's trust. That trust depends in large measure on the public's perception of the museum's integrity. If it is perceived that a museum is being used by a private collector to enhance the value of works in his or her collection, the public trust is diminished. Saatchi had sold works from his collection on a regular basis, including works by artists in *Sensation*. A reasonable person might have concluded that Saatchi was a trader who bought and sold artworks for profit and therefore did what he could to enhance their value. A reasonable person might perceive *Sensation* as having been created by Saatchi to a make an eventual profit for himself.

This does not mean, however, that museums should refuse to exhibit works owned by collectors who have sold works from their collections. For example, Mellon, one of the nation's most distinguished collectors, sold works from time to time, as many other collectors do. But no one would seriously argue that the National Gallery of Art should not have shown works owned by this great patron because of that history of sales.

The issue, therefore, is one that should be decided on a case-by-case basis. The question that needs to be asked is, Would a reasonable person perceive that the primary purpose of a given exhibition is to enhance the market value of the exhibited works or otherwise to confer a financial benefit on a private individual?

It has been suggested that one solution to the problem, which is followed by some museums, is to have the collector agree not to sell works from the collection during the exhibition and for a period of time thereafter. This may well be the answer where an entire collection is exhibited. But how should a museum deal with loans of individual works?

Let us assume that a museum is planning an important exhibition by a prominent artist and that it wishes to borrow several important works from a private collector. In the course of negotiating the loan, the collector informs the museum that he will need to sell those works within the next two years and may offer the works for sale while they are on the museum's wall. Should the museum include the works in its exhibition? To do so could give rise to an allegation that the museum is lending itself to a commercial venture by enhancing the value of works that it knows will be sold.

I have been involved in two such situations. In both cases, the museum included the works in the exhibition because of their art-historical importance even though they were offered for sale at the time of the exhibition.

Similarly, assume that a museum is preparing a group exhibition of contemporary art. The curator in charge has visited studios of the artists to be included and has selected works for the exhibition; some of those works are as yet unexhibited and unsold. The curator understands that those works will be offered for sale during the exhibition or after it closes. Should they nonetheless be included? I doubt that any reasonable curator would refuse to exhibit work that the curator believes to be necessary to an exhibition even though it might be claimed that the museum is enhancing the work's value when it is offered for sale.

And what if a sale results from the museum exhibition? Suppose a collector sees the work on the museum's walls, learns that it is available, and buys it. Is the museum entitled to a commission because it is instrumental in the sale? Should the museum take a commission? Some museums have done so. Is this an improper commercial venture? Does the museum deserve to be compensated? Or is there an appearance of impropriety?

What if the curator selects an artist's work that is in the inventory of a dealer? Could it be claimed that the museum is conferring a direct financial benefit on a dealer by enhancing the value of a work that the dealer is offering for sale? Is there a difference between a work in an artist's studio (which will probably be offered for sale through the artist's dealer) and a work in a dealer's inventory?

It is widely assumed that inclusion in a museum exhibition enhances the reputation of the artist and increases the value of the works exhibited and other works by the artist. I know of no study of the effect of a one-person museum exhibition or inclusion in a group exhibition on the reputation or prices of an artist. There is no question that a one-person exhibition, a retrospective of the works of a living artist, enhances the reputation of the artist. It probably also has a beneficial effect on the artist's prices, although there are questions about how great this effect is and whether and to what extent the effect is long-term.

The benefit is probably less if the artist is one of a number in a group show of contemporary art in a museum. Inclusion in this case is like mother's chicken soup—it doesn't hurt. Clearly it is a credential, a selling tool, a talking point. But it is by no means certain that it has any long-term effect on prices or on an artist's reputation.

Indeed, if one reviews the past catalogues of group shows of contemporary art in museums, such as the Whitney *Biennial*, it is apparent that many of the artists exhibited are not well-known today. It is thus far from certain that any or every museum exhibition enhances the prices of the works of the artists in that exhibition.[5]

Clearly, then, it is not necessarily improper for a museum to borrow from a private collection and to exhibit one or more works that are likely to be sold or offered for sale during or after an exhibition. Once again, the issue turns on reasonable perception: Would a reasonable person perceive that even though, in general, exhibiting a borrowed work may enhance its market value, this is not the motive or purpose in borrowing or exhibiting a given work of art?

Should a Museum Accept Financial Support for an Exhibition from Those Who Have, or Appear to Have, a Financial Interest in the Exhibited Works?

The Brooklyn Museum was also criticized because it sought and accepted financial assistance for the *Sensation* exhibition from the collector, Saatchi; from Christie's, an auction house that had done business both with Saatchi and with the museum; and from dealers who represented artists included in the exhibition.[6] This criticism raises the question of whether a museum should refuse to accept any financial assistance in support of an exhibition from any person who might conceivably benefit financially from it.

The St. Louis Art Museum declined to accept financial assistance from the Herman Miller Company for an exhibition of the furniture of Charles and Ray Eames, the distinguished American designers. This exhibition had previously been shown at the Cooper-Hewitt Museum, a component of the Smithsonian Institution, which had accepted support from the corporate sponsor. The stated reason for the St. Louis Museum's action was that it could not accept financial assistance from Herman Miller because there would have been the appearance that the company would benefit financially from the exhibition.[7]

If museums are to adopt a policy of refusing to accept support for exhibitions that might financially benefit the contributor, how far should the policy extend? For example, assume that a museum is developing an exhibition of impressionist paintings. A trustee of the museum has several important impressionist paintings, which the curator believes should be included in the exhibition. The trustee agrees to lend the requested paintings for the exhibition. Should the museum now be barred from requesting or accepting assistance from the trustee to finance the exhibition?

The Brooklyn Museum was also criticized because it sought financial support for *Sensation* from dealers who represented artists in the show. Dealers were asked to support a dinner benefiting the exhibition, and some did so. Dealers have been long-time supporters of museums, most particularly those in their community. Dealers support the museums generally and support specific exhibitions, especially those in which they are interested. Why not? Does it make any sense to investigate all donors to see whether they might conceivably receive a financial benefit from an exhibition? What is to prevent such an interested party, dealer or collector, from making a cash contribution to the general funds of the museum, thereby presumably freeing up funds to support an exhibition?

Common sense tells us that a museum should be free to solicit contributions from collectors, dealers, or auction houses as long as it retains its curatorial independence. An analogy could be made with a newspaper that reports on, reviews, and promotes a variety of business ventures, including art-gallery exhibitions, while at the same time soliciting advertising support from those businesses. As long as the newspaper retains its editorial independence, there is no reason why it should be barred from soliciting advertising monies from entities about which it also writes.

Similarly, institutions of higher education should be free to solicit funds from corporations to support their research even though that research may ultimately benefit a donor. Here again, as long as the institution controls the work to be done and as long as that work is done independently from the donors, there is nothing improper in soliciting such funds.

Museums, Commerce, and Dealers

The Brooklyn Museum case has also pointed up the increasing involvement by museums in commercial activities. In the past museums resolutely prided themselves on being above mere commercial enterprises. They were, after all, treasure houses where knowledgeable and interested persons could contemplate great works of art in an atmosphere of serenity. Art dealers, interested in making a profit on art, in commercializing art, were, in a sense, asked to use the trade entrance.

In fact, one of this nation's major museums regularly asked dealers to lend works from their private collections for special exhibitions. But the catalogue and the wall label listed those works as from a "private collection." The museum's stated reason for this practice was that the dealer might offer the work for sale while on the wall or, even if this were not the case, that identifying the lending dealer might give the impression to some unsophisticated viewers that the museum was endorsing the dealer. This practice has now changed. In addition, it was the practice of a major museum not to identify dealers in listing the provenance of works of art in its catalogues. This practice has also changed.

Museums have come to realize that they and dealers are members of the same art community, which also includes artists, collectors, critics, auction houses, and others who are involved in the making, exhibiting, selling, discussing, conserving, collecting of works of art. All members of the art community have common interests.

Dealers, of course, are interested in selling works of established artists and introducing works of younger artists to museums. They are important sources of information and expertise; it is unusual to find a catalogue of a museum exhibition that does not acknowledge the assistance of one or more dealers. Dealers are also important sources of financial support for museums.

Contributions of works of art by art dealers are even more significant. For example, the Morgan Library in New York has been the recipient of the Thaw collection of Old Master drawings, perhaps the finest collection of its kind in this country. Klaus Perls has donated what was arguably the world's finest private collection of Benin art to the Metropolitan Museum of Art, together with an important group of School of Paris paintings and sculpture. He has also given a superb group of works by Alexander Calder to the National Gallery of Art. Stephen Hahn has given the National Gallery his collection of more than forty works by Jean Dubuffet. Heinz Bergruuen has given the Metropolitan Museum of Art his great collection of works by Paul Klee. Sidney Janis gave his collection of twentieth-century art to the Museum of Modern Art in New York. These are only a few examples; most major museums have on their wall one or more works that have been donated by dealers. And dealers are frequently instrumental in persuading their clients to make gifts of works of art.

Most museums and their professional staff have enjoyed excellent relations with dealers.[8] But some in the profession and some museum trustees have spoken or unspoken reservations. No doubt some of those reservations derive in part from the fact that dealers are (for the most part) profit-making, a quality that is believed by some in the art community (usually in academe) to be somehow impure, if not corrupting. And there have been and are long-standing prejudices against dealers, some based on pure snobbery. But these prejudices are diminishing with time and with the increasing involvement of museums in commercial activities.

The bedrock problem is, of course, funding for the arts. The United States is the only major nation in the world that does not have a ministry of culture. The arts are almost entirely privately supported; almost all museums are private, not-for-profit corporations. Government funding is minimal, and when there is government money, it is almost always followed by a protesting politician. Taxpayers, we are told, should not be required to support art that they find objectionable but should be required to subsidize wealthy sugar growers whether they like it or not.[9]

The problem of funding is exacerbated by the ever-expanding role of the art museum. No longer a treasure house, the art museum has become a cultural center, a peoples' palace of the arts, with educational programs, films, concerts, tours, lectures, classes, long descriptive labels, and tape recorders through which the museum director carefully explains to the visitor what it is that the visitor is looking at, why he or she should love it, and how to pronounce the artist's name.

Because of their ever-expanding need for money, museums have become increasingly commercialized. What museum worth its salt has not had a consultant tell it how to market itself? What self-respecting museum is without a restaurant for members (haute cuisine) and a café for ordinary visitors (iceberg-lettuce salads and hamburgers)? Without a bookshop? A gift shop? Christmas cards? A mail-order catalogue? A post-Christmas sale? Branch stores? Reproductions of works in the collection? Scarves, ties, cuff links, dishes, tchotchkes? All of course having educational value. One museum advertised in major magazines a "limited edition" of a reproduction of a work in its collection; the reproduction was accompanied by a certificate of authenticity, which assured the buyer that it was a genuine original reproduction

Many museum gift shops sell original and unique works made by craftspeople, such as jewelry, pottery, objets. Those museums are dealers in crafts. At least one major museum regularly publishes and sells original prints and also sells original prints that it receives on consignment from dealers. That museum is a print dealer.

If a museum is a print and craft dealer, why not take the next step up. Be an art dealer. Some museums have taken that step. For example, the Nevada Museum of Art announced a "weeklong exhibition and sale" titled *Wild Women Take Off.* The Wild Women were described as a group of northern Nevada artists whose work "embodies the 'Wild Woman' spirit as defined in *Women Who Run with Wolves*, a book by Clarissa Pinkola Estes." This museum is not alone; others exhibit and sell works by artists in their communities.[10]

In areas of the country where there are few dealers in art and where artists have few venues in which to exhibit, the museum provides a place for artists to show and provides the public with an opportunity to see and acquire original, contemporary works of art. But for the museum, neither the artist nor the public would have this opportunity. It may be that many of the works exhibited and sold at the museum are not of "museum quality"; but one can argue that at least some of the works of contemporary art in major museum exhibitions are also not of "museum quality." And so, in communities that are not major art centers and that have few art dealers, museums have assumed the dealer's role. It is otherwise in major art centers. As Philippe de Montebello said in an interview in the *New York Times* (January 9, 2000): "Here, in the city of New York, the greatest museum of contemporary art is the aggregate of hundreds of commercial galleries. That's the great museum of contemporary art, the galleries."[11]

We do not anticipate that dealers in contemporary art will be invited to join the American Association of Art Museum Directors. We are, nevertheless, pleased to welcome many museums to the ranks of art dealers. We await their application to join the Art Dealers Association of America.[12]

NOTES

1. The Christie's auction catalogue entry for each work by an artist included in the exhibition states, "Other work in this series is included in 'Sensation: Young British Artists from the Saatchi Collection.'"
2. Editorial, *New York Times,* November 2, 1999, p. 26.
3. Patricia Failing, "Following the Money," *ArtNews* 99, no. 1 (January 2000): 150–153.
4. The mayor accused Saatchi and Christie's of conspiring to inflate the prices for a future auction, an accusation that was vigorously denied.
5. There is a difference, for example, between inclusion in an exhibition in a major museum and inclusion in one in a smaller museum.
6. The museum no doubt had difficulty raising money from others for an exhibition of Saatchi's collection. It had no practical choice but to look to Saatchi and others who might have a financial interest in the exhibition.
7. It appears that the museum had the funds to support the exhibition even without a corporate sponsor. One may speculate whether, if no other funds were available, the museum would choose to forego the exhibition and deprive the public of its benefit in order to avoid an appearance of impropriety.
8. William Lieberman of the Metropolitan Museum of Art is said to have observed, "I am particularly in debt to art dealers all over the world. I hear so many of my colleagues say, 'I found this or I found that.' They usually neglect to say that they discovered it at a dealer."
9. Art museums and their directors are and must be continually fundraising from individuals and foundations. Most support for the visual arts comes from collectors. They support museums; and, as members of museum boards, they hire and fire directors and curators, and make museum policy. They also support artists, dealers, and auction houses. Collectors as a group are the real power in the art community.
10. "Advance Exhibition Schedule through December 2000," press release from the Nevada Museum of Art, January 17, 2000, p. 3; http://Ggallery.com/wildwomen.html; http://www.nevadaart.org/exhibitions/index.htm.
11. Deborah Solomon, "Is the Met Phobic about Contemporary Art?" *New York Times,* January 9, 2000, sec. 2, p. 47.
12. The Art Dealers Association of America is a not-for-profit association of the nation's leading dealers in works of fine art.

ANDRÁS SZÁNTÓ

Don't Shoot the Messenger

Why the Art World and the Press Don't Get Along

On Sunday, September 26, 1999, the *New York Times Magazine* ran a generous profile of Charles Saatchi, the advertising mogul and art collector behind *Sensation*. The article did not anticipate that the kind of scandal the exhibition had stirred up in England would spread to these shores. "In Brooklyn, the show will no doubt be less controversial," the magazine prognosticated, "in part because many of the 43 artists in it have already won a loyal following in the New York art world."[1] In a gaping omission, the article didn't even mention Chris Ofili, creator of the much maligned, elephant-dung–embellished *The Holy Virgin Mary*.[2] By the time the magazine hit the newsstands the situation had changed. Mayor Rudolph Giuliani had fired the first salvos in the last culture war of the twentieth century. So that Sunday morning, in section A, the *Times* ran a correction: "An article on page 44 of *The Times Magazine* today about the art collector Charles Saatchi and 'Sensation,' a show of his collection scheduled to open this week at the Brooklyn Museum, includes an outdated reference to the possibility that the show will be less controversial in New York than it was in Europe."[3]

The terse hand wringing of the correction speaks volumes about the precarious minefield of contemporary arts journalism. It shows how a sudden turn of events can disrupt the smooth and orderly flow of reporting. Who could have guessed that the mayor of the most important city in the world would pick a fight about an obscure picture hanging in a musty museum in an outer borough? And who might have imagined that the ensuing court case would ignite a major controversy over museum ethics?

The Travails of Arts Journalism

The issues run deeper. The discrepancy between the magazine and the news section occurred because the former is "put to bed" long before the latter. Owing to the complex logistics of newspaper production, the last pieces in the Sunday magazine are closed about ten days in advance of publication. As such, the magazine has little if anything to do with news, but it is seen as a good place to run arts journalism. Why exactly? Because arts journalism is a "features" enterprise. Within most news organizations, arts journalism is not thought of as news precisely, but as something apart from news, something more relaxed and less timely. News that can wait. Arts generate "soft" news, as distinct from the "hard" news gathered on the metro or foreign desk. In the eyes of many high-level editors, arts writers are like tweedy academics who have infiltrated the hardy fortress of news gathering. They are thought of as aesthetes who have abandoned their quiet calling for the newsroom's adrenaline buzz, but who can't really deliver the goods like true hacks.

The problems arise when arts do become news, as with *Sensation*. At these moments the fault lines beneath arts journalism in the United States come crisply into view. Let's examine them.

Arts Journalists Write for Uninformed Readers

Unlike sports, business, or local-news reporters, arts journalists can't rely on the basic topical competence of their readers, principally because of the lamentable failure of the U.S. education system to impart a rudimentary understanding and appreciation of the arts. For this reason a sports writer can mention a "pinch hitter" in a baseball story, but an arts writer can't include a reference to "trompe l'oeil" in an exhibition review without fear of being misunderstood.

But while education deserves ample blame, so does the press. Readers are apathetic and ignorant because they are not regularly informed about the arts. Arts coverage is spotty and sporadic, and there is a virtual blackout of information about the everyday, steady-state functioning of art worlds. In fact, the news media's main failing when it comes to arts and culture is not the inaccuracy that riddles so much arts reporting but simply the lack of coverage the arts receive.

The prime victim of this neglect is visual art. In a study undertaken by the National Arts Journalism Program, we found in a nationwide sampling of local newspapers that visual arts received half as much editorial space as the performing arts, a third of the newsprint given to books and music, and a quarter of the ink expended on movies.[4] Needless to say, in most papers, all the arts combined received less of the "newshole" than either sports or business. Meanwhile, only five of the fifteen metropolitan newspapers we studied had a full-time visual-arts critic. One out of three lacked any kind of dedicated visual-arts writer on staff. Can it be any wonder that so little accurate, in-depth coverage followed on the trail of *Sensation*?[5]

Arts News Is Easily Hijacked by Those with Non-Arts Agendas

From this foundation of apathy, ignorance, and neglect, all else follows. The reason art makes good fodder for politics is that, absent proper information, the public is easily swayed by rhetoric. The opportunities for demagoguery are particularly rife when we move from wars over artistic content—"Is Ofili's *Virgin* sacrilegious?"—to debates about the professional conduct of arts institutions—"Did the director of the Brooklyn Museum lapse in judgment by agreeing to Saatchi's terms?" Here the public is truly walking on virgin ground. For while Americans can form more or less solid opinions about the offensive nature of a painting (or decide what to do with a politician's view on the matter), what are they to make of claims about the allegedly improper dealings of a museum—that most mysterious of all public institutions?

The news media have not prepared people for this discussion. The ideologically charged claims of misconduct are not counterbalanced by any preexisting sense of what counts as normal and acceptable conduct for such institutions. Americans simply have no idea—because they're never told—what kind of lending practices are customary in arranging museum shows, what sort of individuals foot the bill, how curators work with private patrons in mounting exhibitions, and how museum shows influence the art market. This is a blank check for political interests, at least until specialized media and the art establishment correct the record.

The degree to which *Sensation*—which, it must be remembered, was primarily a controversy over artistic content and only secondarily a story about museum ethics—was hijacked by politics leaps out from a cursory review of the news coverage.[6] A Lexis-Nexis search of articles with "Brooklyn" in the headline or lead sentence and "sensation" and "museum of art" in the text resulted in 420 citations.[7] Six out of seven of these articles—360 to be exact—mentioned Rudolph Giuliani.[8] The mayor's name appeared in more articles than Saatchi's did (191). So drenched with politics was the coverage that Hillary Clinton was mentioned more often (28 articles) than all but three of the featured artists.[9] The towering predominance of Ofili, who appeared in 40 percent of the articles despite being a virtual unknown before Brooklyn, is another indication that the effort to politically appropriate *Sensation* and its coverage was a success.[10]

Arts Journalists Have to Resort to Hype, Dramatics, and Simplification

When it comes to culture wars, several tendencies in press coverage play into the hands of politicians, and none so much as the press's inexorable need to simplify stories and create news pegs for them. The frisson of scandal is a godsend to editors hoping to advance an arts story to the front page. In a newspaper, the measure of a writer or a department is appearance on page A1. Prestige, pay, and promotions depend on it. The need to position art as "news"—which is increasing as the mantra of cost cutting steadily replaces the civic obligation to cover arts—results in the single-minded focus on scandal, money, and death. It is important to see that there is an "elective affinity" between any effort to transform art into politics and the journalistic compulsion to pitch arts as news.

Furthermore, news, like great ideas, must be simple. But contemporary art is notoriously obscure and insular. Arts writers, therefore, are presented with the dilemma of where to begin.

Whatever one's view of the individual works in *Sensation,* the reason the Saatchi collection was interesting from an art-world perspective was that it gave a taste of the surge of activity in the London art scene, which in turn was connected to the fallow quiescence of the early-1990s New York art world, which had much to do with the oversold and supercharged excesses of the 1980s art-market boom, which was intimately connected to all kinds of complicated things, including such weighty matters as the end of modernism and the social transformation of arts patronage. The interpretation of individual artworks presents the journalist with a similar hall of mirrors. Where does one begin to unravel the innuendoes and inside jokes that draw attention to Damien Hirst's sliced-up cows, which—to spin just one wheel-within-a-wheel in this omnidirectionally referential work—is an acerbic comment on the minimalist sculpture of Donald Judd, which was itself a refutation of the expressionism of an earlier generation, the members of which had challenged still earlier sculptural conventions?

Aesthetically speaking, the meaning and value of an artwork is informed by the history that preceded its creation and by the presence of what philosopher Arthur Danto calls an "atmosphere of artistic theory."[11] Trying to fit this historical and theoretical apparatus into a newspaper is like trying to convince a cultural theorist to speak in plain English—it won't work. What is a journalist to do? The framework of scandal, the juicy quotes that can be plucked from the steamy swamp of moral outrage present an easier tack to connect the story with a large body of readers.[12]

This was how reporters at mass-circulation tabloids responded to the ethical questions underlying *Sensation*. Instead of analysis, outrage. And instead of research, a quick and merciless verdict. "You can't shame the shameless," vented the *New York Post's* Rod Dreher. "What about the museum's board members? Are they willing to stand behind this corruption? Are they willing to have their museum known for giving artistic and ethical standards the heave-ho to whore after flash and cash? Unthinkable. Prediction: As soon as 'Sensation' closes, the board will sacrifice [Director Arnold] Lehman to appease the gods for [his] hubris. But the question will remain: What did board members know about Lehman's fund-raising flimflammery, and when did they know it?"[13]

Even well-meaning writers at serious newspapers were caught reacting emotionally to the ethical questions raised in Brooklyn, rather than attempting to flesh out the issues. Kristin Tillotson, a thoughtful arts commentator at the *Minneapolis Star Tribune*, wrote:

> When I pick up a shirt on the sale rack at a department store, I wonder if a starving 8–year-old stitched on the buttons during her 11th straight hour of work in a dingy Salvadoran sweatshop. I wrestle with my conscience over hidden profits and agendas. Now we're forced to do the same with art. It's not enough to struggle with meaning and emotional effect: whether or not I like it, whether I just don't get it, whether I'd understand it if I had only taken that class in contemporary art. Now . . . I have to wonder: Were these pieces chosen because they are representative of an artistic movement, or a moment in a time, or a singular vision? Or did some wealthy dealer stand to skim a little extra off the top? . . . Never mind cultural context, symbolism or statement-making. How many cross-promotional tie-ins are hidden in that piece of dung?[14]

An interesting question, perhaps, but we never got an answer. There was no space or time for that kind of depth.

Count on television, which contends with the harshest time limitations, to play host to the worst kind of reductionism during arts controversies.

While public radio still provides in-depth arts coverage to a national audience, television has reneged on its promise to inform viewers about cultural events with even nominal sophistication. Over the years, arts reporting in the evening newscast—which determines the nation's news agenda—has been steadily eclipsed by "media" reporting, particularly news about the Internet. During *Sensation* television generated some of the crudest examples of boiling a debate down to its bare-knuckled extremes. On the *Today Show*, to quote one florid example, William Donohue, president of the Catholic League for Religious and Civil Rights, avowed: "Our Blessed Mother is very important to Catholics. It's more important to Catholics than Martin Luther King [Jr.] might be to the African American community. And when you throw elephant dung, have pictures of vaginas and anuses surrounding her in this kind of invidious fashion, my answer to that is, 'Go show your filth down the street, find a fat-cat bigot—there's plenty of them—and let them sponsor it.'"[15]

News Organizations Engage in "Pack Journalism" and Stereotyping

Like lemmings, newspapers engage in "pack journalism," mindlessly heaping story on story on a topic deemed newsworthy, then consigning the issue back to oblivion. Try this thought experiment: Before or after *Sensation*, how many times did you read about the Brooklyn Museum or Chris Ofili?

Meanwhile, during that fleeting moment of full exposure only a few hand-picked characters get serious shrift. As we've seen, *Sensation* was pared down to a story involving (apart from the museum) a crafty British collector (191 article mentions), a crusading New York mayor (360) and a young artist caught in the crossfire (167). As with Hollywood, the stars carried the show. There was a small and eclectic supporting cast. Playing good cop to the mayor's bad cop, Hillary Clinton (28). Cast in the role of "historical precedent," Andres Serrano, of *Piss Christ* fame (20). Representing justice, lawyer Floyd Abrams (44). In a cameo role as celebrity news peg, David Bowie (17), who recorded an audio tour in exchange for putting *Sensation* on his website. To keep the coverage "on story" countless key personages remained in the shadows, written out of the script, including nearly all the artists in the exhibit.

Most damaging from the point of view of reporting on museum ethics was the rush to judgment spurred by the news media's need to instantly respond to breaking events. When we omit the *New York Times*, which was able to devote unparalleled resources to these issues, we find that newspapers were quicker to assign blame and pick sides than they were to take a serious look at how museums and exhibitions are usually funded. There was no room or time to fill in the gray areas—and in this story, it was all gray areas—but there was huge pressure to come out with an unambiguous angle on the story.

Stereotyping was rife when it came to artists. *Sensation* artists were sorted into the good and the bad. This journalistic device is frequently used in covering foreign wars, when the press picks "good" and "evil" sides in the conflict in order to simplify obscure realities and drive home moral points about human conflict. There were heroes and villains even in the small cadre of *Sensation* artists who made the news. For all the harangues about Ofili and Hirst, almost unanimous praise was heaped on Rachel Whiteread's resin casts of empty spaces under chairs, Richard Billingham's photos of drunks, and Marc Quinn's human head cast from blood. Putting these artists on a pedestal did not necessarily do justice to their work. It provided a suitable backdrop for the vilification of the "bad" artists in the spotlight of the scandal.

When Art Becomes Politics, It Ceases to Be Arts Journalism

But this kind of journalism is not really about art. When an art story escapes the ghetto of the culture desk and captures the attention of news editors, curious things happen. First, the story ceases to be discussed in artistic terms. Second, more often than not, it ceases to be covered by art writers.

The *Daily News* published no fewer than fifty articles on the exhibition—not one of them a review. The *New York Post* was even more virulent about *Sensation,* but it did not see fit to describe the exhibition in a work of criticism (a reporter was dispatched to file a slam piece based on a "sneak peek" before the opening). When it came to television, commentators tended not to refer to the names of any artists, although of course images of the controversial works were flashed onto the screen.

The Brooklyn exhibit became a city-hall story and was covered as such.[16] But the kind of journalist who covers city government, adroit as he or she may be in exposing the connivance of elected officials, is rarely up to speed about the history and inside workings of the art world. Their investigative reporting style is governed by an intrinsic distrust of authority and a post-Watergate conviction that essential truths are tapped only if you "follow the money." This was certainly the case when it came to "exposing" the alleged conflicts of interest in the Brooklyn Museum's dealings. The problem was that the money trail led to exaggerated claims and biased conclusions about the ethical dilemmas lurking behind *Sensation*.

It was as if the reporters had never considered that money is needed to present art. The tone of the exposés was one of thinly veiled shock that in order to stage exhibitions museums reach out to exactly the kind of people who collect art. An implied presumption of culpability suffused the reports. The coverage did not consciously misrepresent the facts, but few reporters contextualized the findings in the light of history and art-world norms.[17] When the *Boston Globe* finally published a review of *Sensation*, for example, a full six weeks after the opening, the second paragraph (preceding any discussion of the art) staked out the ethical terrain thus: "This is the show owned in its entirety by British advertising mogul Charles Saatchi: In displaying and endorsing it, the Brooklyn Museum enhances its value. And this is the show funded by Christie's, the auction house, which has sold chunks of Saatchi's collections in the past and may do so in the future. Christie's potential profit is the aspect of 'Sensation' that leaps most brazenly across the line."[18] But where exactly was this line, and how do we know if it was crossed? The article raised these tantalizing questions, but left them hanging.

To be fair, it's hard to imagine many art critics as hard-hitting investigative reporters. Different talents and sensibilities are involved. (Editors routinely complain they can't get their critics to pick up the phone and ask tough questions.) But the newspapers did not engage in "enterprise journalism" of the sort that teams up an art critic with a courtroom reporter to draw on the talents of both. Instead news reporters and editorial writers often tried their hand at art criticism. In lieu of a review, the *Daily News* ran a conversation with the curator of *Sensation* along with descriptions of several of the pieces in the show—written by the city-hall bureau chief.[19] The *Post* used its editorial page as a venue for art criticism. The day after the exhibition opened its editorial read: "The work that isn't shocking is boring. And even the shocking stuff gets tedious after a while." The conclusion: "By far the lion's share of the work is ugly, technically incompetent and nihilistic."[20]

The News Media Relax Their Standards When Covering the Arts

You can tell what a news organization thinks about its audience by looking at its errors. A newspaper that makes rudimentary mistakes in describing a work of art is not counting on its readers' seeing the exhibit. This may be one reason why, in the space of three days, the *New York Post* ran five variously incorrect accounts of *The Holy Virgin Mary* and the method of its creation, including: "a portrait with elephant dung tossed across the canvas," "the Virgin Mary stained with elephant dung," "the Virgin Mary covered in elephant dung," "smear elephant dung on the Virgin Mary," and "the Virgin Mary splattered with elephant dung." None of these aptly describe how elephant dung was used in (and under) the picture. No corrections were published.[21] The earlier mentioned *Today Show* report described the Virgin Mary as "splattered with elephant dung" even as a running video clip showed this not to be the case. One of the more egregious errors appeared in the *Cleveland Plain Dealer*. Columnist Dick Feagler claimed that elephant dung was smeared on the Virgin Mary's face in two articles (no corrections). The first column (in which Ofili's name was spelled Ofill) included this gem: "The creative muse visits people according to her whim. And when she visits artists, she often picks sociopaths."[22] It stands to reason that if such blatant inaccuracies can appear in descriptions of artworks that are in plain sight, not much hope can be held out for reports about the financial deals behind art exhibits, which are conducted in secret.

As Feagler's hyperbolic claims demonstrate, when it comes to covering arts, even meritorious news organizations tend to abandon their respect for "objectivity"—the jewel in journalism's crown. A brazen, editorializing, side-taking tone crept into accounts of *Sensation*. In its first published paragraph on the show, the *Washington Post* ranted, "It's got dung, blood and beheadings. It's got cows cut into pieces, blasphemies, mass murderers, dwarfs and tattooed ladies, and penises aplenty. [*Sensation*] is sensational on purpose. Its artists know what works. They've rounded up the usual shocks."[23] This kind of writing, reminiscent of that in a tabloid, would rarely appear in the front section of the paper. *Sensation*, it seems, relieved newspapers' compulsions against sensationalistic coverage. The staid *Boston Globe* went film noir: "A rumbling could be heard in New York's art world yesterday, a nervousness that the genteel structure that has sustained the city as the nation's cultural capital for more than a century might be about to implode."[24]

These departures from journalistic creed and custom bring us to the most troubling fault line beneath arts journalism in the United States: a disinclination to believe that readers care about culture. For years, proprietary, in-house market research has been telling editors that readers are following the arts with mounting interest. Culture is no longer an after-work activity but the bedrock of the new economy. Still, the news media are loath to treat the arts with the seriousness, with the urgency, with the generosity accorded to hard news or even sports. Underlying the arts' pariah status is the condescending notion that Americans are too closed-minded to respond favorably to more and better coverage of the arts, especially arts deemed "difficult." From bad coverage to controversy to more bad coverage and still more controversy, we're left with an endless chain of self-fulfilling prophesies.

The Travails of the Art World

But wait. Blaming the media lets the other parties in this story off the hook. Despite its failings, the press had only limited liability for *Sensation*. And for all the bias and misrepresentation, there were many reasonable and objective reports.[25] The news media can be charged with deepening hysteria, polarizing conflict, or trivializing the issues, but, no matter how divisive and corrosive their conduct, newspapers and broadcasters can go only so far in creating a scandal. To put it another way, the news media cannot solve the problems that fueled the Brooklyn Museum controversy from within the art world.

One problem is the contemporary art world's diminished sense of direction and the resulting confusion about the value of much new art. The reluctance of various art-world figures to line up behind the Brooklyn Museum of Art (BMA) during *Sensation* made it clear that even among them, art insiders, there was no consensus that the art was worth defending. The source of this uncertainty goes beyond Saatchi's artists and their respective merits. It is rooted in a postmodern questioning of values at a moment when art history—the recently concluded trajectory of modernism—no longer offers solid advice about the logical next steps. In an era of aesthetic pluralism, it is harder and harder to agree about what new art is worthy of display in an art museum. "We say that the avant-garde is dead, but it's not clear that we mean it," one *Artforum* critic suggested. "Without movements or a clear progressive direction, what's left? Globalism? The decorative, Apollonian art of stable economic times? The repetition of postmodernism? Random pluralism? The Internet? We're not sure. . . . With no collective dogma, there is no easy route for critics, or for those looking for someone or something to follow."[26] Surely, if the art world sent a clearer message about what it considers valuable and what it considers worthless, the press could do a better job presenting its case to the public.

The same kind of uncertainty hampers reporting about museum ethics. In order to treat museums objectively, journalists would need to have a clearer sense of what museums are or ought to be. But just as contemporary art is struggling to regain a sense of purpose, so museums are feeling their way in a milieu where demands on them are expanding exponentially. Greater clarity and confidence in the project would spur a stronger defense of the means required to reach the ends, and it would dampen criticism from the outside.

The news media's job wasn't helped by the mixed messages emanating from the museum community during *Sensation.* Disagreements among the experts may, in fact, have been directly responsible for some of the misinformation and hysteria later attributed to the press. The first big article on the ethical aspects of *Sensation* in the *New York Times* claimed that "the Brooklyn Museum of Art's particular mix of art and commerce . . . violates no hard-and-fast rules in the precincts of the museum world." The article noted that "the museum director's code says nothing about restrictions on the sale of works in a show" and quoted the director of the Worcester Art Museum to support the claim that the BMA had followed standard art-world practices.[27] A month later, however, another article in the *Times* reached a different conclusion. That article found art-world experts willing to argue that the fundraising in Brooklyn was "practically unheard of and ethically problematic." Without specifying sources, the *Times* claimed that "museums have a public trust to display art on the basis of merit, those experts say, and are sure to suffer if they become viewed as instruments for private financial gain."[28]

So who was right? Those who shrugged Brooklyn off as entirely within the bounds of normal and acceptable conduct or those who condemned the BMA and its director for violating the museum's public trust? If "the experts" had presented a more consistent case to the journalists, the story might not have spun so drastically out of control. But to present such a clear-cut position on matters of appropriate conduct the museum world needs to engage in some self-scrutiny of its own.

It Takes Two to Tango

It is said about railroads that the reason for their demise in the twentieth century was that they assumed they were in the railroad business. They focused on building railroads when in fact they were in the transportation business, where they lost out to cars and airlines. Analogously, it would be a mistake to think that museums are still in the art business. They are now in what may be called the "attention business." Museums are the last major public institutions that still fight for public attention for the sole purpose of edification. But in an era of contested cultural hierarchies and vast cultural conglomerates, the longer museums continue to think they are in the art business the more likely they will end up like railroads and capitulate to the likes of Time-Warner AOL.[29] The point is that now more than ever museums must articulate their missions and agendas for themselves and their audiences. Like it or not, they must engage the press as a partner in this process.

I asked Philippe de Montebello, director of the Metropolitan Museum, why he thought museums are coming under so much fire these days about their collecting and exhibiting practices. Why now, and why not earlier? His answer was that museums are victims of their own success in attracting mass audiences. Even in the early 1970s a museum like the Met was still more like a private club, a rarified precinct of academics and people of privilege. Over the years museums have become a kind of "public square." Along with this new role has come the intrusion of public scrutiny. But this experience is all too recent, and museum managers' relations with the press tend to be extremely distrustful. The proper rules of conduct are yet to be devised. To build these relationships, museums will have to part with their traditional formulas for dealing with the public and the press.

This change in attitude is going to be difficult because at the moment museums are astonishingly inscrutable. Built to serve the secular worship of art, they maintain a strict separation between the ritualistic spaces where objects of value are presented and the mundane service operations that facilitate the devotional activity. (In Brooklyn, these operations were given a rare close look.) All that the visitor sees of what transpires in these back offices is a door with a warning: "Do Not Enter, Staff Only." This fencing off of the sacred from the profane is a legacy of romantic attitudes that informed the creation of museums and are still respected today. Mystery surrounds decisions on acquisitions and deaccessioning and more or less the entire financial and logistical infrastructure of mounting major exhibits.

The museum perfectly exemplifies the distinction sociologist Erving Goffman made between front stage and backstage behavior. The neatly appointed front stage—the viewing gallery—is intended for the public. The backstage—the "real" part of the operation, including all the prosaic decisions and activities that keep a museum going—is hidden from view. Goffman's classic illustration of this separation in *The Presentation of Self in Everyday Life* was the restaurant, where the decorum of the hushed dining room stands in marked contrast to the noisy and disheveled world of the kitchen. It is a quotidian analogy, but it does aptly describe the challenge presently facing art museums (and their commercial counterparts, art galleries and auction houses, as well).

Had you recommended to a four-star chef some twenty years ago that he should knock down the wall between his kitchen and his dining room, he would probably have questioned your sanity. Cuisine was an art, and the messy circumstances of cooking were supposed to be kept strictly off limits to the public. How the world has changed! Today, diners are happy to sit in restaurants where the cooks are in plain view. An open kitchen creates intimacy, not to mention assurance that the ingredients are of high quality and that the chef enforces high sanitary standards.

I'd like to suggest that, in a manner of speaking, museums should open their kitchens to the public. They should do so because we have graduated from Goffman's schizophrenic institutions into a milieu of open kitchens, where transparency is the norm. Theaters have dispensed with curtains. Congress and courtrooms now tolerate cameras at their proceedings. Real-life television is replacing scripted entertainment. Television anchors sit inside open newsrooms filled with reporters. Corporate towers have see-through walls and no private offices. Even computers are being put in translucent casings. Everywhere you look, people are fascinated about "process" and weary of prepackaged "product." Privacy and confidentiality have turned from marks of professionalism into warning signs of complicity and unearned privilege. But amidst all this uncloaking and demystification, one institution has stubbornly kept up the veil. With few exceptions, museums meticulously hide every clue about what it takes to present their collections to the public.[30]

It's time for a new approach, one that lets people in on the action. And there are welcome signs of movement in this direction. Amendments have been added to the American Association of Museums' guidelines insisting on disclosure of support from donors with potential conflicts of interest. The Whitney Museum for American Art has passed a resolution to make public the names of donors who might benefit commercially from exhibitions. These are good first steps, but there is room for more openness; openness that will contribute to the success of museum programming. Why not publish detailed accounts about how artworks were loaned or purchased for a given show (the phone-book size catalogues that are in vogue nowadays could certainly accommodate such information)? What if museums commissioned "the making of the exhibition"-style documentaries, just as Hollywood does with movies? And how about using exhibition websites to provide more detail about provenance and donor support? All this material makes for good copy and even entertainment, and it would enhance the learning experience that lies at the heart of museums' chartered missions in the United States.

Most of all, rather than trying to fend off the inevitable, museums should make it easier for the press to report on their activities: hold press briefings during the planning stages, not just at opening time; invite reporters to curators' meetings, and give them access to donors and collectors; compile candid and exhaustive press packets; learn from others in the "attention business." It may be going too far to put a glass wall between the gallery and the curators' offices, but there are countless ways to promote candor and transparency.

The Risks and the Rewards of Public Scrutiny

Can the prosaic inside workings of museums be exposed without harming their authority? Undeniably, such disclosure is fraught with risks. Museums are faced with a Herculean task: to operate amidst twenty-first-century realities while living up to nineteenth-century ideals of purity. For decades museums have been forced to compete ever more fiercely for attention and funding but still pretend they are unsullied by material concerns.

My own view is that there are no clear-cut ethical standards about exhibition funding practices. The individual cases vary too broadly, and far too much depends on context. Any search for absolutes will likely lead nowhere or, worse, to standards that don't work. Instead, we must accept that—as with most social agreements about right and wrong—ethical standards emerge from an always-shifting consensus. A practice unpardonable in the past may be considered normal today, or tomorrow. A lot depends on how the debate is managed. The more public the discourse over ethical standards of museum management, the more likely we are to see permissive regulation. The more closed and secretive the discussion, the more probable that we will end up with draconian policies and social censure.

Some believe that controversies like that over *Sensation* inflict nothing but damage. Glenn Lowry, director of the Museum of Modern Art in New York, has said, "Any time museums come under the scrutiny that occurred in Brooklyn, it inevitably frays the public trust that museums enjoy."[31] At this early stage the pain of public scrutiny may indeed be more apparent than its salutary effect. But in the long run such scrutiny will foster more trust in museums and not less. It will help museums develop a better sense of what kinds of deals and activities are acceptable, what they must do to avoid allegations of misconduct, and how to manage such crises once they're mired in them. More important, a policy of openness and scrutiny is the only way of assuring that the public gains a proper understanding of museum management and thus of preventing controversies based on political manipulation from erupting in the first place.

The *Sensation* crisis was woefully aggravated by the press, which places a premium on scandal and habitually treats the art world with neglect and distrust. But to move forward from this impasse, museums must acknowledge that the crisis had genuine roots in a host of unresolved problems surrounding contemporary art exhibits and in museums' reluctance to deal with these problems openly. There was no lone culprit here. The lessons of Brooklyn—all immensely valuable—should spur the art world and the press to behave like partners instead of adversaries, to their mutual benefit.

NOTES

1. Deborah Solomon, "The Collector," *New York Times Magazine*, September 26, 1999, p. 44.
2. Eight other artists were mentioned in the article.
3. "Editor's Note," *New York Times*, September 26, 1999, p. A2.
4. Michael Janeway, Daniel S. Levy, András Szántó, and Andrew Tyndall, *Reporting the Arts; News Coverage of Arts and Culture in America* (New York: National Arts Journalism Program, Columbia University, 1999), 21.
5. In all but the largest city papers, *Sensation* ran as a minor story. Arts journalism is typically geared toward local news. Despite its far-reaching implications, the Saatchi controversy was seen as a New York affair in other parts of the country.
6. I gratefully acknowledge the help of Jeremy Simon, who provided research assistance and suggested interpretive criticisms for this article.
7. The search covered articles about *Sensation* appearing in the twelve months following April 1999 in the top fifty U.S. newspapers. Two of the most prolific papers on the exhibit, however, the *New York Post* and *Newsday*, are not included in the Lexis-Nexis database. They were reviewed separately.
8. If advance coverage were taken out of the picture, the percentage would be even higher.
9. The artists were Marc Quinn (twenty-three articles), Rachel Whiteread (nineteen), and the Chapman brothers (thirty-three). In many papers the debate over *Sensation* quickly devolved into a discussion of how the scandal would bolster Mayor Giuliani's chances in his Senate run against Hillary Rodham Clinton (at a time when both candidates had yet to formally announce their entry into the race). A week before *Sensation* opened a *New York Post* column was already proclaiming the exhibit a "political coup" for Giuliani; Rod Dreher, "Bad Art Makes Great Politics for Giuliani," *New York Post*, September 26, 1999.
10. An unusual cast of political characters populated the coverage of the Brooklyn Museum exhibit. Quoted in an article in the *New York Times*, Pat Buchanan had this advice for the mayor: "When we get control of the National Endowment for the Arts, you'll see how it ought to be done. . . . You shut it down, fumigate the building and put the I.R.S. in there"; Kit Roane, "Buchanan Visits Art Museum and Doesn't Like It," November 6, 1999, p. B5. On October 5 presidential hopeful G. W. Bush was quoted as stating, "From what I've read, the exhibit besmirches religion"; William Goldschlag, "Bush Backs Rudy Jihad on 'Sensation,'" *Daily News*, October 5, 1999, p. 6.
11. Arthur Danto, *The Transfiguration of the Commonplace* (Cambridge, Mass.: Harvard University Press, 1981), 135.
12. One way to keep the coverage simple is to abstain from analytical discussion of the works (even though concepts and theories are constitutive of the kind of art featured in *Sensation*) and stick to plain description. A well-intentioned example, from the *Boston Globe*, of sticking to the surface: "This Mary, who more resembles an African earth goddess, is draped in a luminous blue gown against a gold backdrop that glistens. The huge canvas does sit on two clumps of elephant dung, and a highly molded and polished clump of dung represents her breast. But elephant dung is prominent in three other Ofili paintings, which have nothing to do with religious themes"; Fred Kaplan,

"In Brooklyn, Museum Fuss Draws Curious," *Boston Globe*, October 3, 1999, p. A1.

13. Rod Dreher, "Director's Future Has Come Undung," *New York Post*, November 2, 1999, p. 9.
14. Kristin Tillotson, "'Sensation': Bared Flesh, Hidden Cash," *Minneapolis Star Tribune*, November 7, 1999, p. 5F.
15. *Today Show*, NBC, September 27, 1999. This quote also illustrates that as far as the mass media were concerned, the main issue wasn't Saatchi's sponsorship of the Brooklyn Museum of Art but the art that his support presented to the American public. The exchange was with Norman Siegel, executive director of the New York Civil Liberties Union. In discussing Ofili's picture, the morning news show noted this was not the first controversy for *Sensation*: "When it first opened in London two years ago, some were appalled, others disgusted and a few threw eggs." But the controversy in London centered mostly on Marcus Harvey's *Myra*, a painting of a child murderer, and not on any of Ofili's pictures.
16. In an interview conducted for this article by Jeremy Simon, Mila Andre, an arts writer at the *Daily News* for fifteen years, said: "We [the arts department] stayed away from covering the *Sensation* exhibit. . . . First of all, that kind of art does not interest me at all. Secondly, the partitioned cow has been dragged around by the artist for so many years it's old hat. Thirdly, the work referred to as the Virgin Mary . . . to me, it was a very limited piece of work." Did the *Daily News* run a review of the exhibit? "No. It went news side because it became a news-side story, because of Giuliani, basically. If he had kept his mouth shut, I don't think anybody would have flocked to see it."
17. Instead, numerous newspapers employed the polarizing arsenal of campaign-year political reporting, including political polling. Lead reporter Dave Goldiner noted in the *Daily News*: "Sixty percent of those surveyed said they opposed Giuliani's efforts to close the 'Sensation' show which includes a portrait of the Virgin Mary decorated with clumps of elephant dung"; Dave Goldiner, "Apple Turns Sour on Rudy: Poll Shows Most N.Y.ers Back Museum," October 1, 1999, p. 7.
18. Christine Temin, "Review: Sensation Isn't So Much of One," *Boston Globe*, November 24, 1999, p. C1.
19. Michael Blood, "Exhibit Taps into Dark Side of Art, Life," *Daily News*, September 29, 1999, p. 4. The *Daily News* did use its editorial page to discuss the funding controversy. An unsigned editorial took up the issue of Saatchi's donation to the show: "Take Saatchi's pledge of $160,000 to help finance the show. What started out as a donation suddenly became a debt for the museum as Saatchi insisted that he be paid back a portion of it. Profit sharing? Is it a museum or a baseball team? More outrageous than Saatchi's moxie in making the demand is Lehman's agreeing to it." "A Dung Heap Starts to Smell," *Daily News*, December 9, 1999, p. 58. The editorial did not delve into why what's acceptable for sports programming is not acceptable for arts entertainment.
20. Editorial, "One Stink-ular Sensation," *New York Post*, October 3, 1999, p. 30. Oddly enough, despite giving the art this kind of treatment, the *Post* was one of several newspapers decrying the "publicity" the exhibition received. "The museum wins. It gathered more attention than it deserves." Andrea Peyser, "Exhibit a Masterpiece of Generating Publicity," *New York Post*, September 28, 1999, p. 7. By this time the paper had already run eight stories on the exhibit.
21. The articles appeared September 24–26, 1999. The *Post* later made its views clear on the elephant-dung issue: "The baghwan of buffoonery offers a sus-

piciously jerry-built argument holding that dung is sacred to Africans"; Rod Dreher, "Leftist Loonies in Comedy of Manures," *New York Post,* September 30, 1999, p. 22.

22. Dick Feagler, "Our Lady of the 'Sensation,' Pray for Us," *Cleveland Plain Dealer,* September 26, 1999, p. 16.
23. Paul Richard, "A Lot of Wear on the Shocks,' *Washington Post*, September 24, 1999, p. C4.
24. Fred Kaplan, "Difference of Aesthetic Opinion Pits Purse vs. Palette," *Boston Globe*, September 24, 1999, p. A12.
25. One of the more thoughtful assessments was penned by *New York Times* chief art critic Michael Kimmelman: "The problem stems from the puritanical American supposition that culture is pure and money is corrupt. This leads to the notion that self-interest on the part of rich collectors necessarily pollutes the sanctity of the museum, as if American museums were not the result of rich collectors' donations. Collectors' loans of their works to museums for exhibition also benefit the public and are an act of generosity. No one said that generosity cannot exist simultaneously with self-interest"; Michael Kimmelman, "In the End, the 'Sensation' Is Less the Art Than the Money," *New York Times*, November 3, 1999, p. E1.
26. Katy Siegel, "Biennial 2000," *Artforum*, May 2000, 171–173.
27. Judith H. Dobrzynski, "Private Collections Routine at Museums," *New York Times*, October 1, 1999, p. B6.
28. David Barstow, "Brooklyn Museum Recruited Donors Who Stood to Gain." *New York Times*, October 31, 1999, p. A1.
29. Who is to say for-profit culture can't enter the art game? Just as we now have for-profit universities, we also have at least one example of a for-profit museum with real art, the Bellagio casino and resort in Las Vegas.
30. The museums that have experimented with breaking down the walls between their galleries and supporting operations, like the Museum of Anthropology in Vancouver, have garnered enormous success with the public, without sacrificing their academic missions.
31. Quoted in Lee Rosenbaum, "The Battle of Brooklyn Ends, the Controversy Continues," *Art in America*, June 2000, 39.

KIMERLY RORSCHACH

Afterword

As the essays in this volume demonstrate, the Brooklyn Museum *Sensation* controversy raised difficult issues concerning what should be exhibited in a public institution supported by public funds and how museum exhibitions should be funded in a capitalist free-market economy, given the inadequacy of these public funds. Although these issues surfaced under the pressure of an intensely local politics, they are, in a sense, always already implicit in the situation of any publicly (under)funded museum in a democratic society. But other factors, neither ephemeral nor essential to the very idea of a museum in America, may account for the peculiar vulnerability of the museum world at the present time. The more important causes of the present predicament of American museums stem from the vast changes of the 1990s. As the world has moved from the paradigm of the Cold War to that of globalism, assisted by the engines of a powerful world economy, the dominance of free-market capitalism, and new Internet communications, the museum's nature and environment have been transformed in ways that, as the aftermath of the Brooklyn controversy shows, policy is only gradually assimilating.

Broadly speaking, the mission of many art museums in the United States has evolved from collecting, preserving, and displaying the best art judged according to a monolithic Western canon, which was paramount during the Cold War years, to bringing art and people together in the context of an ever-broadening and more diverse set of canons. This pluralist populism was in part a defensive maneuver encouraged by the "culture wars," which exploded in the Robert Mapplethorpe and Andres Serrano controversies of 1989–1990 and led to a dramatic decrease in direct federal grants to art institutions. Much worse than the actual loss of such funding, from the museums' point of view, was the suspicion, planted in the minds of at least some, that the art museum could no longer function as an authoritative cultural arbiter in the matter of the visual arts and that artistic quality was impossible to define in a universal or absolute way. For collecting art museums especially, this was (and remains) a frightening notion and one that the appeal to a more ecumenical canon has not managed to dispel.[1]

In fact, the new respect due to repressed and oppressed cultures and peoples has turned collecting itself, formerly an exciting and intellectually positivist quest, into a minefield of difficulties, from the reporting and return requirements mandated by the Native American Graves Protection and Repatriation Act of 1990 to the rising debates about the international trade in antiquities and other forms of cultural property and on to the issues surrounding works of European art that may have been seized by the Nazis during the Second World War and not properly "restituted" (as we now say) to their rightful owners or their heirs. These issues affect almost every area of museum collections and acquisitions (with the exception of art made after 1945 and art made in this country by artists of European ancestry before that time).

Traditional art museums have also had difficulties in coming to grips with the rapidly changing demographics of our nation and the greater racial, ethnic, and cultural diversity that distinguishes us. Formerly prosperous cities like Brooklyn and Detroit, whose inhabitants had once found meaning in the traditional European-centered aesthetic values embodied in their cities' great art museums, are now different places, with different, or at least much more diverse, cultural concerns. Despite sincere efforts and the very real gains that have been made in attracting more diverse audiences, for many traditional art museums, the great majority of visitors remain white, well-educated, middle-aged, and upper-middle-class. Nor has significant progress been made on increasing staff diversity at high management levels in traditional art museums.[2]

However, the 1990s were also a decade of great opportunity for art museums, at least partly because of the enormous growth of wealth during that time. While philanthropy has not exactly caught up with this vast expansion of wealth, all the trends seem to be up. Many more foundations are being created from this new wealth, and many more wealthy individuals are in need of the tax breaks provided for charitable donations. As a result, museum endowments have ballooned, and many, if not most, art museums seem to be engaged in capital campaigns and building expansions.[3] The Internet has also brought new possibilities for communication, education, and earned income to art museums, although museums have been slow to exploit this resource because of fears surrounding intellectual property rights. Other papers in this volume refer to the great rise in art-museum attendance and consequent rise in entry-fee and museum-shop revenues, which can also be mentioned as a factor here.

As fast as the money comes in, however, it barely keeps pace with the increased costs of bringing it in. As museums have expanded to accommodate larger gift shops, family learning centers, and restaurants, and collections have grown in numbers and value, museums have become vastly more expensive to run. Their large physical plants must be constructed to and maintained at high standards, with exacting environmental and security requirements. They need large and specialized staffs to care for their collections, to manage the ever-increasing numbers of visitors, and to successfully execute the ambitious international exhibitions that the public has come to expect and that museums have come to need to draw in larger audiences and revenues. As in any chicken-and-egg situation, it is difficult to say what came first here, but there is no doubt of the new reality.

The funding and First Amendment issues raised in the Brooklyn controversy must be seen in this larger context of new challenges and opportunities and in the nexus of globalism and the emphasis on diversity of cultures rather than one common culture. Whatever the artistic merits and importance of the *Sensation* exhibition, it represented an effort by Brooklyn to attract broader and more diverse audiences and to capitalize as creatively and effectively as possible on whatever funding sources might be available. By devising an inflammatory advertising campaign that seemed to call the artistic merit of the exhibition's works into question, the museum all but invited protests that one or another work was not just bad but insulting; and when this protest came, the museum's funding strategies, which suggested potential conflicts of interest and a single lender who seemed to be usurping the museum's artistic control of the exhibition, made it difficult to claim that a higher interest was at stake.

But of course a higher interest *was* at stake. And it is the function of policies, whether written into law, promulgated as regulations, or established in codes of ethics, to clarify our responsibility to that higher interest. Since the Brooklyn Museum controversy erupted and subsided, and spurred in part by the findings presented at the University of Chicago's conference, which are collected in this volume, policies have been reaffirmed, undermined, and crafted anew. The museum was vindicated in court: the City of New York was enjoined from withdrawing operating support from the museum and compelled to release substantial capital-improvement funds that had also been withdrawn. The strengths of a First Amendment defense in such matters were thus revealed. As David Strauss's paper on the "false promise of the First Amendment" asserts, however, this victory may be a mixed blessing for publicly funded arts institutions in that governments in the long run may opt not to fund at all rather than fund programs over which they may have no control of content. Recognizing the need for advocacy in such matters, some artists have begun to organize to articulate for a broader audience the social value of what they do, even if it is controversial or shocking.

Despite these efforts at rallying public opinion and the declarations of victory by Brooklyn Museum supporters, there are signs that the controversy has had a chilling effect on museums more generally. The Australian tour of the *Sensation* exhibition was canceled after the public revelations of Charles Saatchi's support of the show. The National Gallery of Australia's director, Brian Kennedy, declared that the exhibition's funding "takes it into an ethical area which is untenable for the National Gallery."[4] And in November 1999, just after the Brooklyn exhibition opened, the Detroit Institute of Arts was featured in the *New York Times* because its new director, Graham Beal, had closed an exhibition of work by the contemporary artist Jef J. Bourgeau ahead of schedule. Works singled out in the article included "a toy Jesus wearing a condom, a pile of human excrement, and a brazil nut labeled with a racial epithet."[5] These cancellations again raised the issue of the artist's rights versus self-censorship in a civil society, and they called into question the museum's authority to determine what is good or worthwhile in the difficult realm of contemporary art. However, the Whitney Museum of American Art, which does not receive general funding from the City of New York, exhibited a deliberately provocative work created in specific response to the Brooklyn controversy. Hans Haacke's installation "Sanitation" responded directly to Mayor Rudolph Giuliani by putting his critical comments about *Sensation* into Nazi-style script. Even here, the museum's director was not aware of the piece's specific content before the installation and expressed shock and dismay at its content, while supporting the artist's "right to express his opinions in our galleries."[6]

These ad hoc responses make it clear that museum directors and curators have work to do to develop policies for dealing with art that may be (or later turns out to be) controversial or even offensive to some but nonetheless has merit and is judged worthy of a museum exhibition. Directors and curators must also be articulate, forceful advocates for the difficult art that they show if they expect to win the approbation of a truly broad public. As institutions that have the ability to bring diverse groups together, museums should have both the autonomy to present art, even difficult art, that positively engages a civil but ever more diverse society and the responsibility to acknowledge the implications of what they are doing. The policies and strategies that emerge should be an important legacy of *Sensation*.

The other important legacy of this controversy will surely be the new anxiety and the new policy debate it has engendered about how the museum enterprise is funded, what Richard Epstein in this book calls "the grubby engines of law and business" that underpin our great art institutions. On May 18, 2000, the Metropolitan Museum of Art's director, Philippe de Montebello, announced that the museum would cancel its planned Coco Chanel retrospective rather than adopt the artistic vision of Chanel head Karl Lagerfeld for the organization of the exhibition, which was to have been underwritten by the couture house. de Montebello said, "I need to be able to assure people that what they see on the walls is not inflected by the money we receive to do an exhibition, and if I can't make that assurance, then I'm not doing it."[7] Aware as never before of the importance of maintaining the public trust, museum associations are busy developing rules about disclosure and "arm's length" relationships with backers to ward off potential conflicts of interest, as well as clearer policies and better information about how museums are and should be funded. The Association of Art Museum Directors, which includes the directors of about two hundred leading art museums in North America, has articulated new policies on these issues in the context of the regular revision of *Professional Practices in Art Museums*, released in 2001. The American Association of Museums, which represents three thousand museums in all disciplines nationwide, has revised its *Guidelines on Exhibiting Borrowed Objects* to include strong recommendations on disclosure of support from donors with potential conflicts of interest.[8] The Whitney Museum of American Art has drafted new policies on program support and sponsorships in potential conflict-of-interest situations, and many other museums will surely follow suit.

One of the greatest strengths of the American system (as opposed to the system in countries where arts institutions are supported largely by public funds) is its diversity, and the healthiest, most robust arts institutions are usually supported by a combination of public subsidies (usually from state or municipal authorities or a parent institution or university), private support in the form of foundation grants and contributions from interested individuals, and earned income in the form of admission fees or ticket sales, retail income, and the like. In this country, except for the Smithsonian Institution museums in Washington, D.C., arts institutions receive only a tiny proportion of direct support from the federal government, as grants from agencies such as the National Endowments for the Arts and Humanities and the Institute of Museum and Library Services. Most crucially, all private giving to such institutions, whether in the form of cash, appreciated assets, or works of art, is stimulated and supported by the U.S. tax laws, which encourage the establishment of private, nonprofit entities such as museums and arts institutions whose ultimate purpose is educational; the tax laws also encourage individual citizens to support these institutions by offering a broad range of federal tax benefits in exchange for contributions. It is for this reason that the maintenance of public trust is so important and that museums and artists must continue to make the case as forcefully and effectively as possible regarding the public and social value of their enterprise.

NOTES

1. It can be argued that these changes began earlier; see Neil Harris's prescient essays, "A Historical Perspective on Museum Advocacy" (first published 1980) and "Museums: The Hidden Agenda" (first published 1987), both reprinted in *Cultural Excursions* (Chicago: University of Chicago Press, 1990), 82–95 and 132–147.
2. On the issue of visitor diversity, see John H. Falk, "Visitors: Who Does, Who Doesn't, and Why," *Museum News* 77 (March/April 1998): 38–43, which cautions against drawing overly simplistic conclusions about the reasons for a lack of greater visitor diversity. See also *Expanding the Market for the Arts in Chicago* (Chicago: Arts Marketing Center of the Arts & Business Council of Chicago, 1996) and *Diversifying Chicago's Arts Audiences: A Progress Report* (Chicago: Arts Marketing Center of the Arts & Business Council of Chicago, 2000). Both these studies point out that, for African American and Hispanic audiences, participation in arts activities generally is as high (or even higher) by percentage of total population as participation by nonminority groups. Only the 1994 study segments findings for different arts activities (art museums, theater, classical music, dance, and ballet). On staff diversity, see Lonnie G. Bunch, "Flies in the Buttermilk: Museums, Diversity, and the Will to Change," *Museum News* 79 (July/August 2000): 32–35.
3. Statistics compiled annually by the Association of Art Museum Directors show that, for 1998–2000, art museums' combined spending on capital improvements hovered between $274 and $306 million annually, a significant jump from earlier years.
4. Radio National, "The Spirit of Things," April 30, 2000; http://www.abc.net.au/m/relig/spirit/stories/5122362.htm.
5. News summary, *New York Times*, November 23, 1999, p. A2.

6. Maxwell L. Anderson, "Director's Statement on Hans Haacke's 'Sanitation,'" March 10, 2000, http://www.echonyc.com/~whitney/exhibition/2kb/director.html.
7. Michael Kimmelman, "At the Met, a Necessary Retreat," *New York Times*, May 28, 2000, sec. 2, p. 31.
8. David Barstow, "After 'Sensation' Furor, Museum Group Adopts Guidelines on Sponsors," *New York Times*, August 3, 2000, p. B1.

About the Contributors

CAROL BECKER is the dean of faculty and a professor at the School of the Art Institute of Chicago. She has edited two collections of essays, *The Subversive Imagination: Artists, Society, and Responsibility* (1994) and *The Artist in Society: Rights, Roles, and Responsibilities* (1995).

HOMI K. BHABHA is the Chester D. Tripp Distinguished Service Professor in the Humanities at the University of Chicago. He is the editor of *Nation and Narration* (1990) and the author of *The Location of Culture* (1994).

JOHN BREWER is the John and Marion Sullivan University Professor of English and History at the University of Chicago. He is the author of *The Pleasures of the Imagination: English Culture in the Eighteenth Century* (1997).

JAMES CUNO is the Elizabeth and John Moors Cabot Director of the Harvard University Art Museums and professor of the history of art and architecture at Harvard.

GILBERT S. EDELSON, Esq., is administrative vice president and counsel of the Art Dealers Association of America.

TERI J. EDELSTEIN is the principal of Teri J. Edelstein Associates, Museum Strategies. Previously director of several university museums, she served most recently as deputy director of the Art Institute of Chicago. Her publications include *The Stage Is All the World: The Theatrical Designs of Tanya Moiseiwitsch* (1993) and *Perspectives on Berthe Morisot* (1990).

RICHARD A. EPSTEIN is James Parker Hall Distinguished Service Professor in the Law School at the University of Chicago. His many books include *Bargaining with the State* (1993) and *Principles for a Free Society: Reconciling Individual Liberty with the Common Good* (1998).

DAVID HALLE is a professor of sociology at UCLA and director of the UCLA LeRoy Neiman Center for the Study of American Society and Culture. He is the author of *Inside Culture: Art and Class in the American Home* (1993) and "The Audience for 'Primitive' Art in Houses in the New York Region," *Art Bulletin* (Fall 1993), and he is the editor of *New York and Los Angeles: Politics, Society and Culture* (2000).

D. CARROLL JOYNES is the executive director of the Cultural Policy Program at the University of Chicago. He holds a Ph.D. from the University of Chicago in European history, and he has taught at both the University of Chicago and the New School for Social Research.

W.J.T. MITCHELL is the Gaylord Donnelley Distinguished Service Professor of English and Art History at the University of Chicago and editor of *Critical Inquiry*. His recent books include *Picture Theory: Essays on Verbal and Visual Representation* (1994) and *The Last Dinosaur Book: The Life and Times of a Cultural Icon* (1998).

STEPHEN B. PRESSER is the Raoul Berger Professor of Legal History at Northwestern University Law School, and he holds a joint appointment as professor of business law in Northwestern University's Kellogg Graduate School of Management, Department of Management and Strategy. He is the author of *Recapturing the Constitution: Race, Religion, and Abortion Reconsidered* (1994) and *Piercing the Corporate Veil* (1991, updated annually), and he is the senior coauthor of *Law and Jurisprudence in American History: Cases and Materials* (4th ed., 2000).

KIMERLY RORSCHACH is the Dana Feitler Director of the Smart Museum of Art at the University of Chicago.

DAVID A. ROSS is the director of the San Francisco Museum of Modern Art. Between 1991 and 1998 he was the director of the Whitney Museum of American Art; he directed Boston's Institute of Contemporary Art from 1982 through 1991. A specialist in new media, Ross has lectured in contemporary art at UC San Diego, the San Francisco Art Institute, Harvard University, and Columbia University.

LAWRENCE ROTHFIELD is an associate professor of English and faculty director of the Cultural Policy Program at the University of Chicago. He is the author of *Vital Signs: Medical Realism in Nineteenth-Century Fiction* (1992).

J. MARK SCHUSTER is a professor of urban cultural policy at MIT. He is the author of *The Geography of Participation in the Arts and Culture* (2000) and *The Audience for American Art Museums* (1991); and he is the coauthor and coeditor of *Preserving the Built Heritage: Tools for Implementation* (1997) and *Who's to Pay for the Arts? The International Search for Models of Arts Support* (1989).

GEOFFREY R. STONE is provost and Harry Kalven, Jr., Distinguished Service Professor of Law at the University of Chicago. He is the editor with Cass Sunstein of *Constitutional Law* (3d ed., 1996) and of *The First Amendment* (1999).

DAVID A. STRAUSS is the Harry N. Wyatt Professor of Law at the University of Chicago. He is the author of a number of articles on freedom of expression and on constitutional interpretation, and he has argued sixteen cases before the U.S. Supreme Court.

CASS R. SUNSTEIN is the Karl N. Llewellyn Distinguished Service Professor of Law and Political Science at the University of Chicago. He is the author of many articles and books, including *Republic.com* (2001), *Free Markets and Social Justice* (1997), and *One Case at a Time* (1999).

ANDRÁS SZÁNTÓ is deputy director of the National Arts Journalism Program, a fellowship program for arts and cultural journalists and academic research center at Columbia University. He earned a Ph.D. in sociology from Columbia; his dissertation examined recent transformations in the New York art world. Szántó has coauthored two books and has published numerous research reports, newspaper articles, and magazine essays on arts, culture, and politics.

ELISABETH TISO graduated from Sarah Lawrence College in 1981 and later studied art history at Columbia University and the City

University of New York. She is currently a freelance art historian living and working in New York City.

GIHONG YI is a Ph.D. student in sociology at UCLA. His research interests are corporate networks, immigration, East Asian economic development, and methodology.

Index

The following typographical conventions are used in the index: *f* identifies a figure; *t* identifies a table.

